Psychological Processes in Social Media

Psychological Processes in Social Media

Why We Click

ROSANNA E. GUADAGNO
OASIS Research Unit
Faculty of Information Technology and Electrical Engineering
University of Oulu
Oulu, Finland

ELSEVIER

ACADEMIC PRESS
An imprint of Elsevier

Academic Press is an imprint of Elsevier
125 London Wall, London EC2Y 5AS, United Kingdom
525 B Street, Suite 1650, San Diego, CA 92101, United States
50 Hampshire Street, 5th Floor, Cambridge, MA 02139, United States

ISBN: 978-0-12-811320-2

For Information on all Academic Press publications
visit our website at https://www.elsevier.com/books-and-journals

Publisher: Nikki Levy
Acquisitions Editor: Joslyn Chaiprasert-Paguio
Editorial Project Manager: Samantha Allard
Production Project Manager: Omer Mukthar Moosa
Cover Designer: Christian Bilbow

Typeset by MPS Limited, Chennai, India

Contents

Preface

> *I think the potential of what the internet is going to do to society, both good and bad, is unimaginable. I think we're actually on the cusp of something exhilarating and terrifying.*
>
> ***David Bowie; YouTube (n.d.)***

My favorite singer, David Bowie, predicted the impact of the Internet on people and their relationships in the quote above. Nowhere has this been more apparent than in people's social media use. In the digital age, social media has woven itself into the fabric of our daily lives, shaping how we communicate, interact, and even perceive the world around us. The allure of a click, a like, or a share has become almost irresistible, drawing billions of users into an intricate web of social connections and content consumption. But what drives these seemingly simple actions? What psychological processes compel us to engage so deeply with these platforms? These are the questions that sparked the journey of this book.

Psychological Processes in Social Media: Why We Click was born out of a deep curiosity about the underlying mechanisms that govern our online behaviors. As an academic, I have spent more than 20 years studying the intersection of psychology and technology, observing how the rise of social media and other Internet technologies have transformed human interactions in ways both profound and subtle. This book is the culmination of that research—a comprehensive exploration of the cognitive and emotional triggers that make social media such a powerful force in our lives.

Throughout this work, I draw on a diverse range of studies and theories to dissect the psychological processes at play in our digital engagements. From the gratification of instant feedback to the social validation of likes and shares, each chapter delves into a specific aspect of social media interaction, offering insights into why we are so captivated by these platforms. By understanding these processes, I think we can better navigate the digital landscape, making more informed choices about how we use social media and how it influences our lives.

Writing this book has not been without its challenges. The rapidly evolving nature of social media platforms means that new developments and trends are constantly emerging, often outpacing the research itself. At times, the rapidity of technological development moved faster than my writing speed. However, these challenges have also reinforced the importance of this work, as understanding the psychological impact of social media becomes ever more critical in our hyperconnected world.

My hope is that this book will serve as a valuable resource for academics, students, and professionals alike, offering a deeper understanding of the psychological underpinnings of social media behavior. Whether you are a researcher looking to explore new avenues of inquiry, a student eager to grasp the complexities of digital psychology, or simply a curious reader, I invite you to join me on this journey into the fascinating world of social media psychology.

As we delve into the reasons why we click, I encourage you to reflect on your own digital habits and consider the broader implications of these behaviors. By the end of this book, I hope you will have gained not only a greater awareness of the psychological processes that drive social media engagement but also a clearer perspective on how we can shape a healthier relationship with the digital world.

Finally, I would like to thank the friends and family who supported this project by listening to my ideas, brainstorming with me, and in the case of my son, Raymond Loewald, who contributed original artwork to this project. Specifically, thank you to the friends and work colleagues who suggested illustrative news stories and other ideas for my book: Angelia Messina, Pat Parmelee, Lucinda Ruch, Gina Fisk, Melanie Green, Danielle Jablanski, Herb Lin, Nicole Mathusa Anderson, Sandra Mercado Guadagno, Paul Koschel, Angel Jones, Ngoc Tran, and Lucy Cuetter Edwards. Thanks to the brilliant Stanford students in my Spring 2020 Psychology and Digital Propaganda class for feedback on Chapter 6. Special thanks go to Eleonore Mellon-Drahon for assistance with copy editing, proofreading, and literature searches. And, thank you to the students in my Fall 2023 Societal and Individual Impacts of Information Systems at the University of Oulu for their helpful feedback on early drafts of this manuscript. Special thanks to my dog, Elsa, who has kept me company through the writing process and has been a huge source of support. To friends and family who supported me during this arduous task, especially: Tonio Loewald, Barbara Yondorf, Cindy Kreek, Tom Yondorf, Annkathrin Weigel, Marina Dalfovo Deon, Janet Emerson, Brad Kearn, and Jaelle Loewald. I am lucky to have you in my life!

Reference

YouTube (n.d.). *David Bowie speaks to Jeremy Paxman on BBC Newsnight (1999)*. YouTube. https://www.youtube.com/watch?v = FiK7s_0tGsg.

CHAPTER 1

Introduction to psychological processes in social media

It was the summer of 2014 when the news stories started to appear. The headlines expressed outrage, shock, resignation, and helplessness in response to the publication of an experiment Facebook conducted on 700,000 users without their knowledge. A sampling of these headlines included "Facebook fiasco: Was Cornell's study of 'emotional contagion' an ethics breach?" (Chambers, 2014; July 1); "Users angered at Facebook emotion-manipulation study" (Murray, 2014; October 14); "Was the Facebook emotion experiment unethical?" (Albertson & Gadarian, 2014; July 1); "Should Facebook Manipulate Users?" (Lanier, 2017; June 30); "Facebook Manipulated 689,003 Users' Emotions for Science" (Hill, 2014; June 28); and "We're all just lab rats in Facebook's laboratory" (Vaughn-Nichols, 2014; June 30), which captured people's varied reactions to this news.

What caused all this outrage? Researchers conducted a week-long experiment in early 2012, in which several hundred thousand participants were randomly selected from Facebook's user database for a study examining whether positive and negative emotions were "contagious" and spread on social media. To examine this research question, the authors carried out two studies, one that altered the content of people's news feeds by reducing the number of positive terms (e.g., love, nice, and sweet; Pennebaker, Chung, Ireland, Gonzales, & Booth, 2007) appearing in their friends' posts, and a second that altered the content to reduce the number of negative terms (e.g., hurt, ugly, and nasty). Each experimental condition was paired with a control condition in which a comparable proportion of words on participants' news feeds were removed at random.

Using text analysis (the Linguistic Inquiry Word Count [LIWC]—described in detail later on in this chapter), the authors analyzed more than 3 million posts to determine whether positive and negative emotions were contagious and would spread through people's social networks on Facebook. The main dependent measures were the quantity of negative and positive emotion words in participants' own posts. Results revealed

Psychological Processes in Social Media
DOI: https://doi.org/10.1016/B978-0-12-811320-2.00002-2

that, as predicted, emotions were contagious and spread throughout the social network. Specifically, people whose news feeds were altered to reduce the number of negative emotion words wrote posts conveying more positive and fewer negative emotions relative to participants in the control condition, while people whose news feeds had the number of positive emotions reduced showed the opposite changes to their posts, using more negative and fewer positive emotion words.

Once the results of this study were published, the public reaction was varied but generally expressed concern at the ethics of the experiment especially given that the sole reference to ethical considerations in the paper stated: "consistent with Facebook's Data Use Policy, to which all users agree to prior to creating an account on Facebook, constituting informed consent for this research" (Kramer, Guillory, & Hancock, 2014, p. 8789). This was particularly the case in the social and personality psychology academic community as well as in related social science disciplines as they pondered whether the procedures employed in this research were ethical with respect to research with human subjects. Indeed, the Editor-in-Chief, Dr. Inder Verma, of the journal, *Proceedings of the National Academy of Sciences*, that published the paper issued an "Editorial Expression of Concern" in which he acknowledged that, while the research may not have followed the principles of informed consent that are (1) standard in research on human subjects and (2) required for all research conducted at institutions that receive federal funding such as universities, corporations such as Facebook are not currently held accountable to the same rules (Verma, 2014).

In telling this story, I am not suggesting that these scholars did anything wrong in this scenario. Instead, I present this as an example of the ways in which corporate interests do not always align with ethical guidelines provided by the university Institutional Review Boards (IRBs; a university committee that reviews, approves, and monitors research involving human participants) nor with people's expectations for privacy when they use the Internet. While thousands of psychologists and other scientists now study social behavior on the Internet, this experiment is unique in that it was one of the first to raise people's awareness that their behavior while using social media is not private and that their experiences are subject to experimentation without their knowledge. This is part of the price people pay for their free social media accounts—many social media companies today make money through advertising and the better able social media companies are to target ads, the more money they make.

What is social media?

While the Internet has long been used by people to socialize and express themselves, in the last decade, social media has enhanced people's ability to use technology for this purpose. Today's social media applications represent the pinnacle of Web 2.0 technologies which center on user-created content more so than previous iterations of the Web (O'Reilly, 2005).

The phrase *social media*, often used synonymously with the phrases *social networking site (SNS)*, *social networking platform*, and *social media platform*, specifically refers to

> *"Web-based services that allow individuals to (1) construct a public or semi-public profile within a bounded system, (2) articulate a list of other users with whom they share a connection, and (3) view and traverse their list of connections and those made by others within the system." (Boyd & Ellison, 2007, p. 211)*

Thus, the common properties of social media include (1) a profile which is created when a person creates an account on an SNS, is customizable, and informs other SNS users and advertisers about the person and (2) suggests connections by browsing people's email inboxes and cell phone contacts and based on the people social media users are already connected with. A person's social media network typically starts by connecting to people in user's offline social networks but expands over time as people encounter new people through the SNS; and (3) a means of navigating through the software program by viewing the content provided by the other users (with whom they are typically connected). Across the various SNSs, people make new friends and find new romantic partners, maintain existing relationships with friends and family, search for information (e.g., product, restaurant, book, and movie reviews) and job leads, and converse with others on a scale larger than that afforded by previous forms of Internet technology. While the details and purpose of social media applications vary widely, their common features include a focus on mapping people's connection with others. The appeal of social media is well known, and its adoption has been widespread globally. See Table 1.1 for a description of the key features and country of origin for the most popular social media applications in 2018.

What types of behaviors do people typically engage in on social media? As indicated earlier, people start off by creating an account which provides a customizable profile that often includes a photograph of the users as well as information on their profession, geographic location, hobbies, and interests. Depending on the specific functionality of the

Table 1.1 Popular social media applications by type.

Social media type	Name	Key features	Country of origin
Personal	Baidu Tieba	Users spend time socializing in virtual bars organized by special interest (e.g., celebrities, pop culture, and books).	China
Personal	Facebook	Largest global social media application centers on the news feed in which people read and interact with their friends' (other users they have mutually connected with) posts (called status updates).	United States
Messaging	Facebook Messenger	Private messaging system spun off from Facebook's chat system. Supports voice and video calls, sharing of photos, videos, and text.	United States
Videosharing	Instagram	Users publicly or privately share video- or photo-centric posts.	United States
Messaging	LINE	Launched as a disaster response system, now more popular for gaming. Users can exchange text, images, video, and audio.	Japan
Business	LinkedIn	Allows users to create a profile highlighting their occupational achievements, search for jobs, and network with colleagues.	United States
Personal	Pinterest	Scrapbooking social network in which users create, organize, and share images (pins) on compilations (pinboards).	United States
Messaging	QQ	Messaging system that supports social games, text and voice chat, shopping, microblogging, and consuming music and film.	China

(Continued)

Table 1.1 (Continued)

Social media type	Name	Key features	Country of origin
Personal	QZone	Users customize their profiles by specifying the music and background décor.	China
News aggregator	Reddit	News aggregator in which people subscribe to user-created interest groups called "subreddits." People's posts are evaluated by others with the most popular featured most prominently.	United States
Microblog	Sina Weibo	"Weibo" means microblog in Chinese. Users share posts with images, news, and videos for other users to comment on.	China
Business	Skype	Primarily used for video and voice calls between two or more individuals. Also supports text messaging.	Sweden, Denmark, and Estonia
Messaging	Snapchat	An image-based messaging system in which the images (called "snaps") are only available for a limited time.	United States
Messaging	Telegram	Instant messaging system that supports the transmission of any file type.	United Kingdom
Microblog	Tumblr	Users can create their own blog and/or follow other users' blogs managed primarily through the dashboard.	United States
Microblog	Twitter[a]	People consume curated news and information as users decide whose posts (tweets) to follow. Tweets are limited in length.	United States
Messaging	Viber	Instant messaging application that supports text, audio, and video chatting	Israel

(*Continued*)

Table 1.1 (Continued)

Social media type	Name	Key features	Country of origin
Messaging	WeChat	Called China's "app for everything," it supports text, image, and video messaging (one-to-one and one-to-many) as well as payments	China
Messaging	WhatsApp	Instant messaging application that supports text, audio, and video chatting as well as location and file sharing	United States
Videosharing	YouTube	People upload videos for sharing with others who view, evaluate, comment on, and share their videos.	United States

[a]Since this writing, Twitter was purchased by Elon Musk and been renamed "X" or "X.com". However, the social media platform is still typically referred to as Twitter.

application and the privacy settings selected, people contact with other SNS either by mutually following or otherwise connecting one another which gives each person reciprocal access to their profile and posts or by following or subscribing to a person's posts which may or may not result in reciprocal access. Once people have social media friends, subscribers, or followers, they have a built-in audience for the information of the post and when following others, this gives people content to interact with as well. Typically, people post messages to share personal or professional photos, videos, and news as well as links to news and information of interest. Other social media users may comment on, share, like, and/or favorite these posts. Some social media applications, such as Facebook, allow users to react to others' posts using emojis expressing emotions such as love, amusement, surprise, sadness, happiness, and anger. These interactions are typically public—depending on privacy settings, this may be restricted to the interactants' friends or open to the entire social media user base—so that others can view their discourse. In addition to the public interactions, many SNSs also have private messaging available for one-on-one or small group conversations.

History of social media

While the earliest social media applications appeared in the late 1990s (e.g., Classmates Online, a social media application that connected people with their current and former classmates from school; SixDegrees, an invitation-only platform based on the premise that most people in the world are connected to others through six people or less), social media did not really enter mainstream consciousness until the mid-2000s when well-known applications such as MySpace, LinkedIn, and Facebook were first introduced. See Fig. 1.1 for a timeline displaying the introduction of social media applications of both historical and contemporary importance.

Initially, users trickled slowly into these applications. For instance, in the United States, only 7% of adults reported using social media in 2005. However, by 2015, that number reached 65%. Among American teenagers, the number is even higher with an estimated 71% on social media (Perrin, 2015; October). Over time, however, the number of social media applications as well as the number of users have grown—some estimates indicate that there are currently hundreds of social media applications today and an estimated 2.62 billion people use social media globally (Statistica, 2018a). Social media has become so popular that some reports suggest that social media use accounts for approximately one-third of the time people currently spend online (Global Web Index, 2017). This is more so the case in developed countries (e.g., North America, China, and Europe); however, as people in less developed parts of the world (e.g., North Africa and the Middle East) gain increasing access to the Internet—particularly through mobile devices, social media use is rapidly gaining users there too (Poushter, 2016, February 22).

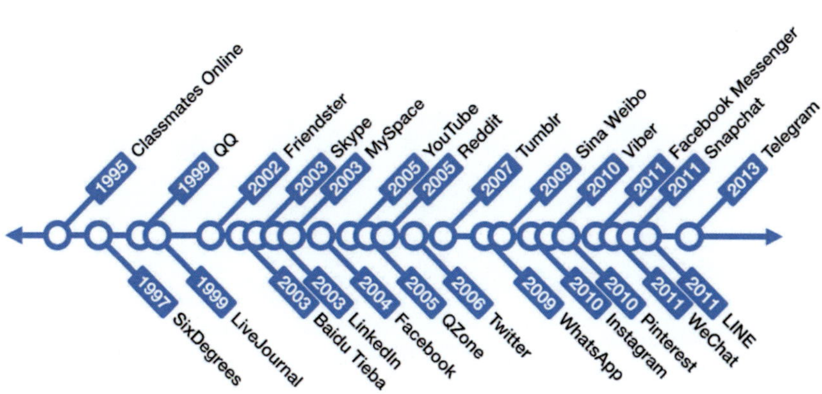

Figure 1.1 Timeline of social media applications.

Types of social media

Are all social media apps the same? The answer is no; many social media applications do have similar functionality and features but differ in purpose, degree of anonyminity, and privacy. Furthermore, the way people use social media varies widely and there are also broad geographic differences in social media use. For instance, the People's Republic of China does not permit the use of American social media applications such as Facebook, Twitter, and YouTube, in their country. Instead, there are quite a few social media applications that have been developed in China (WeChat, QQ, and so on) and are primarily used by people who live in China and surrounding countries. Similarly, Angiani, Fornacciari, Iotti, Mordonini, and Tomaiuolo (2018) propose that there are three main types of social media platforms: (1) business-related (e.g., LinkedIn) in

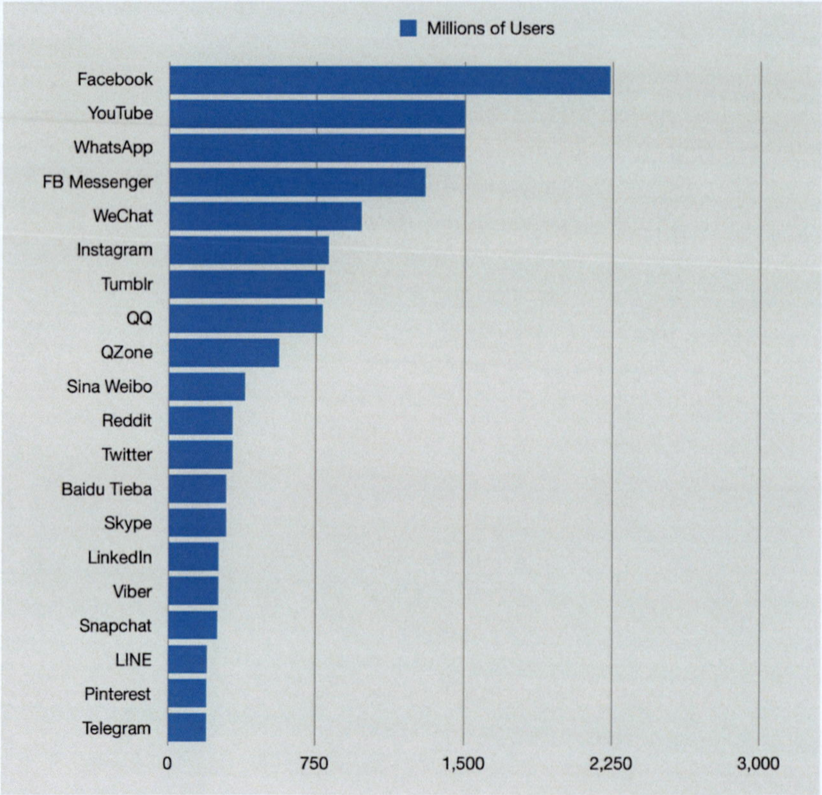

Figure 1.2 The world's most popular social media applications by estimated user base (Statistica, 2018b).

Figure 1.3 The pervasiveness of social media in today's society (Gouw, 2018; Edited by Tonio Loewald, 2018).

which a person's profile is at the forefront and is used largely to promote one's career and/or search for new opportunities; (2) microblogging (e.g., Twitter) in which people largely follow each other and share links to newsworthy (but not necessarily accurate) information and information sharing is the main point; (3) personal (e.g., Facebook) in which people both agree to friend each other in order to be connected. In this case, the emphasis is on user's news feed which presents posts and information from their friends in real time. In addition to these three types of social media, news aggregator, messaging, and media sharing round off the list. See Table 1.1 for a list of the most popular social media applications globally, Fig. 1.2 for estimated usage statistics for them, and Fig. 1.3 for a graphic illustrating the ubiquity of social media in contemporary society.

Psychological processes in the age of social media

Psychology is the scientific study of people's thoughts and behavior. Research in psychology uses the scientific method to enhance our understanding of people. The scientific method involves the development of theories which synthesize knowledge of a particular aspect of human cognition and/or behavior to make broad predictions about the concepts related to understanding a particular psychological phenomenon. Specific studies then test hypotheses derived from these theories by collecting and

Table 1.2 Psychology subdisciplines and typical social media research topics.

Subdiscipline	Description	Potential research topics
Clinical/ counseling	How to help people with mental or behavioral health issues	Does social media use make people depressed?
Cognitive	How to understand people's sensory perception, thoughts, and memory	How does social media use affect people's creativity?
Developmental	How people change over the course of their lifespan from infancy to adulthood	How does social media use affect the emotional growth of children?
Environmental	How people's physical environments affect their thoughts and behaviors	Does viewing environment-friendly products on social media increase people's purchase intentions?
Forensic/law	How psychological processes affects the criminal justice system	What types of crimes do people typically confess to on social media?
Health	The psychological factors that affect people's physical health and illnesses	Does membership in social media support groups improve the health of people with chronic illnesses?
Human factors/ engineering	Applies psychology research to improving people's experiences with technology and design	How can social media be designed to improve people's experiences using the application?
Industrial/ organizational	The psychological factors that affect people's experiences, outcomes, and interactions at work	How does social media use at work affect people's productivity?
Media	How the media (e.g., news, television, videogames, film, and Internet) influence people's thoughts and behavior	Do people's behavior on social media affect their offline behavior?
Neuropsychology	How the brain functions and influences people's thoughts and behavior	Does the amount of time people spend using social media affect their brain chemistry?

(*Continued*)

Table 1.2 (Continued)

Subdiscipline	Description	Potential research topics
Personality	How people's unique characteristics affect their thoughts and behavior	Do introverts (as compared to extroverts) use social media differently?
Physiological	How people's biological systems (e.g., genes, nervous system) affect their thoughts and behavior	How do interactions on social media affect people's cardioactive functioning?
Quantitative	Development of techniques and approaches to study and measure people's thoughts and behavior	Developing new data analysis techniques to extrapolate psychological meaning from people's activities on social media.
Social	How people's thoughts and behavior are influenced by other people	Does the behavior of people's social media friends affect the extent to which they self-disclose personal information in their posts?
Sports	How people's thoughts and behavior affect their performance in sports	How does reading a post on a competitor's tennis win affect a person's subsequent tennis performance?

analyzing data gathered from people. While there are many ways in which psychologists use the scientific method to predict and understand human cognition and behavior, this book focuses on the psychological study of social media. As a result, the research described in this book integrates research findings from a wide range of psychology subdisciplines (see Table 1.2 for a nonexhaustive list and examples of the types of research questions a typical psychologist from each subdiscipline may explore). In addition to psychology, there are other social science fields (e.g., communication, which studies the processes involved in the transmission of meaningful information) that also engage in the study of psychological processes in social media. While this book focuses on the psychological processes inherent in people's social media use, I draw research from all areas of psychology and closely related social science disciplines such as communication.

Research methodology

Research on social media employs many of the same research methodologies and data analysis techniques utilized in other areas of the psychological and social sciences. The key differences involve a shift to the use of social media as a means of directly obtaining samples and for data collection by downloading people's social media activities for analysis. Thus, some research reviewed in this book use self-report measures while others directly examine data captured about people's real-world activities (such as credit card and supermarket purchases) while using social media (also called a "digital footprint"). In the following sections, I review the practices researchers use to sample and collect data on people's social media use as well as some of the ethical considerations inherent in this type of research. The methods I highlight in this section are those that tend to be widely used in scholarship on social media. As a result, understanding the basics of these methodologies is an important foundation for understanding the research reported throughout this book.

Snowball sampling

Much like how snowballs accrue over time to create large snowdrifts, snowball sampling refers to the practice of asking subjects in a study to recruit additional subjects (Goodman, 1961). While asking study participants to recruit additional participants is not a new practice in and of itself, it works exceptionally well on social media in part because of the ease with which information spreads quickly and widely on social media ("going viral," Ellis-Barton, 2016). For example, one study employed snowball sampling to understand how scientists use Twitter (Ke, Ahn, & Sugimoto, 2017). To examine this, scientists were recruited via snowball sampling. The results revealed that social and computer scientists are overrepresented on Twitter relative to other scientists and that women scientists were better represented on Twitter relative to their (under) representation in journal articles. Thus, while this method of sampling is useful for rapidly spreading the call for participation among a population of interest, snowball sampling is not random, and this can impair the validity of research that employs this method.

Social network analysis

Another research methodology often used in studying psychological process in social media is *social network analysis* which examines the interconnections between multiple people (called nodes) within a network (Scott, 1988). For instance, with several colleagues, I recently conducted a study which examined gender differences in communication via Yammer—a social media application developed by Microsoft for use in businesses (Guadagno, Nelson, & Lock Lee, 2018). While previous research indicates that women are more likely to engage in relationship maintenance and less task focused while using social media (e.g., Muscanell & Guadagno, 2012), to date, no one has examined gender difference in social media use within the workplace—a context that has traditionally been male dominated. To examine this, we conducted a social network analysis using data from 6 months of social media communication in an Australian bank with approximately 7500 employees and an equal amount of men and women. Consistent with research on personal social media use, our results revealed that the women in the sample were more collaborative and communicative with one another and had stronger social networks relative to men. Furthermore, the women in our sample were also more likely to initiate communication with their male colleagues than the men were with each other. Thus this is just one example of the many ways in which social network analysis can help social scientists understand the role that social media plays in people's interactions with one another.

Data collection directly from people's behavior

Another new research methodology that has emerged in the era of social media is the use of people's actual behavior (posts, comments, likes, shares, and time in the application) as variables of interest in research on the psychological processes in social media use. Referred to as digital footprints, this method is often used to predict psychological insights from people's social media behavior. This method was initially adopted by statisticians—called data scientists—working in industry settings. For instance, the popular retailer Target used this method to predict the stage of women's pregnancy and child-rearing based on these women's in-store purchases. As someone pregnant with twins at this time (and an avid Target shopper), I was amazed that Target always sent me coupons and store promotions for products relating to pregnancy and babies just as I was starting to think about my future needs. It was as if Target knew my mind and my plans better than I did. It turns out that Target did as my purchasing behavior, along with that of many other moms to predict their pregnancy and child-rearing needs. From my perspective, this was an insightful approach to customer service. Unfortunately, the use of people's data in this manner blew up in Target's face when parents with underage daughters started receiving similar mailings with coupons for products related to babies and pregnancy. Target's helpful, targeted marketing is how many of these parents found out their teenagers were pregnant (e.g., Hill, 2012; February 12).

Since then, the use of digital footprints has been applied to the social media realm both by social media companies that routinely use people's behavior on their applications for research purposes (e.g., Bakshy, Eckles, Yan, & Rosenn, 2012) and by scholars who have developed techniques for downloading or "webscraping" people's posts from different social media platforms including Facebook (e.g., Guadagno et al., 2013a), movie ratings and discussion sites (Lee, Hosanagar, & Tan, 2015), to online dating services (Rudder, 2014). Scholars have also started correlating Google search data with psychological and other social science outcomes (e.g., Stephens-Davidowitz, 2017). For instance, Bakshy et al. (2012) found that people are more likely to like a product in a Facebook ad if their Facebook friends have already liked the ad. Similarly, Lee et al. (2015) found that people's movie preferences were more heavily influenced by their friends' evaluations relative to those of strangers. Thus the use of digital footprints to understand people's thoughts and behavior while using social media examines both people's behavior within a specific application and the relationship between real-world behavior and people's digital activities.

Inferring psychological states from text

While the analysis of the written word to derive psychological meaning from people's writing is not new nor it is specific to social media, this approach has been widely utilized in research on social media and is sometimes called *sentiment analysis* as a reference to the idea that people's affective states can be extrapolated from their writing (Pang & Lee, 2008). In the field of psychology, there is one sentiment analysis program that is the most commonly employed for this purpose, and as a result, it is both highly reliable and has been widely validated. The LIWC, pronounced "Luke," (Pennebaker, Booth, Boyd, & Francis, 2015) has been cited in more than 4900 scholarly works (Boyd & Pennebaker, 2017) and was developed by Professor Jamie Pennebaker and his colleagues at the distinguished University of Texas, Austin. The LIWC was initially designed to analyze people's written journal entries (Pennebaker, Francis, & Booth, 2001) to derive insight into their psychological states (Pennebaker, 2011). The software classifies people's written language on 80 different psychological and grammatical aspects of language (see Pennebaker, Boyd, Jordan, & Blackburn, 2015). Its output also provides aggregate data on the mean words per sentence, total overall words, the proportion of words the built-in dictionary understood, and the proportion of complex terms and determines the extent to which written passages express psychological states (Boyd & Pennebaker, 2015).

Studies utilizing the LIWC for text analysis have demonstrated that people's writing provides insights into their mental and physical well-being, personalities, social behavior, and cognition (see Boyd & Pennebaker, 2015). Specifically, researchers have found that linguistic data analyzed by the LIWC predicts outcomes such as depression (De Choudhury, Gamon, Counts, & Horvitz, 2013) and individual differences such as the five-factor model of personality (also called the "Big Five"; Park et al., 2015) and also captures a positive change in mental health after a victim of sexual harassment tweeted about it (Foster, 2015). Furthermore, research on the LIWC has also shown that people's language use is different with those people whom we are strongly connected to (e.g., close friends and family) relative to weaker ties (e.g., acquaintances and former work colleagues) (Gilbert & Karahalios, 2009; April). Taken together, these short examples illustrate the importance of sentiment analysis broadly and the LIWC specifically to understand the psychological processes in social media.

Ethics of social media research

In my career, I have often taught statistics and research methods—a common teaching assignment for social psychology faculty members. One thing I always discuss with my students (both in courses and in my research lab) is that, as researchers, we are morally and ethically obligated to follow the rules and regulations for research with human subjects that have been established by our field, our IRBs, and our governments. However, I also tell my students that, within those parameters, each individual must make some personal decisions about how much risk they are willing to take with their human research participants in their pursuit of knowledge. This is particularly a concern for psychological scientists. such as myself, who sometimes employ deception in my research as a means of eliciting a certain psychological state (e.g., the argument is that if you tell people you want to make them sad or angry or observe them while they make a new friend, people will alter their behavior in response to the warning, Aronson, Ellsworth, Carlsmith, & Gonzales, 1990). As Aronson et al. states: "experimenters often find themselves in the troublesome position of concealing the truth from their subjects in order to reveal a truth about human behavior (p. 89)."

When studying people's social media use, there are ethical concerns unique to the context (i.e., of conducting research on the Internet) because participants are not known to researchers in the way they are when participants are recruited in person for research. As a result, there are numerous general issues that should be considered when studying people's social media use that pertain to the privacy of participant data, proper consenting and debriefing of research participants, and participant confidentiality and anonymity. Because this area of research is relatively new, guidelines for the ethical treatment of participants whose data is gathered through social media are still emerging. However, there are some relevant organizations, such as the Association of Internet Researchers (AoIR) that have begun to discuss these issues. For instance, AoIR recently published guidelines for conducting research on the Internet more broadly (Markham & Buchanan, 2012). The AoIR guidelines pose questions and provide examples and discussion pertaining to the ethical treatment of participants in the context of social media research and research on the Internet more broadly. Examples of the issues considered in these guidelines include the following: (1) "Is one's digital information an extension of the self?" (p. 7); (2) "Will capturing a person's Tweets cause them harm?" (p. 7); (3) What constitutes public versus private information online?; (4) What are the ethical implications in the short and long term of explicitly stating the content of a person's social media posts?; (5) What are the participant risks associated with technologies that preclude removing information that can identify them (e.g., photographs)?; and (6) How do researchers determine which information posted on social media is public and which is private? In the following sections, I briefly explore these ethical considerations as they ought to be considered when planning and conducting Internet research.

Privacy of participant data

When people post their photographs on social media, who owns the photo? Do social media companies? Does the person who took the photo? Or the person who posted it? What about the people who are in the photo? If they are members of the social media application, a person in a photo can be "tagged" such that other users will find the photo when searching for them by name. Part of the answer to these questions is currently being battled out in court. Specifically, a group of the US Facebook users are suing the company for using their images (i.e., their faces) in photographs for facial recognition research without their consent, therefore violating their privacy. Specifically, the users are arguing that Facebook does not have consent to use their images for this (or any other purposes; Bennett, 2017; July 31). Facebook is also being sued for having collected more than just our data from our use of the app (Ingram, 2018; March 27). These legal cases raise ethical issues surrounding the question of risk to human research subjects when the data gathered by social media renders it impossible to remove people's identifying information as is the case with people's faces.

These concerns are not limited to images—they also have implications for people's posts and other information available on the Internet (e.g., people's health records and the results of people's DNA analyses). For instance, one study reported that people can be identified by the content (i.e., text) of their posts (Dawson, 2014) through the strategic use of Google searches and/or the assistance of an individual with the right technical skills. For instance, using these methods, the researcher identified the individual behind a passage posted online in 11.2% of articles identified as publishing quotes from people's posts. Among this subset of scholarship, only one article stated that the research team had obtained permission from the IRB to quite excerpts directly from their raw (i.e., nonanonymized) data. The majority of remaining articles in this subset failed to explicitly discuss the ethics of publishing direct quotes nor did the authors alter any content of the posts as a means of anonymizing the data. The upshot is that while most scholars who study people's behavior online are careful about protecting the privacy of their participants, this is not yet a universal ethical standard.

Proper consenting and debriefing of research participants

As illustrated in the Facebook contagion study reviewed at the start of this chapter (Kramer et al., 2014), another ethical consideration unique to social media research (and research on the Internet more broadly) pertains to the issue of suitable participant consent and, if deception is used in research, debriefing. With respect to consent, it may be difficult to obtain consent when people's information is being "scraped" (captured by automated ingestion and analysis of web pages by "crawlers" or "bots"; Guadagno et al., 2013a), or when consent is obtained as part of an end-user agreement that the typical person agrees to without reading. Even when people willingly fill out surveys on their social media experiences, consent is still typically obtained remotely much data is collected online.

As some scholars have pointed out, adequately addressing concerns about proper consent and debriefing is difficult when participants are recruited online and remotely rather than brought into a researcher's lab because "researchers have less control over and knowledge of the research environment and cannot monitor the experience of participants, or indeed their true identities" (Gosling & Mason, 2015, p. 894). Specifically, when human subjects participate in an experiment conducted in a researcher's lab, they have a shared physical presence with the researcher. Thus, the researcher can ensure that the subject provides (and understands) informed consent and if a subject withdraws prematurely from a study, the researchers will still debrief them. With data collected via social media, sometimes researchers do not obtain informed consent, nor do they debrief participants, and sometimes it is difficult to ensure that participants have read and comprehended the consent and debriefing. In this context, subjects who terminate their participation prior to the conclusion of the experiment are unlikely to get debriefed (Miller, Crowe, Weiss, Maples-Keller, & Lynam, 2017). This also makes it difficult to reach and assist a participant experiencing psychological distress in response to the experiment.

Social media demographics

Who uses social media? Why do people use social media? Women outnumber men on social media use across all. However, some social media applications have an even larger gender discrepancy in their user base. For instance, 44% of American women but only 16% of men report using Pinterest; and on news aggregator social media applications such as Reddit, there are twice as many male as female users (20% vs 11%) (Anderson, 2015; August 28). Similarly, social media is used more by young adults than older adults—90% of Americans between the ages of 18–29 report using social media, while only 35% over 65 do (Perrin, 2015; October 8).

In other Western, primarily individualistic societies such as Canada, social media usage patterns are quite similar to the United States (Gruzd, Jacobson, Mai, & Dubois, 2018). However, in Eastern, largely collectivistic countries such as China, the usage patterns are somewhat different. For instance, in China, there are more male than female social media users (57% vs. 43%, Gaille, 2017; May 31). Similarly, overall, usage is lower than the United States and Chinese adults between the ages of 26–30 are the most prevalent users (30%). Other data indicates that globally, social media use is quite high—76% of people with Internet access across 40 countries with the highest prevalence of social media use in Jordan (90%) and the lowest in Japan (51%), Germany (50%), and Pakistan (50%) (Poushter, 2016, February 22).

Generally, the evidence indicates that wealthier and more educated people tend to be more fervent social media users (Perrin, 2015; October 8; Poushter, 2016, February 22). However, other data suggest that the biggest determinant in social media use is based on age, with millennials—people born between the early 1980s and the late 1990s/early 2000s—being the heaviest social media users. Illustrative of this, in one of my early social studies, I examined whether homeless young adults differed in their social media use relative to age-matched yet wealthier and more educated college students (Guadagno et al., 2013a). Prior to designing this study, if I had been asked to state my predictions on whether homeless young adults used social media, my response would have been one of puzzlement. While I could imagine a homeless millennial using a library computer to search for a job or keep in touch with family, the idea that someone might be homeless but also on Facebook or another SNS never would have occurred to me.

Thus, when my colleague, Dr. David Pollio, started describing the results of a recent study he had conducted on homeless young adults, I was quite surprised by his findings. Not only did homeless young adults use technology, they owned technology such as an old laptop or phone, and they had a network of friends who were homeless and used technology. He found that homeless young adults trade information on free wireless hotspot locations and regularly use the Internet to keep in touch. As a result of these experiences, Professor Pollio and I, along with one of my graduate students (now a professor), Nicole Muscanell, set out to assess social media use among college students and age-matched homeless young adults. Overall, we found that nearly all college students reported using SNSs, especially Facebook. That would not be surprising to most people who watch technology news. The surprise to us was that nearly 75% of homeless young adults reported using SNSs. We also found little difference relative to freshmen college students in what they use it for Guadagno et al. (2013b).

Overview of the book

The book contains a series of introductory/foundation chapters describing key differences between people and differing contexts that have broad implications for understanding people's thoughts and behavior on social media. It reviews the wide-ranging ways in which social media can be used to influence people's perceptions of reality and alter their attitudes and behavior. It synthesizes the literature on how social media affects interpersonal interactions. Finally, the book analyzes research related to social media as it affects other aspects of life such as people's well-being, romantic relationships, gender roles, and our perception of privacy.

Summary

This chapter introduced the psychological study of social media by reviewing the history of social media, providing a working definition of social media, and analyzing the different popular platforms across the globe. The section "research methodology" reviewed different methodologies unique to social media and/or widely used in this research. Key ethical issues in social media research and practice were explored as were key demographic differences in social media use. Finally, we concluded with an overview of the entire book.

References

Anderson, M. (2015, August 28). *Men catch up with women on overall social media use*. From http://www.pewresearch.org/fact-tank/2015/08/28/men-catch-up-with-women-on-overall-social-media-use/ (Retrieved 22.05.18).

Angiani, G., Fornacciari, P. Iotti, E., Mordonini, M., & Tomaiuolo, M. (in press) Participation in online social networks: Theories and models. *International Journal of Interactive Communication Systems and Technologies (IJICST)*, *8*(2), 36–55.

Albertson, B., & Gadarian, S. (2014, July 1). Was the Facebook emotion experiment unethical? *The Washington Post*. Retrieved from https://www.washingtonpost.com/news/monkey-cage/wp/2014/07/01/was-the-facebook-emotion-experiment-unethical/?utm_term = 0.15088275b53c.

Aronson, E., Ellsworth, P., Carlsmith, J., & Gonzales, M. (1990). *Methods of research in psychology*. New York: McGraw-Hill.

Bakshy, E., Eckles, D., Yan, R., & Rosenn, I. (2012, June). Social influence in social advertising: evidence from field experiments. In *Proceedings of the 13th ACM Conference on Electronic Commerce* (pp. 146−161). ACM.

Bennett, J. (2017, July 31). Facebook: Your face belongs to us. From https://www.thedailybeast.com/how-facebook-fights-to-stop-laws-on-facial-recognition (Retrieved 13.08.18).

Boyd, D. M., & Ellison, N. B. (2007). Social Network Sites: Definition, History, and Scholarship. *Journal of Computer-Mediated Communication*, *13*(1), 210−230. Available from https://doi.org/10.1111/j.1083-6101.2007.00393.x.

Boyd, R. L., & Pennebaker, J. W. (2015). A way with words: Using language for psychological science in the modern era. *Consumer Psychology in a Social Media World*, 222−236.

Boyd, R. L., & Pennebaker, J. W. (2017). Language-based personality: A new approach to personality in a digital world. *Current Opinion in Behavioral Sciences*, *18*, 63−68. Available from https://doi.org/10.1016/j.cobeha.2017.07.017.

Chambers, C. (2014, July 1). Facebook fiasco: Has Cornell's study of 'emotional contagion' an ethics breach? *The Guardian*. Retrieved from: https://www.theguardian.com/science/head-quarters/2014/jul/01/facebook-cornell-study-emotional-contagion-ethics-breach.

Dawson, P. (2014). Our anonymous online research participants are not always anonymous: Is this a problem? *British Journal of Educational Technology*, *45*(3), 428−437. Available from https://doi.org/10.1111/bjet.12144.

De Choudhury, M., Gamon, M., Counts, S., & Horvitz, E. (2013). Predicting depression via social media. *ICWSM*, *13*, 1−10.

Ellis-Barton, C. (2016). Ethical considerations in research participation virality. *Journal of Empirical Research on Human Research Ethics*, *11*(3), 281−285. Available from https://doi.org/10.1177/1556264616661632.

Foster, M. D. (2015). Tweeting about sexism: The well-being benefits of a social media collective action. *British Journal of Social Psychology*, *54*(4), 629−647. Available from https://doi.org/10.1111/bjso.12101.

Gaille, B. (2017, May 31). *29 Cool China social media statistics, demographics and trends*. From https://brandongaille.com/27-cool-china-social-media-statistics-demographics-and-trends/ (Retrieved 22.05.18).

Gilbert, E., & Karahalios, K. (2009, April). Predicting tie strength with social media. In *Proceedings of the SIGCHI conference on human factors in computing systems* (pp. 211-220). ACM.

Global Web Index (2017, September 11). *Social media captures over 30% of online time*. From https://blog.globalwebindex.com/chart-of-the-day/social-media-captures-30-of-online-time/ (Retrieved August 12, 2018).

Goodman, L. A. (1961). Snowball sampling. *The Annals of Mathematical Statistics*, *32*(1), 148−170. Available from https://doi.org/10.1214/aoms/1177705148.

Gosling, S. D., & Mason, W. (2015). Internet research in psychology. *Annual Review of Psychology*, *66*, 877−902. Available from https://doi.org/10.1146/annurev-psych-010814-015321.

Gruzd, A. Jacobson, J., Mai, P., & Dubois, E. (2018, February 26). The state of social media in Canada 2017: A new report from @SMLabTO. From http://socialmedialab.ca/2018/state-of-social-media-in-canada/ (Retrieved 23.05.18).

Hill, K. (2012, February 12). How target figured out a teen girl was pregnant before her father did. *Forbes*. Retrieved from https://www.forbes.com/sites/kashmirhill/2012/02/16/how-target-figured-out-a-teen-girl-was-pregnant-before-her-father-did/#72d076516668.

Hill, K. (2014, June 28). Facebook manipulated 689,003 users' emotions for science. *Forbes*. Retrieved from https://www.forbes.com/sites/kashmirhill/2014/06/28/facebook-manipulated-689003-users-emotions-for-science/#593f5cbf197c.

Ingram, D. (2018, March 27). Three Facebook users sue over collection of call, text history. *Reuters*. From: https://www.reuters.com/article/us-facebook-data-history/three-facebook-users-sue-over-collection-of-call-text-history-idUSKBN1H4032 (Retrieved 22.05.18).

Gouw, T. (2018). Adult city clothes clothing daytime enjoyment fun. Retrieved from https://all-free-download.com/free-photos/download/adult_city_clothes_clothing_daytime_enjoyment_fun_599902.html.

Guadagno, R. E., Loewald, T. A., Muscanell, N. L., Barth, J. M., Goodwin, M. K., & Yang, Y. L. (2013a). Facebook history collector: A new method for directly collecting data from Facebook. *International Journal of Interactive Communication Systems and Technologies*, *3*, 57–67.

Guadagno, R. E., Muscanell, N. L., & Pollio, D. E. (2013b). The homeless use Facebook?! Similarities of social network use between college students and homeless young adults. *Computers in Human Behavior*, *29*, 86–89.

Guadagno, R. E., Nelson, M., & Lock Lee, L. (2018). Peace data standard: A practical and theoretical framework for using technology to examine intergroup interactions. *Frontiers in Psychology*, *9*. Available from https://doi.org/10.3389/fpsyg.2018.00734.

Ke, Q., Ahn, Y. Y., & Sugimoto, C. R. (2017). A systematic identification and analysis of scientists on Twitter. *PLoS One*, *12*(4), e0175368.

Kramer, A. D., Guillory, J. E., & Hancock, J. T. (2014). Experimental evidence of massive-scale emotional contagion through social networks. *Proceedings of the National Academy of Sciences*, *111*(24), 8788–8790.

Lanier, J. (2017, December 20). Opinion | Should Facebook manipulate users? *The New York Times*. Retrieved from https://www.nytimes.com/2014/07/01/opinion/jaron-lanier-on-lack-of-transparency-in-facebook-study.html.

Lee, Y. J., Hosanagar, K., & Tan, Y. (2015). Do I follow my friends or the crowd? Information cascades in online movie ratings. *Management Science*, *61*, 2241–2258.

Markham, A. N., & Buchanan, E. A. (2012). *Recommendations from the AoIR Ethics Working Committee (Version 2.0)*. Retrieved from: http://aoir.org/reports/ethics2.pdf.

Miller, J. D., Crowe, M., Weiss, B., Maples-Keller, J. L., & Lynam, D. R. (2017). Using online, crowdsourcing platforms for data collection in personality disorder research: The example of Amazon's Mechanical Turk. *Personality Disorders: Theory, Research, and Treatment*, *8*(1), 26–34.

Murray, M. (2014, October 14). Users angered at Facebook emotion-manipulation study. *Today*. Retrieved from https://www.today.com/health/users-angered-facebook-emotion-manipulation-study-1D79863049.

Muscanell, N. L., & Guadagno, R. E. (2012). Make new friends or keep the old: Gender and personality differences in social networking use. *Computers in Human Behavior*, *28*(1), 107–112.

O'Reilly, T. (2005). What is web 2.0. Retrieved from: https://www.oreilly.com/pub/a/web2/archive/what-is-web-20.html.

Pang, B., & Lee, L. (2008). Opinion mining and sentiment analysis. *Foundations and Trends in Information Retrieval*, *2*(1-2), 1–135.

Park, G., et al. (2015). Automatic personality assessment through social media language. *Journal of Personality and Social Psychology*, *108*(6), 934–952.

Pennebaker, J. W. (2011). *The secret life of pronouns: How our words reflect who we are*. New York, NY: Bloomsbury.

Pennebaker, J. W., Booth, R. J., Boyd, R. L., & Francis, M. E. (2015). *Linguistic Inquiry and Word Count: LIWC 2015 [Computer software]*. Pennebaker Conglomerates.

Pennebaker, J. W., Boyd, R. L., Jordan, K., & Blackburn, K. (2015). *The development and psychometric properties of LIWC2015*.

Pennebaker, J. W., Chung, C. K., Ireland, M., Gonzales, A., & Booth, R. J. (2007). *The Development and Psychometric Properties of LIWC2007*.

Pennebaker, J. W., Francis, M. E., & Booth, R. J. (2001). *Linguistic inquiry and word count: LIWC 2001*. Mahway: Lawrence Erlbaum Associates.

Perrin, A. (2015, October 8). *Social media usage: 2005-2015*. From <http://www.pewinternet.org/2015/10/08/social-networking-usage-2005-2015/> (Retrieved 02.05.18).

Poushter, J. (2016, February 22). 3. Social networking very popular among adult internet users in emerging and developing nations. *Pew Research Center's Global Attitudes Project*. http://www.pewglobal.org/2016/02/22/social-networking-very-popular-among-adult-internet-users-in-emerging-and-developing-nations/.

Rudder, C. (2014). *Dataclysm: Who we are (when we think no one's looking)*. Random House Canada.

Scott, J. (1988). Social network analysis. *Sociology*, *22*(1), 109–127. Available from https://doi.org/10.1177/0038038588022001007.

Statistica (2018a). *Number of social media users worldwide 2010–2021*. From https://www.statista.com/statistics/278414/number-of-worldwide-social-network-users/ (Retrieved 12.08.18).

Statistica (2018b). *Leading global social networks 2018*. From https://www.statista.com/statistics/272014/global-social-networks-ranked-by-number-of-users/ (Retrieved 27.04.18).

Stephens-Davidowitz, S. (2017). *Everybody lies: Big data, new data, and what the Internet can tell us about who we really are*. New York: Harper Collins.

Vaughn-Nichols, S.J. (2014, June 30). We're all just lab rats in Facebook's laboratory. *ZDNet*. Retrieved from http://www.zdnet.com/article/were-all-just-lab-rats-in-facebooks-laboratory/.

Verma, I. M. (2014). Editorial expression of concern: Experimental evidence of massive scale emotional contagion through social networks. *Proceedings of the National Academy of Sciences*, *111*(29), 10779.

CHAPTER 2

The self in social media

All the world's a stage and the men and women merely players

Shakespeare & Marshall, 2004

Essena O'Neil had it all—she was beautiful, stylish, and had a fabulous life. Her amazing life was chronicled on her Instagram page which featured photo after photo of Essena wearing fashionable clothing, looking happy, while visiting beautiful places in her native country of Australia. To Essena's more than 500,000 followers, Essena's life was perfect, something to envy; something to aspire to. Then one day it all changed. It turned out that Essena's beautiful life was all a lie. As Essena explained in messages on her Instagram feed, she was "addicted to Social Media fame" (as cited in O'Neil, 2015, November 3) In her final messages, she explained that she was given money and clothing in exchange for the fabulous life she fabricated on her Instagram page, stating: "There is nothing cool about spending all your time taking edited pictures of yourself to prove to the world "you are enough"" (as cited in Roy, 2015, November 3). See Fig. 2.1 for additional comments on her motivations and Fig. 2.2 (Loewald, 2018) for a reproduction of one of her photos she took solely for the purpose of promoting her clothing. Today, there is one post on her Instagram account that states: "Social Media is NOT real life" (O'Neill, n.d.) (see Fig. 2.3). In today's social media environement, Essena would be described as one of the early social media *influencers*.

Essenaoneill Not real life. Only reason we went to the beach this morning was to shoot these bikinis because the company paid me and also I looked good to society's current standards. I was born and won the genetic lottery. Why else would I have uploaded this photo? Read between the lines, or ask yourself "why does someone post a photo....What is the outcome for them? To make a change> To look hot? Sell something> I thought I was helping young girls get fit and healthy. But I only realised at 19 that placing any amount of self worth on your physical form is so limiting! I could have been writing, exploring, playing, anything beautiful and real...Not trying to validate my worth through a bikini shot with not substance #celebrityconstruct

Figure 2.1 Quote from Essena O'Neill's now-defunct Instagram account in which she explains the truth behind one of her photos (O'Neill, n.d.).

Psychological Processes in Social Media
DOI: https://doi.org/10.1016/B978-0-12-811320-2.00003-4

Figure 2.2 Reproduction of one of Essena O'Neill's now-defunct Instagram images that she posted as a candid image but later admitted she was paid to advertise the shirt and jeans. *Photo credit: Loewald, T. A. (2018) Recreation of Essena O'Neil photo. (photograph). Half Moon Bay, CA, USA.*

Why would this beautiful young woman work so hard to convey a false impression of her life? Even more puzzling, once she became successful—rising to fame on social media, earning money, obtaining free products, and garnering hundreds of thousands of followers—why did she give it up and walk away from it all? Is Ms. O'Neill correct in her supposition that Social Media is fake and not reflective of real life? Do most people lie in their social media profiles and posts? While existing research indicates that people's online behavior can reflect certain aspects of themselves (e.g., Dunn & Guadagno, 2012; Guadagno, Muscanell, Okdie, Burke, & Ward, 2011), the ways in which people engage in self-expression on social media differ from previous forms of

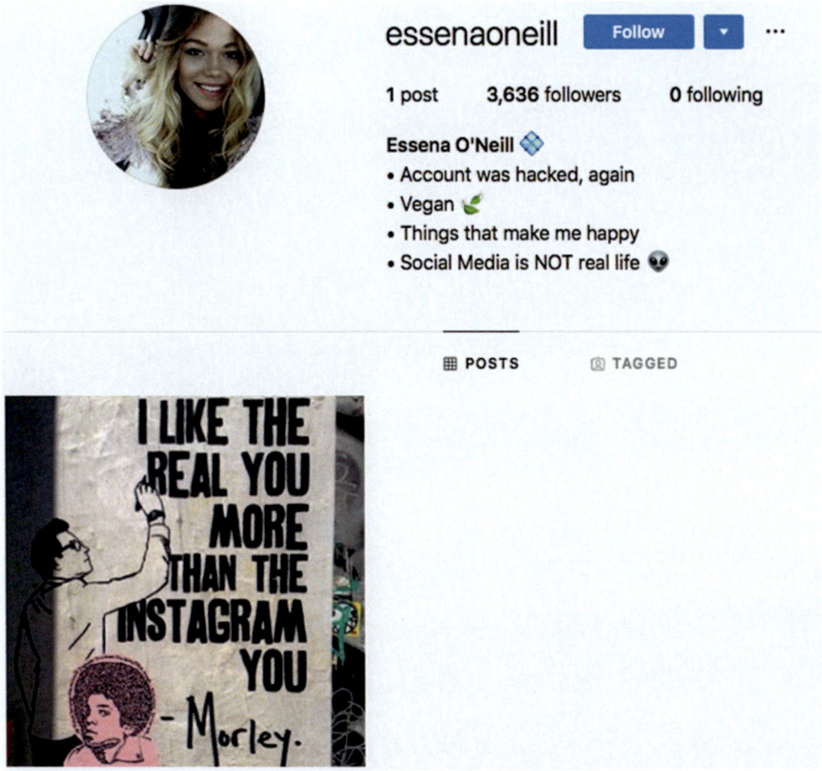

Figure 2.3 Screenshot of Essena O'Neill's Instagram page.

technology-mediated communication. This chapter explores the question of self-expression and social media to understand the extent to which people's social media use is an accurate (vs distorted or idealized) reflection of their selves. Furthermore, this chapter will examine whether people form accurate impressions of others based on their social media profiles and activities. Implicit in these issues is the question of impression formation, self-presentation, and social comparison. A unique aspect of social media is that many users' networks are composed of people from disparate parts of a person's life (e.g., childhood friends and family, coworkers, supervisors, and current and past romantic partners), many of whom hold conflicting thoughts, opinions, and beliefs on topics as wide ranging as politics to parenting. This requires individuals to manage multiple identities at once. Table 2.1 provides definitions and social media examples of the key concepts related to the self in social media.

Table 2.1 Definitions and social media examples of psychological concepts related to the self.

Concept	Definition	Social media example
Downward social comparison	When people compare themselves to less fortunate others as a means of feeling better about themselves	Cheryl did not get the promotion to vice president she wanted at work, so she spends time viewing Facebook pages of friends with minimum wage jobs
Impression formation	The characteristics people ascribe to people based on our observations and/or third-party descriptions	Thomas sees pictures of Frank drinking heavily posted on his Instagram page and forms the impression that he has a drinking problem
Self-concept clarity	The extent to which people have an easy to imagine mental representation of themselves	Tinga responds to a request to donate to her favorite senator on Twitter by quickly donating because she sees herself as the type of person who does such things
Self-consciousness	The extent to which people direct attention to themselves that can be private or public	Corey removes a post from Facebook after it became clear that his friends formed a negative opinion of him based on its content
Self-enhancement	People's motivation to create and project an inflated positive self-image	Lucy bought herself a new car with her annual bonus and posts pictures of herself posing with the new car with a bow tried around it on Pinterest
Self-esteem	People's (positive or negative) feelings about themselves	Joseph feels great about himself after he opens Facebook to hundreds of birthday greetings from his friends

(*Continued*)

Table 2.1 (Continued)

Concept	Definition	Social media example
Self-perception	How people see themselves; based in part by the inferences people draw about themselves after observing their own behavior	Gina notices that she "likes" a lot of political news stories on Twitter and this leads her to infer that she is a political activist
Self-presentation	The process individuals use to attempt to control the impressions others form of them, which also referred to as *impression management*	Anna posts a picture of herself next to the Google sign on her first day of work at the corporation to appear successful and competent to her social media followers
Social comparison	When people compare themselves to others based on social standing, skills, abilities, and other characteristics	Steve wonders how successful he is relative to his friends from college, so he compares his LinkedIn profile to his closest college friends to see who is the most successful
Upward social comparison	When people compare themselves to more successful others and it makes them feel bad about themselves	Sally reads Anna's post about her new job at Google and it makes her feel bad about herself

Self-presentation defined

Also called *impression management*, self-presentation is the process through which people attempt to influence the impressions others form of them (Goffman, 1959; Jones, 1990; Leary, 1995; Schlenker, 1980). While not typically deceptive, when people engage in self-presentation, they alter their behavior in the presence of others in an attempt to make a good impression. To accomplish this, people emphasize different personal characteristics to convey specific impressions to their audience based on their specific goals for the interaction. Thus people's self-presentational goals vary by context and are sometimes intended to convey the impression that they are likeable, competent, or have high status and are therefore powerful (Smith, Cody, Lovette, & Candry, 1990). Research suggests that people engage in self-presentation to obtain resources they desire (e.g., a new job, a raise in salary, or a favor), be perceived as likable, create a desired self-perception, or to influence others how to treat them (e.g., Levine & Feldman, 1997; Neuberg, Judice, Virdin, & Carrillo, 1993; Nezlek, Schütz, & Sellin, 2007). Illustrative of this, Goffman (1959) suggested that people must not only possess a certain status level but also dress for the part. He expressed this idea as part of his dramaturgical perspective in which he conceptualized social interactions as a theatrical performance in which people self-present through the use props and preplanned actions intended to create a desired impression. As Goffman asserted: "All the world is not, of course, a stage, but the crucial ways in which it isn't are not easy to specify."

Self-presentation on social media

How does social media use affect people's *self-presentation*? How do people engage in self-presentation on social media? Conveying the desired impression successfully is more complicated because self-presentation attempts through social media are typically seen by many more people than the intended audience. For instance, if a person wishes to share good news (e.g., a change in job or promotion, a new car, or the birth of a baby) with their families and posts this news on social media, the number of people likely to see their status update may be far larger depending on the size and composition of the person's network and their privacy settings. Furthermore, depending on the relational dynamics between the poster and their social media connections, good news such as the examples described above may not create the desired impression. Indeed, I had one particular nasty experience along these lines after sharing a positive teaching experience on Facebook which had the effect of *teaching me* that while many of my Facebook connections thought well of me as an instructor, this is not a universally held opinion. Thus the answer to the question of how social media use affects self-presentation is a complex one that will be explored in the literature reviewed in this chapter.

In one paper exploring these issues, Vogel and Rose (2016) reviewed the literature on people's self-presentation on social media. The authors theorized that people: "selectively present the most positive aspects of their lives, such that their lives appear unrealistically and successful (p. 294)."

This process is often referred to as an idealized[1] self-presentation, an allusion to the carefully selected nature of many people's social media postings. The authors hypothesized that to understand the positive and negative psychological impact of social media self-presentation, people's self-versus-other focus must also be examined. Specifically, Vogel and Rose argued that people who focus on their own social media self-images will experience positive well-being, while people who focus on others' curated self-presentations will experience detriments to their well-being. While I will have a lot to say about well-being later on in Chapter 9, the differences in the way people use social media will often be related to increased or decreased well-being. Illustrative of this latter point, Bazarova, Taft, Choi, and Cosley (2013) found that people with greater concerns about their self-presentation used more positive emotion words in their status updates, suggesting that greater self-focus is associated with more positive self-presentation.

Yang and Brown (2016) conducted a longitudinal study of self-presentation on social media among college students in the Midwestern United States by sampling them once at the beginning and again at the end of their first semester in school. The amount of time participants spent on Facebook, the number of Facebook friends, and dimensions of self-presentation on Facebook were assessed. Specifically, the amount of information participants self-disclosed, including the breadth (i.e., "What I put on Facebook was a fairly comprehensive representation of myself."), depth (i.e., "I openly shared my emotions."), positivity (i.e., "I normally express positive feelings about myself on Facebook."), authenticity (i.e., "My statements about my feelings on Facebook were always honest."), and intentionality (i.e., whether participants thought about the consequences of their posts) of this information, was assessed. In addition to these self-presentational dimensions, the authors also asked participants to provide input on their perceptions of their Facebook friends' responses to their posts. Finally, the authors assessed individual differences in participants' self-esteem, self-concept clarity, and self-reflection. Results revealed that 72% of participants in this study were experienced social media users with three or more years of Facebook use, while 28% were novice users and had used the site for less than 6 months. Between Time 1 and Time 2, self-reported self-presentational behaviors became broader, deeper, and

[1] This has also been colloquially referred to as a "curated self-presentation." This will be discussed in greater detail in the next sections.

less positive. While there was no difference with respect to authenticity and intentionality, engagement in self-presentation on social media predicted self-reflection and supportive feedback. Results also indicated that self-reflection negatively predicted self-concept clarity, while supportive audience feedback predicted increased self-esteem. Taken together, the overall results of this study demonstrate the dynamic manner of self-presentation on social media as it changes both over time and in response to interactions with people's social media connections.

Other research on social media and self-presentation has examined the role of culture (covered more thoroughly in Chapter 4) in this process. For instance, Lee-Won, Shim, Joo, and Park (2014) examined the role of self-consciousness and the proportion of IRL (In Real Life) friends—friendsships formed in people's offline lives—on people's Facebook connections on strategic social media self-presentation among individuals from Western, individualistic cultures (i.e., the United States, Canada, and Western Europe), as well as people from Eastern, collectivistic cultures (i.e., China, Central and South America, and South Korea; Lee-Won et al., 2014). In this case, the authors conceptualized strategic self-presentation as protective—in which the primary goal is to avoid looking bad—and acquisitive—in which the primary goal is to appear in a positive light (Rosenfeld, Giacalone, & Riordan, 1995) and suggested that this type of strategic self-presentation is associated with two potential forms of communication behaviors. Specifically, Lee-Won and colleagues argued that protective self-presentation involves: "controlling negative other-provided information about the self (p. 414)," while acquisitive self-presentation involves "disclosing or sharing positive self-provided information (p. 414)." Data were collected in the United States and South Korea. Their results revealed that culture did affect the type of strategic self-presentation people engaged in. Specifically, relative to South Korean participants, the US participants were more likely to report engaging in acquisitive strategic self-presentation. South Korean participants were more affected by the proportion of IRL friends in their social media networks. In this case, the fewer IRL friends in their Facebook networks, the more participants engaged in acquisitive self-presentation. Furthermore, among the South Korean sample, public self-consciousness also predicted engagement in this type of strategic self-presentation. Thus these participants spent more time curating their Facebook profiles when their audience comprised fewer people who actually knew them in their offline worlds and when they were high in public self-consciousness.

Stephens-Davidowitz (2017) noted that there is a discrepancy between what people post (publicly) on social media versus what they search for (privately) on Google. For example, he described a hypothetical young woman who publicly posts happy photos of her recent vacation with her boyfriend, while privately searches Google for relationship advice (e.g., "Why won't my boyfriend have sex with me?"). In another example of this, Stephens-Davidowitz uses big data techniques to illustrate the extent to which tabloid magazines and celebrity gossip are a guilty pleasure for many people (myself included!). He does this by comparing that the subscription rates and Google searches for Atlantic magazine—a credible and esteemed periodical—and the National Enquirer—a low credibility tabloid largely known to publish falsehoods—to the number of Facebook likes and shares of articles from each publication. There were just as many subscriptions and Google searches for the Atlantic as the National Enquirer. However, the Facebook data revealed that there were 27 likes and/or shares of an Atlantic article as there were for a National Enquirer article. Thus, as this data suggests, there may be a disconnect between people's actual online behavior and the behaviors that they promote publicly on their social media pages as a means of making a positive impression on their audience.

Motivations for using social media for self-presentation

According to the evidence reviewed earlier, most people use social media to engage in self-presentation. However, this evidence does not address the question of *why* people do this or what motivates people to engage in self-presentation on social media. Certainly, based on the evidence reviewed before, making a good impression is part of it. Illustrative of this, Nadkarni and Hofmann (2012) found that some of people's motivation to use Facebook can be explained by their desire to engage in positive self-presentation. Similarly, Vogel and Rose (2016) theorized that other-focused social media use leads to social comparison, a phenomenon in which people compare themselves to others based on characteristics such as social standing, skills, and abilities to evaluate and/or enhance the self (Suls, Martin, & Wheeler, 2002), but self-focused social media use leads to self-affirmation, in which people remind themselves of important and positive details about themselves and/or their lives (Sherman, 2013). Specifically, Vogel and Rose (2016) stated: "although the SNS profiles typically do reflect users' true selves (Back et al., 2010), users tend to emphasize the positive aspects of their lives (Chou & Edge, 2012; Qiu, Lin, Leong, & Tov, 2012) and portray themselves as popular, well-rounded, and thoughtful (Zhao, Grasmuck, & Martin, 2008)." Thus one way to understand the ways in which people use social media for self-presentation is that they generally attempt to be accurate in the information presented about themselves but selectively edit the information they disclose such that only generally positive news and information on themselves and their lives is shared with followers.

Park and Lee (2014) also examined social media use among college students, uncovering four motivations that predicted self-presentation on social media: entertainment, relationship maintenance, self-expression, and communication. They further found that these four factors plus concern for impression management predicted the intensity of Facebook use, defined as the extent to which people use Facebook to achieve relational goals such as communication and relationship maintenance. Facebook intensity was positively predictive of a sense of belonging in college. Belonging and impression management concern both positively predicted satisfaction with campus life. These results suggest that college's social media, particularly the extent to which they use it for interpersonal communication, is an important aspect of a rewarding college experience—a finding that has been shown in other studies as well (e.g., Jung, Youn, & McClung, 2007; Raacke & Bonds-Raacke, 2008).

Finally, much of the existing research on social media and self-presentation indicates that self-enhancement—people's motivation to convey a positive image—plays a large role in people's self-presentation on social media. For instance, evidence from research suggests that exhibitionism is the primary self-presentational motive for social media use (Mäntymäki & Islam, 2016; Wang & Stefanone, 2013).

The threatened self

What happens when people's self-images are threatened by others who hold differing (and often negative) impressions and are not afraid to publicly express this on social media? Wohn and Spottswood (2016) examined how people respond to such threats which they referred to as face threats, defined by Goffman (1967) as "a situation that occurs when a person's desired image [i.e., "face"] is challenged (p. 187)." The authors theorized that the features or *affordances* of social media, especially the "persistence and scalability take control away from the victim who is trying to save face (p. 189)" (Wohn & Spottswood, 2016). They hypothesized that people generally respond to face threats in one of four ways: (1) disengagement strategies, in which the person escapes or ignores the face threat; (2) redirective strategies, in which the victim engages but also deflects with a joke, an apology, or an excuse; (3) subtractive strategies, in which the target removes tags and asks the social media company for help; and (4) and addressive strategies, in which the victim confronts the offender. The authors predicted that the more severe face threats and the greater participants' perception that others were intending to inflict harm, the lower the perceived relationship closeness. To examine this, participants filled out a survey assessing these four different strategies in dealing with face threats. Results revealed that most participants (60%) reported engaging in subtractive strategies than the other types of response to face threats. The second most common response was addressive strategies, with half the sample reporting engaging in this type of response to face threats. Next, 34% of participants reported using redirective strategies and 29% of participants reported using disengagement strategies. See Table 2.2 for stories from participants on their different experiences.

The aftermath of a face threat affected the interpersonal dynamics between the target and perpetrator of face threats. Specifically, Wohn and Spottswood's (2016) study revealed that post–face threat, negative relationship outcomes included a decrease in communication frequency and an increase in redirective and subtractive strategies. Overall, the authors concluded that there was tension between the concerns of broadly managing self-presentation and managing relationships with others. I also suspect that these issues are not unique to interpersonal relationships as the same could be said for corporate, political, or government entities. Finally, the authors noted that because of the affordances of social media, people employ different responses to face threats when they occur on social media relative to when they occur offline.

Social comparison and curated self-presentation

As is illustrated by the abovementioned research, an important aspect of self-presentation on social media is that—as in people's offline, face-to-face interactions—attempts at self-presentation on social media entail the transmission of overwhelmingly positive self-relevant information. However, these attempts are also heavily curated to selectively emphasize only the most positive aspects of a person's life (see Fig. 2.4) (Loewald, 2024).

Table 2.2 Participant examples of responses to face threats (Wohn & Spottswood, 2016).

Strategy	Definition	Example reported by participant
Disengagement	A person escapes or ignores the face threat	"Some high school classmates of mine posted some photos of me bare chest naked in tight shorts with two other male classmates with the same attire. One of the guys in the photo "came out of the closet" proclaiming he was gay during the college years. I felt embarrassed with the photo because some people might misinterpret it. I am not gay but I don't want to seem homo-phobic demanding to take down that photo. (Daniel, 41)" (p. 190)
Redirective	The victim engages but also deflects with a joke, an apology, or an excuse subtracting strategies	"I thought it was an adorable thing to post for Valentine's Day but given my tumultuous, uncertain relationship with my ex-boyfriend/current best friend, it was especially awkward when he commented on it, alluding to my interest in getting back together with him. I commented in response to his comment on my post, trying to minimize his comment." (Gwen, 23) (p. 190)
Subtractive	The target removes tags and may ask the social media company for help	"There have been a number of times when I was tagged in embarrassing or unflattering photos. One extreme situation occurred

(*Continued*)

Table 2.2 (Continued)

Strategy	**Definition**	**Example reported by participant**
		during my junior year of high school when I joined the high school swim team. I, like all the other swimmers, was required to wear a Speedo, which showed off my amazingly white thighs. I immediately untagged myself and asked my friend to remove the photo altogether. (Peter, 20)" (p. 191)
Addressive	The victim confronts the offender	"I was out with a friend of mine drinking, and there was a really hot girl where we were having the drinks. I was trying to talk to her, but I was really drunk! I ended up puking all over her, and even on myself! I saw my friend, and I made him promise not tell anyone. The next day I heard he put some comments on Facebook about what happened. I called him up, and he laughed at me. I felt like a fool! I have not talked to him, or even seen him ever since, and I deleted him as a friend on Facebook. (Cliff, 20)" (p. 191)

As a result, there is an absence of well-rounded details about the person engaging in self-presentation and observers form the impression that their social media friends' lives are uniformly better than theirs. In doing so, there are social costs of this type of curated self-presentation—in terms of perceptions of trustworthiness, lost opportunities for social support, and

Figure 2.4 Social media as a exaggerated reflection of ourselves Loewald, R. J. (2024). Curated Self-presentation. (digital art). Oulu, Finland.

because this type of behavior makes other people feel bad about their own lives. Selective sharing of the most positive aspects of one's life makes other people feel bad about themselves and denies the self-presenter social support when they need it.

Social comparison on social media

That said, people do engage in this kind of curated self-presentation on social media. This begs the following questions: Why do people engage in such behaviors? And, what is the overall impact of such behaviors? One often-mentioned explanation for people's overly positive self-presentation on social media is a form of social comparison. These comparisons can be either upward, in which people compare themselves to successful others, or downward, in which the comparison against someone fairing more poorly in life. Research on social comparison has demonstrated that social comparison helps people gauge whether they are likely to be successful in a new endeavor (Wheeler, Martin, & Suls, 1997), generally serves to give people feedback on how well they are doing in life relative to others, and has been linked to psychological well-being (Wood, Taylor, & Lichtman, 1985). Similarly, Vogel, Rose, Roberts, and Eckles (2014) make the point that both upward and downward social comparison will sometimes make people feel better and other times make people feel worse (Vogel et al., 2014).

In the context of social media, research has established that people to engage in social comparison with people in their social networks (Vogel, Rose, Okdie, Eckles, & Franz, 2015). Furthermore, the existing literature suggests that individual differences in self-esteem, gender, engagement with (i.e., the amount of time spent using) a social media application, and propensity to engage in social comparison affect the extent to which people engage in social comparison with their social media friends. For instance, in two studies, Vogel et al. (2014) examined how engaging in upward social media comparisons affected people's self-esteem. Their first study revealed that, based on self-reports, increased Facebook use was negatively correlated with self-esteem. Greater Facebook use was also related to an increased propensity for both upward and downward social comparison. The propensity to engage in upward but not downward social comparison mediated the relationship between Facebook use and self-esteem. In Study 2, the authors conceptually replicated Study 1 in an experiment that varied the direction of social comparison information (upward vs downward) and whether the social comparison information was based on either: (1) information provided in another Facebook user's profile revealing that this target individual engaged in healthy (upward social comparison) or unhealthy behavior (downward social comparison) or (2) based on their social media activity levels (high vs low), defined as the extent to which the target person liked, shared, and posted. Social networking activity but not user profile information affected participants' self-esteem. Specifically, after viewing a high-activity target individual, participants' self-esteem decreased. Participants also rated the comparison person higher than themselves in the upward comparison conditions. Thus these results illustrate the close connection between people's social media use and their resulting feelings about themselves.

The results of a natural experiment also highlight the impact that social media use has on people's propensity to engage in social comparison processes and also link social comparison to negative psychological outcomes. Specifically, Arad, Barzilay, and Perchick (2017) examined the impact of social media use on social comparison and happiness among employees in an Israeli security firm. As part of this firm's terms of employment, employees were initially prohibited from having a Facebook account. This policy lasted for several years and then company policy shifted such that, regardless of occupational role, people on some projects were permitted to open (or reopen) Facebook accounts. After this change in corporate policy, the authors were permitted to assess the extent to which employees engaged in social comparison, their overall happiness, and their Facebook use. Results revealed that Facebook users were significantly less happy than nonusers and that this relationship was mediated by greater levels of social comparison. Interestingly, their results also revealed that this finding was also affected by age such that younger employees—18 to 24 years old—were more affected than were older employees.

Similarly, Hanna et al. (2017) reported that increased Facebook use was associated with increased social comparison and self-objectification. These self-related factors were then predictive of decreased self-esteem, poorer mental well-being, and increased body shame. Evidence also suggests that men and women vary in the type of information they use for social comparison. For instance, Haferkamp and Krämer (2011) examined people's domain-relevant social comparison processes. Their initial pilot study revealed gender differences in the source of information used for social comparison such that men reported comparing themselves more to the details in other people's profiles (e.g., achievements, occupation, and education) while women reported comparing themselves more to others' profile pictures. Next, the authors conducted two small follow-up studies in which they varied the level of comparison other occupational success in the first study and the physical attractiveness of comparison others in the second study. Study 1 failed to find any differences with respect to social comparison when the target dimension was occupational success. However, the authors reported that their occupational success manipulation interacted with gender such that men, but not women, reported a greater discrepancy in their real versus ideal physical appearance when viewing the successful rather than unsuccessful target profile. However, in the second study, when physical attractiveness was manipulated through the attractiveness of other's profile pictures, the results revealed that downward social comparison—the condition in which participants viewed the physically attractive profile pictures—resulted in decreased reported positive affect and a greater discrepancy between participants' real versus idealized physical appearance. Thus, as the research reviewed in this section suggests, social media use can affect the positive regard people have for themselves as a result of social comparison processes. I will have more to say about the impact of social comparison of images and the differential impact this has on women and girls relative to men and boys in Chapter 4.

Managing multiple identities

As established earlier in this chapter, as part of the self-presentation process, people emphasize different traits depending on the context as a means of making the right impression (Goffman, 1959; Guadagno & Cialdini, 2007; Jones, 1990; Leary, 1995; Schlenker, 1980). For instance, when visiting our parents, a person may try to emphasize their maturity and self-sufficiency. When spending time with friends, people may be more willing to show their goofy sides. In the workplace, people focus more on establishing their competence. Depending on how we know someone, our impressions of them will be based in part on different information. This presents a challenge on social media because, based on the composition of people's social media connections, it is possible to simultaneously be a parent, child, sibling, friend, supervisor, coworker, and more all at once.

The features of a typical social media platform blend people from all the different domains of our existence together, making it difficult to manage multiple identities, referred to by some scholars as the online multiple audience problem (OMAP; Marder, Joinson, & Thirlaway, 2016). In such a context, how do people choose to present themselves? One of my students examined this issue in her dissertation (Muscanell, Guadagno, & Hamilton, 2014, July). Across three studies, the factors that affect the extent to which people engage in self-presentation, operationalized as sharing risky behaviors (e.g., alcohol consumption, negative comments about one's job, or other potentially inflammatory information), on social media were examined. In the first study, we found that people's willingness to report posting such information depended on their levels of self-control (i.e., the ability to self-regulate by inhibiting or changing impulses; Tangney, Baumeister, & Boone, 2004). In our second study, we found that the composition (similar others vs similar plus high-status others) and presence of an audience—the people likely to view participant's posts—only affected the degree of risky self-disclosures in people's mock social media posts when had sufficient mental resources available.

When they did not—after a manipulation that reduced participants' self-regulation ability—participants did not differentiate between the two audiences. In our third study, we found that presenting participants with an audience comprised people from multiple aspects of one's life (e.g., professors + students or just fellow students) lowered participants' performance on a series of math and English standard test questions. Taken together, these results indicate that people are aware of the presence of multiple audiences and this affects their self-presentation on social media in different ways depending on the extent to which people have the mental resources available to notice the composition of their audience.

Other research on the impact of multiple audiences has yielded evidence indicating that people are most motivated to tailor their self-presentation attempts to connections with the most reward power (Marder, Joinson, Shankar, & Thirlaway, 2016). Specifically, Marder and colleagues argue that in order for OMAP to affect people's self-presentation on social media, three conditions need to be met. First, the social networking account includes multiple audiences such as friends, boss, employees, and family. Second, the different audiences hold varying standards for appropriate self-presentation. Third, privacy settings (e.g., grouping circles which allow people to create subsets of their social media followers to better control the posts and other content audience members view) are not in use. To examine OMAP, Marder et al. examined whether the strength of audience—defined as social and economic reward power—impacted self-presentation in a study of nearly 400 students who were primarily British women. Their results indicated that the strongest audience predicted increased levels of self-censorship and social anxiety. Thus, when the OMAP arises, self-presentation attempts may be successful in making a positive impression on some audiences (e.g., family) but not on others (e.g., coworkers).

OMAP is also something that most social media users are generally aware of. For instance, one study also revealed that the majority of social media users—75% on Facebook—are aware of the OMAP as indicated by their admissions of self-censorship (Das & Kramer, 2013, June). OMAP was also a theme that arose in the study of Wohn and Spottswood (2016) reviewed before as well. In their work, participants reported resorting to juggling multiple identities, with some indicating tension between a response to a perceived face threat from one social media connection against concerns about the impact such a response would have on their larger audience.

Similarly, Marwick & boyd (2010) examined the multiple audience problem on Twitter. The affordances of Twitter are such that it is far easier for strangers with no connection to interact as most people do not have to approve followers' requests unless their account is locked such that only approved followers can read people's tweets (this is unusual – estimates suggest that approximately 10% of all Twitter users have locked accounts). As a result, most people do not have a good feel for the composition of their followers, many of whom do not connect to their offline social networks. Marwick and boyd referred to the ways in which Twitter's features do not allow users to easily distinguish and differentiate followers from the different spheres of life as "context collapse." Additionally, on Twitter, a person does not need to have an account or follow a person to read their tweets and people can tweet to one another without following each other. In illustration of these dynamics, the authors stated:

> *Twitter users negotiate multiple, overlapping audiences by strategically concealing information, targeting tweets to different audiences and attempting to portray both an authentic self and an interesting personality. (p. 122).*

Thus, owing to the affordances of Twitter, along with people's typical usage behavior, the OMAP is more of an issue because much of people's interactions are widely available to a broad audience. As a result, self-presentation attempts may only be successful at creating a desired impression among a subset of people's Twitter audience.

Impression formation on social media

While the earlier sections reviewed the literature on the ways in which people attempt to make a good—albeit curated—impression on others through social media, this chapter would not be complete without a discussion on the ways in which communicating via technology affects the impressions people form of others. In other words, how do people's attempts at self-presentation through social media affect the impressions others form of them? What can we infer about people's characteristics (e.g., Is he nice? Is she smart? Are they honest? Is he wealthy? Is she highly educated? Are they successful?) based on their behavior on social media? And do, people form accurate impressions of individuals based on their social media posts? The extant evidence can be summarized as follows (Carpentier, Parrott, and Northup. 2014): "First impressions are formed very quickly and based on relatively little information (Taylor, Peplau, & Sears, 2000)."

The most widely cited theory of impression formation online is Walther's hyperpersonal model of interpersonal communication (Walther, Van Der Heide, Ramirez, Burgoon, & Peña, 2015). According to this model, asynchronous, text-based communication creates a context in which interpersonal interactions are more positive owing to the affordances of the communication technology. That is, because people interacting over social media generally use text to communicate, the social and nonverbal cues typically transmitted during a face-to-face interaction are missing and instead replaced with idealization (i.e., people fill in the unknowns about another person with overly positive, desirable information) and, as reviewed above, selective self-presentation. As a result of this, over time face-to-face versus computer-mediated impression formation processes have the same general outcomes (Tidwell & Walther, 2002). Unfortunately, to date, there is no published research that has examined the generalizability of this model to interpersonal interactions over social media.

However, there have been some studies that have investigated the accuracy of impressions formed from viewing people's profiles and interacting with them on social media. For instance, Carpentier et al. (2014) argued that because of the differing information available about other people on social media relative to face-to-face, impressions of others formed via their social media profiles and posts may be more heavily influenced by contextual cues. Illustrative of this, Tong, Van Der Heide, Langwell, and Walther (2008) examined the impact that the number of Facebook friends had on impression formation. Participants viewed identical Facebook profiles with one key difference: the number of friends which ranged from a low of 102 to a high of 902. After viewing the profile, participants evaluated targets on social attractiveness, physical attractiveness, and extraversion. Results revealed that a moderate number of friends garnered the most positive impressions on social attractiveness (302 friends) and extroversion (502 friends). There was no difference in impressions of physical attractiveness based on the number of Facebook friends. Notably, the number of friends that yielded the most positive impressions were also the conditions closest to participants' own average friend count which was 395.02. This suggests that what perceived similarity with the target individual may be the underlying mechanism explaining these findings. It is also important to note that the raw numbers reported in this study may not generalize given that the study is over a decade old – an eternity in social media years.

Other research has continued to isolate the factors that most clearly predict impression formation on social media. For instance, Levordashka and Utz (2016) introduced the idea of ambivalent awareness, which they defined as peripheral impression formation over social media that accrues over time and exposure. They proposed that ambivalent awareness underlies impressions of approachability formed through interactions between people and their social media connections that they do not know in person. Illustrative of this, example items on this measure include the following: "I feel like I know what (social media only friend) is like as a person"; "I am aware of (social media only friend's) profession or personal interests." This suggests that people are attending to the content of others' social media profiles and may use it rather than interpersonal interactions to form initial impressions. Furthermore, there is also evidence that people who are likable in person also have likeable social media profiles (Weisbuch, Ivcevic, & Ambady, 2009), suggesting that generally people's social media profiles contain information helpful in forming accurate impressions of others. Consistent with this suggestion, other research has shown that certain personality traits, such as extroversion, are also accurately transmitted via social media (Back et al., 2010; Utz, 2010), a body of research that I will discuss in detail in Chapter 3. The following is the summary statement.

Summary

"Choose your self-presentations carefully, for what starts out as a mask may become your face." Goffman (1959). I started this chapter by questioning whether people's activity on social media reflects accurate self-perceptions. As the words and actions of Essena O'Neill illustrate, some people use social media as a money-making scheme without initially realizing the negative psychological impact this choice has on herself and her audience. Based on the extant literature, was Ms. O'Neill right? Is social media fake? Does everyone lie on social media? These are hard questions to answer because there are so many ways in which people's perceptions are distorted by self-enhancement processes and by people's propensity to curate their social media posts to focus on positive but not negative aspects of life, owing to social comparison processes. However, overall, as the research reviewed in this chapter suggests, people's behavior online does reflect certain aspects of their true selves. This chapter explored the literature on self-expression online and examined the extent to which people's social media use is reflective of their true selves and how self-presenting to more than one audience at once affects people. Finally, this chapter also examined whether people form accurate impressions of others based on their social media profiles and activities. Overall, the literature indicates that people can detect accurate impressions on some dimensions, especially those linked to sociability. Finally, the ways in which people engage in self-presentation on their social media profiles have implications for people's well-being, both on the part of the poster and his or her audience. We will revisit this issue in Chapter 9.

References

Arad, A., Barzilay, O., & Perchick, M. (2017). *The impact of Facebook on social comparison and happiness: Evidence from a natural experiment*. Unpublished Manuscript, Tel Aviv University. Retrieved from: https://papers.ssrn.com/sol3/papers.cfm?abstract_id = 2916158.

Back, M. D., Stopfer, J. M., Vazire, S., Gaddis, S., Schmukle, S. C., Egloff, B., & Gosling, S. D. (2010). Facebook profiles reflect actual personality, not self-idealization. *Psychological Science, 21*(3), 372–374.

Bazarova, N. N., Taft, J. G., Choi, Y. H., & Cosley, D. (2013). Managing impressions and relationships on Facebook: Self-presentational and relational concerns revealed through the analysis of language style. *Journal of Language and Social Psychology, 32*(2), 121–141.

Carpentier, F. R. D., Parrott, M. S., & Northup, C. T. (2014). When first comes love (or lust): How romantic and sexual cues bias first impressions in online social networking. *The Journal of Social Psychology, 154*(5), 423–440.

Chou, H. T. G., & Edge, N. (2012). "They are happier and having better lives than I am": the impact of using Facebook on perceptions of others' lives. *Cyberpsychology, Behavior, and Social Networking, 15*(2), 117–121.

Das, S., & Kramer, A. (2013, June). Self-censorship on Facebook. In *Seventh international AAAI conference on weblogs and social media*.

Dunn, R. A., & Guadagno, R. E. (2012). My avatar and me? Gender and personality predictors of avatar-self discrepancy. *Computers in Human Behavior, 28*, 97–106.

Goffman, E. (1959). *The presentation of self in everyday life*. Garden City, NY: Doubleday.

Goffman, E. (1967). On face-work. Interaction ritual, pp. 5–45.

Guadagno, R. E., & Cialdini, R. B. (2007). Gender differences in impression management in organizations: A qualitative review. *Sex Roles, 56*(7–8), 483–494.

Guadagno, R. E., Muscanell, N. L., Okdie, B. M., Burke, N. M., & Ward, T. B. (2011). Even in virtual environments women shop and men build: Gender differences in Second Life. *Computers in Human Behavior, 27*, 304–308.

Haferkamp, N., & Krämer, N. C. (2011). Social comparison 2.0: Examining the effects of online profiles on social-networking sites. *Cyberpsychology, Behavior, and Social Networking, 14*(5), 309–314.

Hanna, E., et al. (2017). Contributions of social comparison and self-objectification in mediating associations between Facebook use and emergent adults' psychological well-being. *Cyberpsychology, Behavior, and Social Networking, 20*(3), 172–179.

Jones, E. E. (1990). *Interpersonal perception*. New York: Freeman.

Jung, T., Youn, H., & McClung, S. (2007). Motivations and self-presentation strategies on Korean-based "Cyworld" weblog format personal homepages. *CyberPsychology & Behavior, 10*(1), 24–31.

Leary, M. R. (1995). *Self-presentation: Impression management and interpersonal behavior.* Madison, WI: Brown & Benchmark.

Lee-Won, R. J., Shim, M., Joo, Y. K., & Park, S. G. (2014). Who puts the best "face" forward on Facebook? Positive self-presentation in online social networking and the role of self-consciousness, actual-to-total Friends ratio, and culture. *Computers in Human Behavior, 39*, 413–423.

Levine, S. P., & Feldman, R. S. (1997). Self-presentational goals, self-monitoring, and nonverbal behavior. *Basic and Applied Social Psychology, 19*(4), 505–518.

Levordashka, A., & Utz, S. (2016). Ambient awareness: From random noise to digital closeness in online social networks. *Computers in Human Behavior, 60*, 147–154.

Loewald, T.A. (2018) Recreation of Essena O'Neil photo. (photograph). Half Moon Bay, CA, USA.

Loewald, R.J. (2024). Curated Self-presentation. (digital art). Oulu, Finland.

Mäntymäki, M., & Islam, A. N. (2016). The Janus face of Facebook: Positive and negative sides of social networking site use. *Computers in Human Behavior, 61*, 14–26.

Marder, B., Joinson, A., Shankar, A., & Thirlaway, K. (2016). Strength matters: Self-presentation to the strongest audience rather than lowest common denominator when faced with multiple audiences in social network sites. *Computers in Human Behavior, 61*, 56–62.

Muscanell, N.L., Guadagno, R.E., & Hamilton, J.C. (2014, July). *Losing face on Facebook: A self-regulation perspective on inappropriate self-presentation in social media environments.* Talk presented at the annual meeting for the European Association of Social Psychology, Amsterdam, The Netherlands.

Marwick, A. E., & boyd, D. (2011). I tweet honestly, I tweet passionately: Twitter users, context collapse, and the imagined audience. *New media & society, 13*(1), 114–133.

Nadkarni, A., & Hofmann, S. G. (2012). Why do people use Facebook? *Personality and Individual Differences, 52*(3), 243–249.

Neuberg, S. L., Judice, T. N., Virdin, L. M., & Carrillo, M. A. (1993). Perceiver self-presentational goals as moderators of expectancy influences: Ingratiation and the disconfirmation of negative expectancies. *Journal of Personality and Social Psychology, 64*(3), 409–420.

Nezlek, J. B., Schütz, A., & Sellin, I. (2007). Self-presentational success in daily social interaction. *Self and Identity, 6*(4), 361–379.

O'Neil, L. (2015, November 3). *Teen Instagram star Essena O'Neill hailed as a 'revolutionary' for quitting social media.* Retrieved from: https://www.cbc.ca/news/trending/instagram-essena-o-neill-social-media-isn-t-real-1.3302045.

O'Neill, E. [@essenaoneill]. (n.d.). Essena O'Neill. Retrieved from: https://www.instagram.com/essenaoneill/?hl = en.

Park, N., & Lee, S. (2014). College students' motivations for Facebook use and psychological outcomes. *Journal of Broad casting & Electronic Media, 58*(4), 601–620.

Qiu, L., Lin, H., Leung, A. K., & Tov, W. (2012). Putting their best foot forward: emotional disclosure on facebook. *Cyberpsychology, Behavior, and Social Networking, 15*(10), 569–572.

Raacke, J., & Bonds-Raacke, J. (2008). Myspace and Facebook: Applying the uses and gratifi- cations theory to exploring friend-networking sites. *CyberPsychology & Behavior, 11*, 169–174.

Rosenfeld, P., Giacalone, R. A., & Riordan, C. A. (1995). *Impression management in organizations.* London: Routledge.

Roy, J. (2015, November 3). *Famous Instagram teen Essena O'Neill posts new video to social media swearing off social media*. Retrieved from: https://www.thecut.com/2015/11/essena-oneill-shares-tearful-new-video.html.

Schlenker, B. R. (1980). *Impression management: The self-concept, social identity, and interpersonal relationships*. Monterey, CA: Brooks/Cole.

Shakespeare, W., & Marshall, C. (2004). *As you like it*. New York: Cambridge University Press.

Sherman, D. K. (2013). Self-affirmation: Understanding the effects. *Social and Personality Psychology Compass*, 7(11), 834–845.

Smith, S. W., Cody, M. J., Lovette, S., & Candry, D. J. (1990). Self-monitoring, gender, and compliance-gaining goals. In M. J. Cody, & M. L. McLaughlin (Eds.), *The psychology of tactical communication* (pp. 91–135). Clevedon, UK: Multilingual Matters.

Stephens-Davidowitz, S. (2017). *Everybody lies: Big data, new data, and what the Internet can tell us about who we really are*. New York: Harper Collins.

Suls, J., Martin, R., & Wheeler, L. (2002). Social comparison: Why, with whom, and with what effect? *Current Directions in Psychological Science*, *11*(5), 159–163.

Tangney, J. P., Baumeister, R. F., & Boone, A. L. (2004). High self-control predicts good adjustment, less pathology, better grades, and interpersonal success. *Journal of Personality*, *72*(2), 271–324.

Taylor, S. E., Peplau, L., & Sears, D. O. (2000). Person perception: Forming impressions of others. In N. Roberts, B. Webber, & J. Cohen (Eds.), *Social Psychology* (pp. 62–97). Upper Saddle River, NJ: Prentice Hall.

Tong, S. T., Van Der Heide, B., Langwell, L., & Walther, J. B. (2008). Too much of a good thing? The relationship between number of friends and interpersonal impressions on Facebook. *Journal of Computer-Mediated Communication*, *13*(3), 531–549.

Tidwell, L. C., & Walther, J. B. (2002). Computer-mediated communication effects on disclosure, impressions, and interpersonal evaluations: Getting to know one another a bit at a time. *Human Communication Research*, *28*(3), 317–348.

Utz, S. (2010). Show me your friends and I will tell you what type of person you are: How one's profile, number of friends, and type of friends influence impression formation on social network sites. *Journal of Computer-Mediated Communication*, *15*(2), 314–335.

Vogel, E. A., & Rose, J. P. (2016). Self-reflection and interpersonal connection: Making the most of self-presentation on social media. *Translational Issues in Psychological Science*, *2*(3), 294.

Vogel, E. A., Rose, J. P., Okdie, B. M., Eckles, K., & Franz, B. (2015). Who compares and despairs? The effect of social comparison orientation on social media use and its outcomes. *Personality and Individual Differences*, *86*, 249–256.

Vogel, E. A., Rose, J. P., Roberts, L. R., & Eckles, K. (2014). Social comparison, social media, and self-esteem. *Psychology of Popular Media Culture*, *3*(4), 206.

Walther, J. B., Van Der Heide, B., Ramirez, A., Burgoon, J. K., & Peña, J. (2015). Interpersonal and hyperpersonal dimensions of computer-mediated communication. In S. S. Sundar (Ed.), *The handbook of the psychology of communication technology* (pp. 1–22). Wiley.

Wang, S. S., & Stefanone, M. A. (2013). Showing off? Human mobility and the interplay of traits, self-disclosure, and Facebook check-ins. *Social Science Computer Review*, *31*(4), 437–457.

Weisbuch, M., Ivcevic, Z., & Ambady, N. (2009). On being liked on the web and in the "real world": Consistency in first impressions across personal webpages and spontaneous behavior. *Journal of Experimental Social Psychology*, *45*(3), 573–576.

Wheeler, L., Martin, R., & Suls, J. (1997). The proxy model of social comparison for self-assessment of ability. *Personality and Social Psychology Review*, *1*(1), 54–61.

Wohn, D. Y., & Spottswood, E. L. (2016). Reactions to other-generated face threats on Facebook and their relational consequences. *Computers in Human Behavior, 57*, 187–194.

Wood, J. V., Taylor, S. E., & Lichtman, R. R. (1985). Social comparison in adjustment to breast cancer. *Journal of Personality and Social Psychology, 49*(5), 1169.

Yang, C. C., & Brown, B. B. (2016). Online self-presentation on Facebook and self development during the college transition. *Journal of Youth and Adolescence, 45*(2), 402–416.

Zhao, S., Grasmuck, S., & Martin, J. (2008). Identity construction on facebook: digital empowerment in anchored relationships. *Computers in human behavior, 24*(5), 1816–1836.

CHAPTER 3

Personality in social media

The things that make me different are the things that make me.

—Piglet from Winnie the Pooh (Katona & Wexler, 1999)

I have a confession to make. While I am a fervent social media user, I do not use Facebook—I shut down my account a couple of years ago[1]. However, when I did use Facebook, I often spent time filling out various tests that circulated on my news feed. I wanted to know which Hogwarts house I should join, whether I would be more likely to become a Jedi or a Sith, and which Avenger or Disney princess matched up to my characteristics. Generally, people are interested in learning about themselves and, despite my training as a social psychologist (or maybe because of it), I was not immune. While I realized that these tests were not psychologically nor psychometrically valid and did not take my results seriously, I also failed to realize that there was a nefarious purpose for these quizzes: to gather information about me and my social media friends for advertising purposes. These tests gained popularity because they tapped into people's desire to learn about themselves and, in particular, how they are different from others. Psychologists refer to this as *personality*. Personality describes people based on the characteristics that remain stable across contexts and distinguish people from one another (Burger, 1986). This includes various emotional, motivational, and cognitive processes that influence people's feelings and actions. Furthermore, research indicates that people's personality characteristics have been shown to predict different long-term outcomes in people's educational outcomes, career achievements, romantic relationships, happiness, and political ideology (Azucar, Marengo, & Settanni, 2018).

In addition to these silly and fun personality quizzes, I would occasionally see a more serious and psychologically valid option appear on my news feed. One such application was called MyPersonality (MyPersonality.org), developed by Professors Michal Kosinski and David Stillwell as students. This app offered to provide people with their

[1] The reasons why will become clear as you read this chapter and the chapters in subsequent chapters.

Psychological Processes in Social Media
DOI: https://doi.org/10.1016/B978-0-12-811320-2.00001-0

personality scores on many different scientifically valid assessments (Stillwell & Kosinski, 2012). Anonymously and with participant's consent, MyPersonality also collected data on people's digital footprints and, across unique empirical papers derived from this data, demonstrated that these footprints could predict people's personality, preferences, as well as some physical characteristics (Stillwell & Kosinski, n.d.). More than six million people participated in this research and the resulting new methodology has been widely adopted by many large tech companies who created their own versions and collected data to infer people's personality and preferences. This information was then used to decide what advertisements people see on the social media and more broadly on the Internet. One such example of this became headline news shortly after the 2016 US presidential election. Through no fault of their own[2], Stillwell and Kosinski's methods were adopted by Cambridge Analytica (CA), a now infamous (and defunct) data analytics firm. Specifically, CA developed their own personality quiz app and collected the digital footprints of participants and their unsuspecting Facebook friends, resulting in a database of 87 million Facebook users, many of whom had not consented to have their data harvested (Davies, 2015). This information was then used to target political advertisements developed to appeal to people based on their personality profiles and was used to attempt to influence people's voting behavior in several countries, including by the Republican candidate in the 2016 US presidential election.

People's behavior—both on social media and more broadly—is driven in part by the situation (e.g., the software design and the behavior of people's social media friends) and in part by these unique aspects of each individual's personality (e.g., how outgoing, organized, kind, and self-centered they are). Social psychologists such as myself refer to this as the person-by-situation interaction (Buss, 1977), indicating that human behavior results from a combination of normative expectations set by the situation (e.g., students in class know that they should not text their friends while their session is going on, people know to pull over for an emergency vehicle when the sirens are on, and people generally copy the behavior of others in an unknown environment) and people's personality and other unique, individual difference.

[2] Indeed, when initially approached by then Oxford Professor, Dr. Alexsandr Kogan (who legally changed his name to Dr. Spectre), Kosinski turned down the offer to share his MyPersonality database and instead reported his concerns to Cambridge University—his doctoral granting institution (Grassegger & Krogerus, 2017; January 28).

While much of this book focuses on the context-specific or situational aspects of people's social media use, this chapter and Chapter 4 will review the research work on individual differences in social media use.

While there are numerous personality traits upon which people differ, research has generally shown that there are five key factors of personality that explain much of the variability in people's behavior: The "Big Five" Factors of personality (BFF; Digman, 1990; John & Srivastava, 1999; McCrae & Costa, 1997). The BFF assesses openness to new experiences, conscientiousness, extroversion, agreeableness, and neuroticism (easy to remember as OCEAN) and it has been widely shown to affect people's technology use. Similarly, other research has focused on the Dark Triad of Personality (Paulhus & Williams, 2002) which assesses psychopathy, narcissism, and Machiavellianism, personality traits that are conceptually similar to one another and reflect the extent to which people are prone to engaging in malevolent, callous, and self-aggrandizing behavior. As with the Big Five, the Dark Triad has been shown to predict the ways in which people's behavior online varies as a function of their scores on this measure. See Table 3.1 for definitions of each personality characteristic with examples of how the trait manifests on social media.

This chapter focuses on the Big Five and the Dark Triad because they are central to understanding how people's personality affects their social media use and, as a result, have been widely studied in this domain (Settanni, Azucar, & Marengo, 2018). As indicated in Chapter 1, there are several different methods used by scholars to draw psychological insights from research on people's social media use. These include self-reported behavior and digital footprints assessed from people's posts and actions (e.g., likes and shares). As the work of Kosinski and others indicates (e.g., Kern, McCarthy, Chakrabarty, & Rizoiu, 2019; Kosinski, Stillwell, & Graepel, 2013), people's digital footprints predict individual differences, including people's personality, gender, relationship status, ethnicity, sexual orientation, political affiliation, occupation, and the size and density of their friendship network. Furthermore, as scholars have shown, people's language use is reflective of their personality (Boyd & Pennebaker, 2017) and, as a result, digital footprints are often deeply revealing.

The "Big Five" Factors of personality

As specified before, the BFF assesses the five traits that describe the core aspects of personality (Digman, 1990; John & Srivastava, 1999; McCrae &

Table 3.1 Individual differences in social media use.

Personality factor	Description	Differences in social media use
Big Five Factor model:		
Openness	Assesses people's willingness to try new things and explore new ideas. Higher scores indicate greater willingness.	People high in openness are more likely to make new friends through social media.
Conscientiousness	Assesses people's level of organization and self-discipline. Higher scores indicate greater organization and self-discipline.	People high in conscientiousness spend less overall time social media.
Extroversion	Assesses the extent to which people enjoy socializing with others and spending time in stimulating environments. Higher scores indicate a greater interest in socializing.	People high in extroversion tend to be heavier social media users.
Agreeableness	Assesses the extent to which people prioritize kindness, cooperation and group prosperity. Higher scores indicate a great focus on kindness and group outcomes.	People high in agreeableness express more positive and fewer negative emotions in their social media posts.
Neuroticism	Assesses the extent to which people's moods and emotions fluctuate. Higher scores indicate greater fluxuation.	People high in Neuroticism tend to make more frequent social media posts.
Dark Triad:		
Psychopathy	Assesses the extent to which people engage in reckless and impulsive behavior without consideration for others. Higher scores indicate greater recklessness, callousness, and impulsivity.	People high in psychopathy tend to use more swearwords and express more negative emotions in their social media posts.

(*Continued*)

Table 3.1 (Continued)

Personality factor	**Description**	**Differences in social media use**
Machiavellianism	Assesses the extent to which people are willing to manipulate others to achieve their goals. Higher scores indicate a greater willingness to manipulate others.	People high in Machiavellianism troll others and report that they enjoy doing so.
Narcissism	Assesses the extent to which people are self-absorbed and entitled. Higher scores indicate greater levels of entitlement and self-absorption.	People high in narcissism tend to be more intense social media users and write longer posts than others.

Costa, 1997). These traits are also referred to as the OCEAN model because people's personalities vary on (1) *openness to new experience* which assesses people's inclination to try new things, especially those that engage their imaginations and are novel, creative, and unorthodox; (2) *conscientiousness* which measures people's propensity for organization, planning, and self-discipline; (3) *extroversion* which describes the extent that people enjoy socializing with others, spending time in stimulating environments, and are focused on the world outside themselves; (4) *agreeableness* which measures people's focus on kindness, cooperation, and group prosperity; and (5) *neuroticism* which assesses emotional instability—the extent to which people experience negative emotions and fluctuating moods. Decades of research on the BFF has demonstrated that these traits are stable across age, time, and culture and differentiate people's responses across a wide variety of situations (Digman, 1989; McCrae & Costa, 1997).

Research has also established that people's BFF scores on self-report measures are remarkably consistent with the characteristics ascribed to them by their friends, teachers, and parents (Back et al., 2010; Botwin & Buss, 1989; Digman & Inouye, 1986; Digman, 1989; Goldberg, 1990). Thus, the evidence suggests that individual differences such as the Big Five provide a taxonomy for understanding people's unique traits and characteristics that differentiate them from other people. See Table 3.2 for an example measure of the BFF developed by Gosling, Rentfrow, and Swann (2003). This

Table 3.2 An example of measure of the big five factors of personality developed by Gosling et al. (2003).

Ten-Item Personality Inventory (TIPI)

Instructions: Here are a number of personality traits that may or may not apply to you. Please write a number next to each statement to indicate the extent to which you agree or disagree with that statement. You should rate the extent to which the pair of traits applies to you, even if one characteristic applies more strongly than the other.

1 = Disagree strongly
2 = Disagree moderately
3 = Disagree a little
4 = Neither agree nor disagree
5 = Agree a little
6 = Agree moderately
7 = Agree strongly

I see myself as:

1. _____ Extraverted, enthusiastic.
2. _____ Critical, quarrelsome.
3. _____ Dependable, self-disciplined.
4. _____ Anxious, easily upset.
5. _____ Open to new experiences, complex.
6. _____ Reserved, quiet.
7. _____ Sympathetic, warm.
8. _____ Disorganized, careless.
9. _____ Calm, emotionally stable.
10. _____ Conventional, uncreative.

Scoring instructions: TIPI scale scoring ("R" denotes reverse-scored items). This means that if at item is labeled R, then flip the number on the scale as follows: 1 = 7, 2 = 6, 3 = 5, 4 = 4, 5 = 3, 6 = 2, 7 = 1.

To score, take the average of the two items: extraversion: 1, 6R; agreeableness: 2R, 7; conscientiousness; 3, 8R; emotional stability: 4R, 9; openness to experiences: 5, 10R.

framework has been widely employed in studies examining people's social media use. Early research focused on individual differences in overall Internet use had previously shown that the BFF model differentiated people by how they spent time online (Hamburger & Ben-Artzi, 2000), the extent to which they felt that they could be genuine when socializing online (Amichai-Hamburger, Wainapel, & Fox, 2002), the portion of time spent online socializing versus seeking information (Amichai-Hamburger & Ben-Artzi, 2003), and even their preferred type of social media platform (Gazit, Aharony, & Amichai-Hamburger, 2019).

Openness

This Big Five factor assesses the extent to which people are open to new ideas and experiences and is associated with compassion, freethinking, and expression (Costa & McCrae, 1992; Goldberg, 1993). Research generally shows that people who are high in openness enjoy exploring novel or unconventional ideas, partake in artistic and other creative endeavors, and are avid explorers. People who are low in openness to new experience spend their time focusing on practical matters and conforming to the expectations of those around them—especially authorities and tend to avoid the unexpected. Starting with self-report findings, then transitioning to the research on digital footprints, the next sections review research examining the extent to which openness has been shown to differentiate the patterns of people's social media use.

Self-report findings

While some studies have reported that openness to new experience is unrelated to self-reported social media use (e.g., Moore & McElroy, 2012; Seidman, 2013; Stoughton, Thompson, & Meade, 2013), others have found that people high in openness are more likely to use social media. In some of the earliest research on this question, my graduate students and I examined the extent to which the BFFs predicted whether people blogged (Guadagno, Okdie, & Eno, 2008; Okdie, Guadagno, Rempala, & Eno, 2011). Specifically, across several studies, we found that openness to new experience was a significant predictor of blogging such that people higher in openness were more likely to blog. Similarly, Correa, Hinsley, and De Zuniga (2010) found that in a national sample of Americans, people high in openness were more frequent social media users (when gender was examined, this was only the case for women—explored in detail in Chapter 4). Finally, Brailovskaia and Margraf (2018) reported that in a sample of German university students, openness was positively correlated with Tumblr use.

Other research has examined how openness to new experience affects people's social media behavior. For instance, across two samples—a typical American sample obtained through online crowdsourcing and a sample drawn from a mental health clinic—Stanton, Ellickson-Larew, and Watson (2016) examined whether personality affected the extent to which people engaged in deceptive self-presentation and the formation of intimate relationships through social media. They reported that Openness was unrelated to deceptive behavior but was related to relationship formation such that people high in openness to new experience were more likely to report that they enjoy forming relationships with others through social media. This finding is consistent with the notion that personality may differentiate people based on what activities they find enjoyable across the various types of social media. Supportive of this, Hughes, Rowe, Batey, and Lee (2012) sampled European and American adults from the general population to examine personality and motivations for using Twitter/X and Facebook. For Twitter/X, results revealed that openness to new experience was positively correlated with socializing but not with not information exchange. The opposite pattern occurred when examining people's Facebook use: openness to new experience was positively correlated with information exchange but not social interaction. Finally, Liu and Campbell (2017) examined the relationship between personality and self-reported social media use meta-analytically. With a sample of 38 studies drawn from 11 countries, they reported that openness was one of the strongest predictors of social media use and that openness was positively correlated with social media activities such as gaming, information seeking, posting pictures, and posting status updates.

Digital footprints

The research on the relationship between openness to new experience and people's digital footprints (their actions and words on social media) suggests that people high in openness tend to have larger social networks (Quercia, Lambiotte, Stillwell, Kosinski, & Crowcroft, 2012) and engage in more frequent use of their like buttons (Bachrach, Kosinski, Graepel, Kohli, & Stillwell, 2012) relative to people low in openness to new experience. Kosinski, Bachrach, Kohli, Stillwell, and Graepel (2014, Study 1) demonstrated that openness predicts a preference for "liking" websites focused on arts/animation and arts/photography. In their second study, the authors assessed correlations between BFFs and Facebook profile details, finding that openness was positively correlated with social media activities such as the aforementioned likes, as well as status updates posted, and groups joined. Schwartz et al. (2013) examined individual differences in the linguistic characteristics of Facebook status updates from more than 75,000 research participants. Controlling for gender and age, they found that openness positively predicted the use of more creative (e.g., art, music, and reading) and imaginative (e.g., dream, universe, and soul) words. This study also demonstrated that people's level of openness to new experience could be predicted from the language used in their status updates. Similar results were found in a meta-analysis—a data analysis technique that aggregates the findings from multiple studies—and support what the results from the individual studies suggested—that people's digital footprints provide strong associations between people's online behavior and their personalities (Azucar et al., 2018).

Conscientiousness

As reviewed earlier, the BF factor of conscientiousness reflects the extent to which people are organized, meticulous, and disciplined. People high in conscientiousness are achievement-oriented, planful, reliable, and well-organized, while those individuals on the other side of the spectrum are laidback, imaginative, impulsive, and less likely to follow rules and plans (Costa & McCrae, 1992). The following sections review research examining the extent to which conscientiousness differentiates people based on the patterns of their social media use.

Self-report findings

Research generally shows that highly conscientious people spend less time using social media (Brailovskaia & Margraf, 2018; Carrier, Cheever, Rosen, Benitez, & Chang, 2009; Wilson, Fornasier, & White, 2010). However, among people who do use social media, conscientiousness predicts a decreased motivation to use social media as a means of fulfilling belongingness and self-presentation needs (Seidman, 2013). Similarly, other research has shown that highly conscientious people report engaging in greater amounts of private, direct messaging through their social media applications (Muscanell & Guadagno, 2012). Consistent with this, Seigfried-Spellar and Lankford (2018) examined the impact of the BFF and Dark Triad on behavior while using Yik Yak, a now-defunct anonymous, location-based social media platform. Their results revealed that conscientiousness predicted lurking (passively reading posts and no communication with the other users) such that people high in conscientiousness were more likely to lurk. Furthermore, Stanton et al. (2016) found that people high in conscientiousness did not tend to form intimate relationships with people through social media nor did they tend to engage in deceptive self-presentation. Consistent with this, people high in conscientiousness are less likely to post pictures on their social media profiles (Amichai-Hamburger & Vinitzky, 2010).

These effects are also differed by the type of social media platform. For instance, in the study of Hughes et al. (2012), information seeking on Twitter was positively correlated with conscientiousness, while both seeking information on Facebook and socializing with others on Twitter were negatively correlated with conscientiousness. Finally, the results of the meta-analysis of Liu and Campbell (2017) on the BFFs and self-reported social media use described earlier show that conscientiousness was negatively correlated with most social networking site activities, notably gaming and information seeking. Overall, the self-report research in this area suggests that conscientious people spend less time using social media and when they do, it is primarily to engage in passive and private activities such as lurking and seeking information. This points toward a cautious approach to social media use and, as indicated later, is consistent with the research examining digital footprints instead of self-reporting. However, these findings also provide some initial evidence that the functionality of the different applications also interacts with people's personality to produce different usage patterns.

Digital footprints

While the research examining the relationship between conscientiousness and social media use is much more limited than the scholarship utilizing self-report data, the extant research is consistent with self-report findings. For instance, Kosinski et al. (2014) reported that conscientiousness was negatively correlated with joining groups and liking social media content. Similarly, this research also found that people high in conscientiousness had a preference for websites that provided information (e.g., reference and education sources). In Schwartz et al.'s (2013) examination of individual differences in language used in status updates on Facebook, their results revealed that status updates predicted conscientiousness such that people high in consciousness wrote about their daily activities such as exercise and work and expressed positivity and forethought, while people low in conscientiousness wrote about boredom and video games and swore more. Finally, the meta-analysis of Azucar et al. (2018) also found that people's digital footprints were effective at predicting their level of conscientiousness.

Extroversion

As indicated earlier, extroversion is the BFF trait that assesses the extent to which people seek out and enjoy input from external stimuli. As a result, extroverts—the people who score high on this personality trait—enjoy being around other people, prefer spending time in exciting environments, and tend to express much positivity. They are seen as sociable, demonstrative, and fun. People on the other end of this spectrum are referred to as *introverts* and they prefer quiet environments, solitary time, and are generally more serious and reserved. These descriptions fit people who score on the extreme ends of the scale—most people fall somewhere in the middle of this continuum.

Self-report findings

The literature consistently finds that extroverts use social media more than introverted people do (Annisette & Lafreniere, 2017; Hart, Nailling, Bizer, & Collins, 2015; Wilson et al., 2010). This relationship has been reported in samples drawn from across the globe, including the United States (Correa et al., 2010), Singapore (Ong et al., 2011), and Germany (Brailovskaia & Margraf, 2018). Furthermore, this finding is strongest among the forms of social media used most commonly for socializing rather than microblogging or information sharing. Not only does this literature suggest that extroverts are heavier social media users than introverts, extroverts also have a more outgoing approach to using different social media features. For instance, Muscanell and Guadagno (2012) found that people high in extroversion were more likely to report posting photos on Facebook. Similarly, Kim and Chock (2017) examined personality predictors of selfie behaviors on social media and found that, after controlling for gender and age, extroversion predicted posting group selfies. Furthermore, the study by Ong et al. (2011) reported that people high in extroversion generally reported engaging in greater use of Facebook's different features and this resulted in a greater overall impact on their social networks. Specifically, they had more Facebook friends, were featured more often in photographs, and posted more frequent status updates relative to more introverted participants.

Overall, these findings are consistent with the literature on personality and people's friendships, such that extroverts are generally overrepresented on people's list of closest friends (Feiler & Kleinbaum, 2015). These results are also consistent with the results of the meta-analysis of Liu and Campbell (2017) on the BFF and self-reported social media use in that extraversion was among the strongest predictors of SNS activities, both globally and with respect to the use of specific social media features such as total number of friends, posting pics, and interacting with others. One notable exception to the research findings described before pertains to extroversion differences in Twitter use. Unlike the findings on more socialization-focused forms of social media (e.g., Facebook and Instagram) which consistently report that extroverts use these applications more, Brailovskaia and Margraf (2018) found that extroversion was negatively correlated with Twitter/X use. Additionally, in the study of Hughes et al. (2012), information seeking on Twitter/X was negatively correlated with extraversion indicating that it was the more introverted participants who used Twitter/X more for this purpose.

This literature also documents the ways in which personality differences in social media use also affect key psychological outcomes such as self-presentation, the need to belong, and attention seeking. For instance, in addition to the abovementioned findings, Hart et al. (2015) examined whether extroversion predicted (1) the extent to which people sought feedback on Facebook by posting status updates and (2) how feedback received affected the participant. Their results revealed that people higher in extroversion wanted more frequent feedback from their social media friends but were not differentially sensitive to any feedback they received. Similarly, Seidman (2013) reported that extroversion predicted a greater reliance on social media to fulfill belongingness and self-presentational needs. Consistent with these results, Stanton et al. (2016) reported that extroversion was positively related to the formation of close interpersonal relationships through social media. Finally, Stoughton et al. (2013) examined job applicants' self-reported social media behavior and found that extroversion was positively correlated with self-reported alcohol and drug use.

Digital footprints

The finding that extroverts report engaging in greater social media use relative to more introverted individuals has been borne out in the digital footprint literature as well. This has been reported with respect to general activity (e.g., Blackwell, Leaman, Tramposch, Osborne, & Liss, 2017) as well as specific activities such as the quantity of social media friends, groups joined, status updates posted, and events attended (e.g., Kosinski et al., 2014; Study 2). Other studies have shown that extroversion predicts language use such that people higher in extroversion use more social words, while those low in extroversion use more solitary words (Schwartz et al., 2013). See Fig. 3.1 for a visual illustrating this finding. Research also shows that web browsing preferences vary by extroversion such that

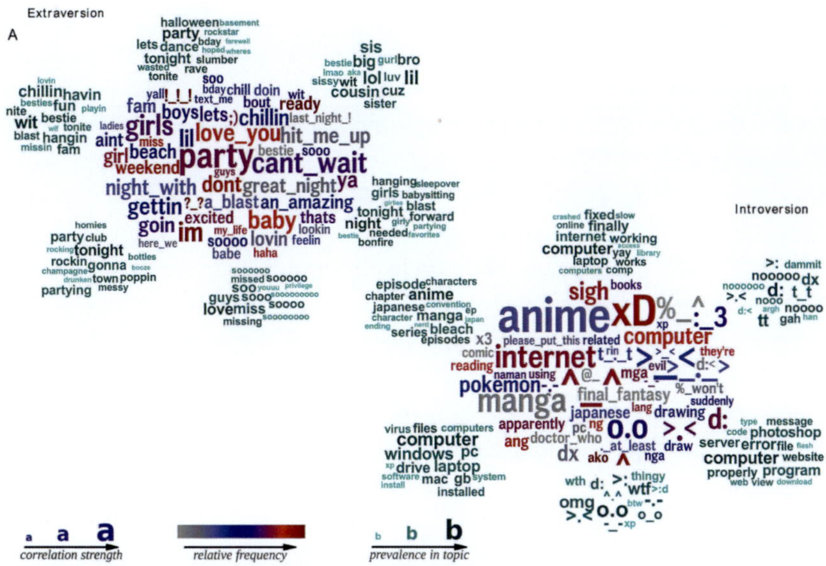

Figure 3.1 Word cloud visualization contrasting common words use in Facebook posts by extroverted and introverted people in the sample of Schwartz et al. (2013). Note that larger words indicate greater frequency of use.

extroverts preferred websites focused on science, arts and music, and computers and the Internet (Kosinski et al., 2014; Study 1). Finally, as with the research on self-reported social media use, the literature on personality and digital footprints indicates that people higher in extroversion consume more social media and this has been shown meta-analytically too (Azucar et al., 2018).

Agreeableness

The BFF trait of agreeableness assesses the extent to which people are oriented toward preserving group welfare (Costa & McCrae, 1992; Goldberg, 1993; Russell & Karol, 1994). People high in agreeableness tend to be kind, trusting, cooperative, and friendly and they prioritize the needs of others, often ignoring their own needs or sacrificing truthfulness in the process. Those low in agreeableness tend to be better at prioritizing their needs as they are less focused on others, more apprehensive of others, stubborn, and unyielding. This individual difference in approach to interpersonal relationships has also led to a consistent finding that people high in agreeableness are more likely to help other people (Habashi, Graziano, & Hoover, 2016).

Self-report findings

Generally, the literature indicates that people high in agreeableness are more likely to report high levels of online interactions and engage in more activities on social media with their offline friends. For instance, Kim and Chock (2017) reported that people high in agreeableness were more likely to post group selfies. Similarly, the meta-analysis of Liu and Campbell (2017) on the BFF and self-reported social media use found that agreeableness was positively correlated with photo sharing and negatively correlated with gaming. Unlike some of the other BFFs such as extroversion, there are some exceptions to this general finding. For instance, Hughes et al. (2012) reported that agreeableness was unrelated to social media use. Similarly, in the self-report study of German College students by Brailovskaia and Margraf (2018), they found that agreeableness was negatively correlated with Twitter/X use.

As with the other BFF factors, individual differences in agreeableness levels have also been shown to produce different outcomes in terms of people's social media behavior. For instance, the study of Seidman (2013) reported that agreeableness was positively predictive of behaviors oriented toward facilitating belongingness (e.g., communication, connection, and caring) and negatively predictive of self-presentation behaviors such as attention seeking. Similarly, in the study of Stoughton et al. (2013), agreeableness was negatively correlated with badmouthing behavior such that people low in agreeableness were more likely to admit to badmouthing classmates or coworkers. Consistent with this, the study on people's Yik Yak use reported that people low in agreeableness were likely to troll others (Seigfried-Spellar & Lankford, 2018). Finally, the study of Stanton et al. (2016) reported that in their second, nationally representative sample, agreeableness was negatively related to people's willingness to deceive others or try to form close relationships with them through social media. Taken together, the evidence from self-report studies suggests that people high in agreeableness use social media for maintaining existing relationships, rather than forming new ones.

Digital footprints

Insights drawn from digital footprints on the relationship between agreeableness and social media use illustrate how this personality factor affects people's digital expression. For instance, Schwartz et al. (2013) reported that status updates for people high in agreeableness contained more positive emotion words (e.g., wonderful, awesome, blessed, and thank you) and fewer negative emotion words—in particular swear words—relative to their lower agreeableness counterparts. This is consistent with the psychological differences in the personality dimension and reflects the focus on positive social interactions that typify people high in agreeableness. Finally, Kosinski et al. (2014) found that people high in agreeableness tended to like websites on Facebook that focused on business and health—perhaps reflecting the focus on others indicative of people high in agreeableness. Finally, as with the previous BFF traits, the meta-analysis of Azucar et al. (2018) reported that agreeableness could be predicted from people's digital footprints.

Neuroticism

Neuroticism assesses emotional reactivity—the extent which people experience variability in moods and emotions (Costa & McCrae, 1992; Goldberg, 1993; Russell & Karol, 1994). People high on this BFF dimension experience more variability, particularly, in the experience of negative emotions (e.g., guilt, shame, and anger) and tend to be more stressed and anxious as well. People low in neuroticism experience more stable moods and emotions and tend to be calm and self-assured, and at the extreme end of the continuum, these characteristics can lead them to appear standoffish. Given this, it should be unsurprising that people high in neuroticism are less satisfied overall in their friendships relative to their lower neuroticism counterparts (Wilson, Harris, & Vazire, 2015).

Self-report findings

People high in neuroticism report a greater frequency of status updates on their social media walls (Moore & McElroy, 2012). Other research has reported similar findings, the motivations behind this increased use vary by the type of social media. For instance, in the study of Seidman (2013), participants high in neuroticism were more interested in seeking out belongingness through communication, seeking information, and engaging in self-presentation behaviors on Facebook relative to participants lower in neuroticism. Similarly, Hughes et al. (2012) found that the relationship between information seeking and neuroticism varied by the type of social media platform such that information seeking was negatively correlated with neuroticism on Twitter/X but positively correlated on Facebook. Furthermore, participants high in neuroticism also preferred Facebook to Twitter. On Yik Yak, users high in neuroticism were likely to confess by self-disclosing personal information anonymously

(Seigfried-Spellar & Lankford, 2018). Stanton et al. (2016) reported that people high in neuroticism were more likely to report a greater frequency of engaging in deceptive behavior and forming new relationships on social media relative to those lower in neuroticism. Finally, in their meta-analysis on BFF and self-reported social media use, Liu and Campbell (2017) found that like extraversion, neuroticism was also predictive with global SNS use such that people higher in Neuroticism were more likely to use social media. They also found that, as reported by some individual studies, neuroticism was positively associated with posting status updates.

Digital footprints

As indicated earlier, Schwartz et al. (2013) examined individual differences (gender, age, BFF) in language used in status updates on Facebook, finding that status updates did predict personality such that people high in neuroticism used far more negative emotion words (lonely, pissed, shit, bored, and depression), while those low in neuroticism used more positive emotion words and wrote appositively bout their activities. See Fig. 3.2 for a visual illustrating these language differences. Similarly, in an analysis of people's Facebook profiles, Kosinski et al. (2014) reported that people

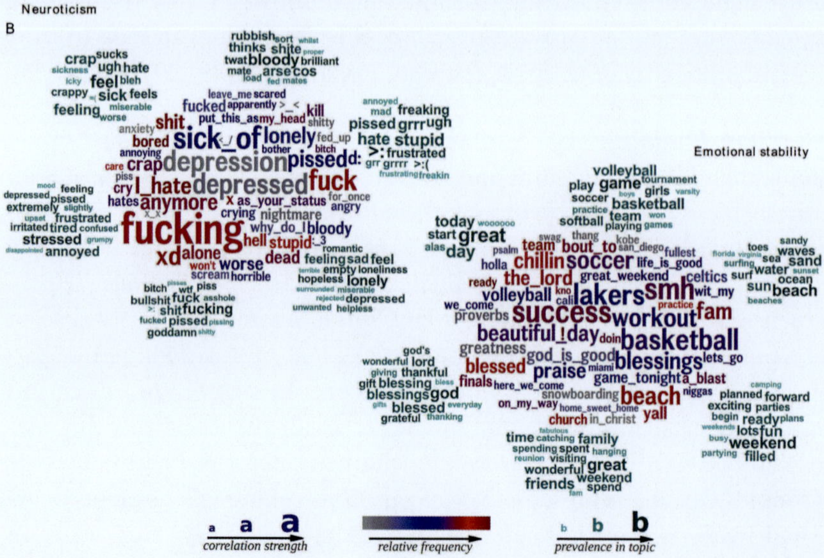

Figure 3.2 Word cloud visualization contrasting common words use in Facebook posts by people on each side of the emotional stability continuum in the study of Schwartz et al. (2013). Note that larger words indicate greater frequency of use.

high in neuroticism tended to like websites focused on animals and pets and that people's level of neuroticism could be predicted from their pattern of likes and status updates. Finally, the meta-analysis of Azucar et al. (2018) reported that the more detailed the footprint or the total number of footprints used to predict personality, the more strongly the behaviors predicted participants' neuroticism levels.

The darker side of personality

While the Big Five Factors of personality model assesses people's overall personality, the Dark Triad[3] assesses people's personality on three intercorrelated but distinct personality traits that capture the darker side of human behavior: narcissism, Machiavellianism, and psychopathy. Previously, scholars described the Dark Triad as "offensive yet nonpathological" and "social aversive," this measure has been used widely to study individual differences in people's behavior on social media and has also been demonstrated to predict people's propensity to engage in antisocial conduct (Paulhus & Williams, 2002), both offline and online (Buckels, Trapnell, & Paulhus, 2014). Table 3.3 displays the most widely accepted measure of the Dark Triad. Men score higher than women on all three measures (Jonason & Webster, 2010).

Narcissism assesses the extent to which people are self-absorbed and see themselves as entitled to more than their fair share (Bogolyubova, Panicheva, Tikhonov, Ivanov, & Ledovaya, 2018). People high in narcissism are vain, superficially charming, and willing to exploit, manipulate, and deceive others to achieve their objectives (Jakobwitz & Egan, 2006). In BFF parlance, people high in narcissism are extroverted, disagreeable, and open to new experiences (Paulhus & Williams, 2002). Machiavellianism assesses the extent to which people are willing to manipulate others to achieve their goals by showing indifference to people and their feelings, behaving in an amoral manner, and are typically perceived as cold and calculating (Bogolyubova et al., 2018). Research has shown that people high in this personality characteristic are low in agreeableness and also low in conscientiousness (Paulhus & Williams, 2002).

[3] Note that another measure of these darker traits also includes sadism and is called the dark tetrad (Chabrol, Van Leeuwen, Rodgers, & Sejourne, 2009). Unfortunately, this has been less used in research on social media and personality so it will not be reviewed in this chapter.

Table 3.3 The Short Dark Triad (SD3; Paulus & Jones, 2014). Instructions: Please indicate how much you agree with each of the following statements using the scale: Strongly disagree (1), Disagree (2), Neither agree nor disagree (3), Agree (4), and Strongly agree (5).

Machiavellianism	Narcissism	Psychopathy
1. It's not wise to tell your secrets. 2. I like to use clever manipulation to get my way. 3. Whatever it takes, you must get the important people on your side. 4. Avoid direct conflict with others because they may be useful in the future. 5. It's wise to keep track of information that you can use against people later. 6. You should wait for the right time to get back at people. 7. There are things you should hide from other people to preserve your reputation. 8. Make sure your plans benefit yourself, not others. 9. Most people can be manipulated.	1. People see me as a natural leader. 2. I hate being the center of attention. (R) 3. Many group activities tend to be dull without me. 4. I know that I am special because everyone keeps telling me so. 5. I like to get acquainted with important people. 6. I feel embarrassed if someone compliments me. (R) 7. I have been compared to famous people. 8. I am an average person. (R) 9. I insist on getting the respect I deserve.	1. I like to get revenge on authorities. 2. I avoid dangerous situations. (R) 3. Payback needs to be quick and nasty. 4. People often say I'm out of control. 5. It's true that I can be mean to others. 6. People who mess with me always regret it. 7. I have never gotten into trouble with the law. (R) 8. I enjoy having sex with people I hardly know 9. I'll say anything to get what I want.

Note: Items should be kept in the same order. Reversals are indicated with (R).

Finally, psychopathy assesses the extent to which people engage in impulsive and reckless conduct without any concern for other people. People high in psychopathy are generally seen as heartless and brash and have been shown to be extroverted, disagreeable, unconscientious, low in neuroticism, and high in openess to new experiences (Paulhus & Williams, 2002). Vander Molen, Kaplan, Choi, and Montoya (2018) argue that callousness is the primary commonality between all three Dark Triad factors and they further suggest that people high in Dark Triad traits find social media particularly appealing owing to the features that allow them to maximize strategic self-presentation. As with the abovementioned sections on the BFFs, the below sections on the Dark Triad review the literature on each personality characteristic and examine how people's social media actions—both self-report and digital footprints—are affected by each facet of the Dark Triad.

Narcissism

The word Narcissist stems from Greek mythology and is based on the fable of Narcissus, a young man who was so entranced by his image reflected in a pool of water that he fell in love with himself. See Fig. 3.3 for a visual of Narcissus for the social media age. As illustrated by this myth, narcissism is typified by an exaggerated sense of self-importance, self-absorption, and boasting. Thus narcissism is characterized by a propensity to regulate self-esteem by seeking external validation, praise, and acceptance from relationships and social situations (Pincus & Lukowitsky, 2010). To some extent, everyone exhibits narcissistic characteristics and some evidence suggests that nonpathological levels of narcissism have been linked to high self-esteem (Campbell, Rudich, & Sedikides, 2002). What makes narcissism as a personality characteristic different from the psychological disorder (Narcissistic personality disorder [NPD]) is the

Figure 3.3 A modern-day Narcissus gazes into his social media reflection (Loewald, 2020).

presence of pathological narcissistic traits such as a lack of empathy for others, callousness, and a willingness to exploit others to achieve personal gains. NPD is thought to affect less than 10% of people (Pincus & Lukowitsky, 2010). Thus "normal" narcissism is common, and most people have moments in which they act in narcissistic ways.

Research has also shown that there is more than one subtype of narcissism and that this personality dimension manifests differently by culture. For instance, personality scholars distinguish between grandiose and vulnerable narcissism (McCain & Campbell, 2018. The characteristics of grandiose narcissism most closely match the characters of NPD (Miller et al., 2014), have been described as the more unfeeling and outgoing version of narcissism, and are typified by an inflated self-concept coupled with behaviors oriented toward maintaining this grandiose self-view. Wink (1991) also described the second type of narcissism—vulnerable narcissism—as being comprised of introversion, defensiveness, anxiety, and vulnerability to life stresses). Similarly, narcissism as typically understood in popular culture is the more western (i.e., United States, Canada, and Europe), individualistic, grandiose variant. People from collectivistic cultures (i.e., China, Mexico, and Japan) tend to have lower average levels of narcissism (Meisel, Ning, Campbell, & Goodie, 2016) and some scholars (Gebauer, Sedikides, Verplanken, & Maio, 2012) argue that communal narcissists focus their efforts to enhance the outcomes of their groups. As a result, a communal narcissist may brag about how much they help other people instead of bragging about their personal qualities such as intelligence or attractiveness.

Self-report findings

Owing to the different narcissism subtypes and the myriad ways to measure narcissism (Pincus & Lukowitsky, 2010), the scholarship on narcissism and social media use is broad and has resulted in somewhat conflicting findings (e.g., Bergman, Fearrington, Davenport, & Bergman, 2011; (Buffardi & Campbell, 2008); Fox & Rooney, 2015). As a result, this section will focus more on meta-analytic results. For instance, Liu and Baumeister (2016) conducted an early meta-analysis on narcissism and social media use across 19 studies. Overall, they found that (global) narcissism was positively associated with the following social media activities: overall use, number of friends, number of photos posted, frequency of status updates, and interactions through likes and comments. These findings were stronger in samples from Eastern, collectivistic cultures and weaker in samples with more women participants.

Grandiose narcissism, typified as a combination of extroversion, self-centeredness, and a lack of empathy, has been the most widely studied form of narcissism with respect to social media use. When Liu and Baumeister (2016) examined their findings by narcissism subtype, their meta-analysis revealed that image uploads were more frequent for people scoring higher on the subscale assessing grandiose narcissism. A later meta-analysis on narcissism and social media use included 62 studies (78% based on self-reported social media behaviors) and a total of 13,430 participants (McCain & Campbell, 2018). Overall, their findings revealed a significant relationship between social media use and grandiose narcissism but not for vulnerable narcissism—the more introverted and emotionally reactive variant. Specifically, the results of this meta-analysis revealed that grandiose narcissists spent more time on social media, posted more frequent status updates, had more social media friends, and posted more pictures and selfies. Most of the studies included in this meta-analysis were from Western samples and examined people's use of Facebook with Twitter/X and Instagram as the other common social media applications. A second meta-analysis replicated these findings and also reported that the relationship between narcissism and social media use was stronger when the culture was collectivistic with a larger power differential or hierarchy incorporated into the cultural norms for behavior (e.g., China and India; Gnambs & Appel, 2018).

Overall, it should not be surprising that people with a predisposition to enhance their self-importance are the more active social media users. As Liu and Baumeister (2016) states: "These patterns reflect the narcissistic assumption that other people will be eager to learn about the lives of the narcissists, presumably because the narcissists think their lives are fascinating and important (p. 85)." This point is further illustrated by the understandable research finding that social media applications designed to provide few options for anonymity are more popular among grandiose narcissists. It also highlights the importance of considering the gender and cultural composition of a sample when evaluating research results—a topic that will be covered broadly in Chapter 4.

Digital footprints

From the research reviewed earlier, it is clear that people who have narcissistic tendencies are generally heavier social media users, especially on platforms that offer less anonymity (e.g., Facebook vs. Reddit). This is unsurprising given the ease with which social media can facilitate self-presentation and the amount of control that people have over self-presentation processes when using social media. Research examining people's language use and other digital footprints on social media further illustrates the ways in which people's personalities are reflected in their social media use. For instance, Garcia and Sikström (2014) examined the linguistic content of people's Facebook status updates and found that the words people use in these posts reflect their personalities and significantly predicted narcissism such that people who scored high on narcissism used more odd phrasing and words that conveyed negative effect. Similarly, Bogolyubova et al. (2018) had Russian participants to fill out short Dark Triad scale and downloaded their Facebook profile details (demographics and posts). In their study, they examined three kinds of harmful online behavior: sending threats/insults, sharing personal information (of someone else?) without consent (including photos/videos), and posting information derogatory on SNS. Results revealed that narcissism was positively correlated with longer average posts and the concepts, including social interaction, self-image, social status, and reasoning.

One assumption about people high in narcissism is that all they talk about is themselves. Does this mean that their social media postings feature a lot of first-person pronouns (e.g., I, me, and mine)? Despite popular culture perceptions that this should be the case, the research has not supported this idea. For instance, DeWall, Buffardi, Bonser, and Campbell (2011) collected the Facebook profile information—both photos and text-based self-descriptions—of 80 college students. They analyzed the text using the Linguistic Inquiry Word Count (LIWC) and has a group of five judges evaluated the pictures with respect to self-promotion and sexiness. While the overall level of narcissism did not predict the extent to which participants used first-person singular pronouns (I/me) in their profile descriptions, the authors reported among people high in narcissism, those who used fewer first-person singular pronouns had more sexy and self-aggrandizing profile pictures. This is particularly notable since later on a series of wide-scale studies revealed that, generally, there is no relationship between narcissism and the use of first-person pronouns (Carey et al., 2015). The authors suggested that these results are reflective of the notion that people high in narcissism use photos more so than words to attract people's attention on social media. Similarly, an examination of personality and Twitter use revealed that people high in narcissism were more likely to have profile photos with one person shown rather than a group and that they also tended to express a lot of positivity and commentary on daily life in their tweets (Preotiuc-Pietro, Carpenter, Giorgi, & Ungar, 2016; October). Consistent with the notion that people high in narcissism seek praise and positive input from others.

One final aspect of the relationship between narcissism and social media use pertains to the reactions of other people. As the evidence indicates before, people high in narcissism are heavier social media users, especially when the social media platform provides less anonymity (McCain & Campbell, 2018). Furthermore, the literature reviewed also suggests that people high in narcissism do so to seek attention. While few studies have examined the reactions of perceivers to these efforts but the limited research that exists suggests that people's narcissistic actions are perceived poorly by others. For instance, Vander Molen et al. (2018) reported that observers used specific cues to infer that someone was narcissistic such as having more than 500 friends, using a "sexy" profile pic, and extensive use of likes. Similarly, Taylor, Hinck, and Lim (2017) reported that hypothetical posts that included selfies were perceived as more narcissistic, inappropriate, and lower in social attractiveness.

Machiavellianism

The term Machiavellianism, the second personality trait assessed by the Dark Triad, stems from the 16th century book entitled *The Prince* by Machiavelli which focuses on political power and generally endorses the idea that power should be obtained and then maintained by any necessary means, regardless of the ethics of the actions. Machiavellianism is characterized by manipulative and deceptive patterns of behavior as the preferred means of attaining self-relevant objectives (Jakobwitz & Egan, 2006). People high in Machiavellianism have been described as unwilling to act in accordance with social conventions, especially if doing so provides an opportunity for personal gain. Furthermore, when making decisions, Machiavellians are able to distance themselves from their own moral convictions when engaging in decision-making (Ciulla, Rojas, Kimbrough, & Guadagno, 2020). Thus, Machiavellianism is different from narcissism in that the defining characteristic centers around personal gain rather than self-esteem maintenance.

Self-report findings

Unlike narcissism, the relationship between Machiavellianism and social media use has not been thoroughly investigated. The extant scholarship has shown that Machiavellianism predicts different usage patterns in anonymous social media platforms such as Yik Yak such that those high in Machiavellianism were likely to confess, while people low in Machiavellianism were more likely to be lurkers (Seigfried-Spellar & Lankford, 2018). Machiavellianism has also been shown to predict participation in trolling and enjoying it (Buckels et al., 2014).

Similarly, research on Machiavellianism and social media use has also revealed gender differences. For instance, Fox and Rooney (2015) surveyed the personality characteristics and social media use of a nationally representative sample of 1000 US men, finding that Machiavellianism correlated with time spent on social media. Abell and Brewer (2014) reported that Machiavellianism predicted greater self-monitoring and self-promotion in men's Facebook use but more dishonest self-promotion and relational aggression among women.

Digital footprints

The literature on the relationship between Machiavellianism and people's digital footprints generally shows that there are distinctive features associated with their social media use. For instance, research in this area indicates that across social media platforms, Machiavellians use few personal pronouns, write shorter posts, express fewer positive emotions, express more negative emotions—especially anger, and use more swearwords (Bogolyubova et al., 2018; Sumner, Byers, Boochever, & Park, 2012; Vander Molen et al., 2018). Consistent with this, an analysis of Twitter/X use demonstrated that Machiavellians posted more advertisements and spam and fewer original posts (Preotiuc-Pietro et al., 2016).

Psychopathy

As indicated earlier, psychopathy, the third facet of the Dark Triad, refers to actions typified by the inability to empathize with other people (Ciulla et al., 2020). This callousness often manifests along with aggressive behaviors (Stellwagen et al., 2011). People high in psychopathy have also been found to be extremely manipulative, violate social norms, and engage in other types of antisocial behaviors and generally do not show remorse for harming other people. Indeed, some scholars assert that psychopaths are extremely disengaged from typical emotional reactions and may instead show pleasure at harm that they have caused others. Furthermore, people high in psychopathy have poor impulse control and difficulty delaying gratification. As with the other facets of the Dark Triad, researchers do distinguish between having psychopathic personality characteristics and being diagnosed with its pathological counterpart: antisocial personality disorder (American Psychiatric Association, 2013; Jonason, Sitnikova, & Oshio, 2018).

Self-report findings

Research has shown that people high in psychopathy are more likely to troll other people online and also report enjoying it (Bogolyubova et al., 2018; Buckels et al., 2014; Seigfried-Spellar & Lankford, 2018). They have also been shown to report higher agreement with other troll comments relative to those lower in psychopathy, especially when the troll target was more successful (Lopes & Yu, 2017). Finally, among men, psychopathy predicts greater time spent using social media and more frequent selfie posting (Fox & Rooney, 2015).

Digital footprints

In terms of digital footprints, research has established that the linguistic content of people's social media posts accurately predicts their level of psychopathy (Garcia & Sikström, 2014). Furthermore, as with the literature on Machiavellianism, psychopathy predicted the expression of negative emotions—especially anger—as well as a greater use of swearwords and expressions of violence (Bogolyubova et al., 2018; Sumner et al., 2012). Finally, with respect to personality differences as reflected in other aspects of people's social media profiles, Vander Molen et al. (2018) found that psychopathy positively predicted the presence of other people in people's main profile picture.

Summary

The obvious upshot of this chapter is that individual differences such as the Big Five Factors of personality (openness, conscientiousness, extroversion, agreeableness, and neuroticism) and the Dark Triad (narcissism, Machiavellianism, and psychopathy) affect the way in which people use social media. While there are other personality traits that have been examined in the literature—some of which will be covered in other chapters—the traits reviewed in this chapter are generally the most widely investigated. Furthermore, because these traits predict differential patterns of social media use, the research reviewed in this chapter also demonstrates that people's personality traits can be estimated from their digital footprints. Overall, these findings illustrate an important theme that emerges from this research: some of the personality findings are general to social media use and others are specific to the type of social media platform and its features.

These new methods of predicting meaningful psychological insights and individual differences from our online behavior behaviors raise important questions regarding people's rights and privacy—an issue that is currently under debate globally. Revisiting the story of CA reviewed at the beginning of the chapter, one issue left unaddressed is whether their tactics were effective. Prior to CA's downfall, they claimed success for electing Trump, passing Brexit, and coining the term "Crooked Hillary." But as I discuss in detail later in Chapter 5, assessing the impact is not easy. However, evidence from one of Cambridge University's whistleblowers (and my former colleague at Stanford), Michal Kosinski and his colleagues, suggests that these types of targeting advertising are effective (Matz, Kosinski, Nave, & Stillwell, 2017) despite the questionable handling of people's data. Indeed, Facebook was fined $5 billion for the CA data breach (Wong, 2019; July 12) and this scandal has inspired much debate as well as changes in privacy laws across the globe. "No," says Kosinski, quietly and shaking his head. "This is not my fault. I did not build the bomb. I only showed that it exists." (Grassegger & Krogerus, 2017; January 28).

References

Abell, L., & Brewer, G. (2014). Machiavellianism, self-monitoring, self-promotion and relational aggression on Facebook. *Computers in Human Behavior, 36*, 258–262.

American Psychiatric Association. (2013). *Diagnostic and statistical manual of mental disorders* (5th ed). Arlington, VA: American Psychiatric Association.

Amichai-Hamburger, Y., & Ben-Artzi, E. (2003). Loneliness and Internet use. *Computers in Human Behavior, 19*(1), 71–80.

Amichai-Hamburger, Y., & Vinitzky, G. (2010). Social network use and personality. *Computers in Human Behavior, 26*(6), 1289–1295.

Amichai-Hamburger, Y., Wainapel, G., & Fox, S. (2002). On the Internet no one knows I'm an introvert": Extroversion, neuroticism, and Internet interaction. *Cyberpsychology & Behavior, 5*(2), 125–128.

Annisette, L. E., & Lafreniere, K. D. (2017). Social media, texting, and personality: A test of the shallowing hypothesis. *Personality and Individual Differences, 115*, 154–158.

Azucar, D., Marengo, D., & Settanni, M. (2018). Predicting the Big 5 personality traits from digital footprints on social media: A meta-analysis. *Personality and Individual Differences, 124*, 150–159.

Bachrach, Y., Kosinski, M., Graepel, T., Kohli, P., & Stillwell, D. (2012, June). Personality and patterns of Facebook usage. In Proceedings of the 4th annual ACM web science conference (pp. 24–32). Evanston, IL.

Back, M. D., Stopfer, J. M., Vazire, S., Gaddis, S., Schmukle, S. C., Egloff, B., & Gosling, S. D. (2010). Facebook profiles reflect actual personality, not self-idealization. *Psychological Science*, *21*(3), 372–374.

Bergman, S. M., Fearrington, M. E., Davenport, S. W., & Bergman, J. Z. (2011). Millennials, narcissism, and social networking: What narcissists do on social networking sites and why. *Personality and Individual Differences*, *50*(5), 706–711.

Blackwell, D., Leaman, C., Tramposch, R., Osborne, C., & Liss, M. (2017). Extraversion, neuroticism, attachment style and fear of missing out as predictors of social media use and addiction. *Personality and Individual Differences*, *116*, 69–72.

Bogolyubova, O., Panicheva, P., Tikhonov, R., Ivanov, V., & Ledovaya, Y. (2018). Dark personalities on Facebook: Harmful online behaviors and language. *Computers in Human Behavior*, *78*, 151–159.

Botwin, M. D., & Buss, D. M. (1989). Structure of act-report data: Is the five-factor model of personality recaptured? *Journal of Personality and Social Psychology*, *56*(6), 988.

Boyd, R. L., & Pennebaker, J. W. (2017). Language-based personality: a new approach to personality in a digital world. *Current Opinion in Behavioral Sciences*, *18*, 63–68.

Brailovskaia, J., & Margraf, J. (2018). What does media use reveal about personality and mental health? An exploratory investigation among German students. *PLoS One*, *13* (1).

Buckels, E. E., Trapnell, P. D., & Paulhus, D. L. (2014). Trolls just want to have fun. *Personality and Individual Differences*, *67*, 97–102.

Buffardi, L. E., & Campbell, W. K. (2008). Narcissism and social networking web sites. *Personality and Social Psychology Bulletin*, *34*(10), 1303–1314.

Burger, J. M. (1986). *Personality: Theory and research*. Wadsworth Publishing Company.

Buss, A. R. (1977). The trait-situation controversy and the concept of interaction. *Personality and Social Psychology Bulletin*, *3*(2), 196–201.

Campbell, W. K., Rudich, E. A., & Sedikides, C. (2002). Narcissism, self-esteem, and the positivity of self-views: Two portraits of self-love. *Personality and Social Psychology Bulletin*, *28*(3), 358–368.

Carey, A. L., et al. (2015). Narcissism and the use of personal pronouns revisited. *Journal of Personality and Social Psychology*, *109*(3), e1–e15.

Carrier, L. M., Cheever, N. A., Rosen, L. D., Benitez, S., & Chang, J. (2009). Multitasking across generations: Multitasking choices and difficulty ratings in three generations of Americans. *Computers in Human Behavior*, *25*(2), 483–489.

Chabrol, H., Van Leeuwen, N., Rodgers, R., & Séjourné, N. (2009). Contributions of psychopathic, narcissistic, Machiavellian, and sadistic personality traits to juvenile delinquency. *Personality and Individual Differences*, *47*(7), 734–739.

Ciulla, C., Rojas, L., Kimbrough, A. M., & Guadagno, R. E. (2020). Antisocial Behavior. In *Encyclopedia of Personality and Individual Differences* (pp. 196–206). Cham: Springer International Publishing.

Correa, T., Hinsley, A. W., & De Zuniga, H. G. (2010). Who interacts on the Web? The intersection of users' personality and social media use. *Computers in Human Behavior*, *26*(2), 247–253.

Costa, P. T., & McCrae, R. R. (1992). Normal personality assessment in clinical practice: The NEO Personality Inventory. *Psychological Assessment*, *4*(1), 5–13.

Davies, H. (2015, December 11). Ted Cruz using firm that harvested data on millions of unwitting Facebook users. *The Guardian*. Retrieved from https://www.theguardian.com/us-news/2015/dec/11/senator-ted-cruz-president-campaign-facebook-user-data.

DeWall, C. N., Buffardi, L. E., Bonser, I., & Campbell, W. K. (2011). Narcissism and implicit attention seeking: Evidence from linguistic analyses of social networking and online presentation. *Personality and Individual Differences*, *51*(1), 57–62.

Digman, J. M. (1989). Five robust trait dimensions: Development, stability, and utility. *Journal of Personality*, *57*(2), 195–214.
Digman, J. M. (1990). Personality structure: Emergence of the five-factor model. *Annual Review of Psychology*, *41*, 417–440.
Digman, J. M., & Inouye, J. (1986). Further specification of the five robust factors of personality. *Journal of Personality and Social Psychology*, *50*(1), 116.
Feiler, D. C., & Kleinbaum, A. M. (2015). Popularity, similarity, and the network extraversion bias. *Psychological Science*, *26*(5), 593–603.
Fox, J., & Rooney, M. C. (2015). The Dark Triad and trait self-objectification as predictors of men's use and self-presentation behaviors on social networking sites. *Personality and Individual Differences*, *76*, 161–165.
Garcia, D., & Sikström, S. (2014). The dark side of Facebook: Semantic representations of status updates predict the Dark Triad of personality. *Personality and Individual Differences*, *67*, 92–96.
Gazit, T., Aharony, N., & Amichai-Hamburger, Y. (2019). Tell me who you are and I will tell you which SNS you use: SNSs participation. *Online Information Review*, *44*, 139–161.
Gebauer, J. E., Sedikides, C., Verplanken, B., & Maio, G. R. (2012). Communal narcissism. *Journal of Personality and Social Psychology*, *103*(5), 854.
Gnambs, T., & Appel, M. (2018). Narcissism and social networking behavior: A meta-analysis. *Journal of Personality*, *86*(2), 200–212.
Goldberg, L. R. (1990). An alternative "description of personality": the big-five factor structure. *Journal of Personality and Social Psychology*, *59*(6), 1216.
Goldberg, L. R. (1993). The structure of phenotypic personality traits. *American Psychologist*, *48*(1), 26.
Gosling, S. D., Rentfrow, P. J., & Swann, W. B., Jr. (2003). A Very Brief Measure of the Big Five Personality Domains. *Journal of Research in Personality*, *37*, 504–528.
Grassegger, H., & Krogerus, M. (2017, January 28). The data that turned the world upside down. *The Guardian*. Retrieved from: https://www.vice.com/en_us/article/mg9vvn/how-our-likes-helped-trump-win.
Guadagno, R. E., Okdie, B. M., & Eno, C. A. (2008). Who blogs? Personality predictors of blogging. *Computers in Human Behavior*, *24*(5), 1993–2004.
Habashi, M. M., Graziano, W. G., & Hoover, A. E. (2016). Searching for the prosocial personality: A Big Five approach to linking personality and prosocial behavior. *Personality and Social Psychology Bulletin*, *42*(9), 1177–1192.
Hamburger, Y. A., & Ben-Artzi, E. (2000). The relationship between extraversion and neuroticism and the different uses of the Internet. *Computers in Human Behavior*, *16*(4), 441–449.
Hart, J., Nailling, E., Bizer, G. Y., & Collins, C. K. (2015). Attachment theory as a framework for explaining engagement with Facebook. *Personality and Individual Differences*, *77*, 33–40.
Hughes, D. J., Rowe, M., Batey, M., & Lee, A. (2012). A tale of two sites: Twitter vs. Facebook and the personality predictors of social media usage. *Computers in Human Behavior*, *28*(2), 561–569.
Jakobwitz, S., & Egan, V. (2006). The dark triad and normal personality traits. *Personality and Individual Differences*, *40*(2), 331–339.
John, O. P., & Srivastava, S. (1999). The Big Five trait taxonomy: History, measurement, and theoretical perspectives. In L. A. Pervin, & O. P. John (Eds.), *Handbook of personality: Theory and research* (2nd ed., pp. 102–138). New York: Springer.
Jonason, P. K., Sitnikova, M., & Oshio, A. (2018). The Dark Triad traits and views of time in three countries. *Personality and Individual Differences*, *120*, 107–111.
Jonason, P. K., & Webster, G. D. (2010). The dirty dozen: A concise measure of the dark triad. *Psychological Assessment*, *22*(2), 420–432.

Katona, K., & Wexler, E. (Directors). (1999). Sing *along songs*: Sing *a song with pooh bear and piglet too* [Film]. The Walt Disney Company.

Kern, M. L., McCarthy, P. X., Chakrabarty, D., & Rizoiu, M. A. (2019). Social media-predicted personality traits and values can help match people to their ideal jobs. *Proceedings of the National Academy of Sciences, 116*(52), 26459–26464.

Kim, J. W., & Chock, T. M. (2017). Personality traits and psychological motivations predicting selfie posting behaviors on social networking sites. *Telematics and Informatics, 34* (5), 560–571.

Kosinski, M., Bachrach, Y., Kohli, P., Stillwell, D., & Graepel, T. (2014). Manifestations of user personality in website choice and behaviour on online social networks. *Machine learning, 95*(3), 357–380.

Kosinski, M., Stillwell, D., & Graepel, T. (2013). Private traits and attributes are predictable from digital records of human behavior. *Proceedings of the national academy of sciences, 110*(15), 5802–5805.

Liu, D., & Baumeister, R. F. (2016). Social networking online and personality of self-worth: A meta-analysis. *Journal of Research in Personality, 64*, 79–89.

Liu, D., & Campbell, W. K. (2017). The Big Five personality traits, Big Two metatraits and social media: A meta-analysis. *Journal of Research in Personality, 70*, 229–240.

Loewald, R. J. (2020). *Narcissus gazes into his social media reflection. Original artwork created for use in this book*. CA: Half Moon Bay.

Lopes, B., & Yu, H. (2017). Who do you troll and Why: An investigation into the relationship between the Dark Triad Personalities and online trolling behaviours towards popular and less popular Facebook profiles. *Computers in Human Behavior, 77*, 69–76.

Matz, S. C., Kosinski, M., Nave, G., & Stillwell, D. J. (2017). Psychological targeting as an effective approach to digital mass persuasion. *Proceedings of the National Academy of Sciences, 114*(48), 12714–12719.

McCain, J. L., & Campbell, W. K. (2018). Narcissism and social media use: A meta-analytic review. *Psychology of Popular Media Culture*, 7(3), 308.

McCrae, R. R., & Costa, P. T. (1997). Personality trait structure as a human universal. *American Psychologist, 52*, 509–516.

Meisel, M. K., Ning, H., Campbell, W. K., & Goodie, A. S. (2016). Narcissism, overconfidence, and risk taking in US and Chinese student samples. *Journal of Cross-Cultural Psychology, 47*(3), 385–400.

Miller, J. D., McCain, J., Lynam, D. R., Few, L. R., Gentile, B., MacKillop, J., & Campbell, W. K. (2014). A comparison of the criterion validity of popular measures of narcissism and narcissistic personality disorder via the use of expert ratings. *Psychological Assessment, 26*(3), 958–969, http:/doi.org.oca.ucsc.edu/10.1037/a0036613.

Moore, K., & McElroy, J. C. (2012). The influence of personality on Facebook usage, wall postings, and regret. *Computers in Human Behavior, 28*(1), 267–274.

Muscanell, N. L., & Guadagno, R. E. (2012). Make new friends or keep the old: Gender and personality differences in social networking use. *Computers in Human Behavior, 28* (1), 107–112.

Okdie, B. M., Guadagno, R. E., Rempala, D. M., & Eno, C. A. (2011). Who blogs in 2010? An updated look at individual differences in blogging. *International Journal of Interactive Communication Systems and Technologies (IJICST), 1*(2), 1–13.

Ong, E. Y., et al. (2011). Narcissism, extraversion and adolescents' self-presentation on Facebook. *Personality and Individual Differences, 50*(2), 180–185.

Paulhus, D. L., & Williams, K. M. (2002). The Dark Triad of personality: Narcissism, Machiavellianism and psychopathy. *Journal of Research in Personality, 36*, 556–563, doi:10.1016/S0092-6566(02)00505-6.

Pincus, A. L., & Lukowitsky, M. R. (2010). Pathological narcissism and narcissistic personality disorder. *Annual Review of Clinical Psychology, 6*, 421–446.

Preotiuc-Pietro, D., Carpenter, J., Giorgi, S., & Ungar, L. (2016, October). Studying the Dark Triad of personality through Twitter behavior. In *Proceedings of the 25th ACM international on conference on information and knowledge management* (pp. 761–770).

Quercia, D., Lambiotte, R., Stillwell, D., Kosinski, M., & Crowcroft, J. (2012). The personality of popular facebook users, February *In Proceedings of the ACM 2012 conference on computer supported cooperative work*, 955–964.

Russell, M., & Karol, D. (1994). *16PF, administrator's manual*. Champaign, IL: Institute for Personality and Ability Testing.

Schwartz, H. A., et al. (2013). Personality, gender, and age in the language of social media: The open-vocabulary approach. *PLoS One*, *8*(9), e73791. Available from https://doi.org/10.1371/journal.pone.0073791.

Seidman, G. (2013). Self-presentation and belonging on Facebook: How personality influences social media use and motivations. *Personality and Individual Differences*, *54*(3), 402–407.

Seigfried-Spellar, K. C., & Lankford, C. M. (2018). Personality and online environment factors differ for posters, trolls, lurkers, and confessors on Yik Yak. *Personality and Individual Differences*, *124*, 54–56.

Settanni, M., Azucar, D., & Marengo, D. (2018). Predicting individual characteristics from digital traces on social media: A meta-analysis. *Cyberpsychology, Behavior, and Social Networking*, *21*(4), 217–228.

Stanton, K., Ellickson-Larew, S., & Watson, D. (2016). Development and validation of a measure of online deception and intimacy. *Personality and Individual Differences*, *88*, 187–196.

Stellwagen, K. K. (2011). Psychopathy, narcissism, and Machiavellianism: Distinct yet intertwining personality constructs. In C. T. Barry, P. K. Kerig, K. K. Stellwagen, & T. D. Barry (Eds.), *Narcissism and machiavellianism in youth: Implications for the development of adaptive and maladaptive behavior*. American Psychological Association. Available from http://doi.org/10.1037/12352-002.

Stillwell, D.J., & Kosinski, M. (2012). *myPersonality project: Example of successful utilization of online social networks for large-scale social research*. Unpublished manuscript retrieved from: https://www.gsb.stanford.edu/sites/gsb/files/conf-presentations/stillwell_and_kosinski_2012.pdf.

Stillwell, D.J., & Kosinski, M. (n.d.). *Publications*. MyPersonality. Retrieved from: https://sites.google.com/michalkosinski.com/mypersonality/publications.

Stoughton, J. W., Thompson, L. F., & Meade, A. W. (2013). Big five personality traits reflected in job applicants' social media postings. *Cyberpsychology, Behavior, and Social Networking*, *16*(11), 800–805.

Sumner, C., Byers, A., Boochever, R., & Park, G. J. (2012). *Predicting dark triad personality traits from twitter usage and a linguistic analysis of tweets, 2012 11th International Conference on Machine Learning and Applications* (Vol. 2, pp. 386–393). IEEE, December.

Taylor, S. H., Hinck, A. S., & Lim, H. (2017). An experimental test of how selfies change social judgments on Facebook. *Cyberpsychology, Behavior, and Social Networking*, *20*(10), 610–614.

Vander Molen, R. J., Kaplan, S., Choi, E., & Montoya, D. (2018). Judgments of the Dark Triad based on Facebook profiles. *Journal of Research in Personality*, *73*, 150–163.

Wilson, K., Fornasier, S., & White, K. M. (2010). Psychological predictors of young adults' use of social networking sites. *Cyberpsychology, Behavior, and Social Networking*, *13*(2), 173–177.

Wilson, R. E., Harris, K., & Vazire, S. (2015). Personality and friendship satisfaction in daily life: Do everyday social interactions account for individual differences in friendship satisfaction? *European Journal of Personality*, *29*(2), 173–186.

Wink, P. (1991). Two faces of narcissism. *Journal of Personality and Social Psychology*, *61*(4), 590.

Wong, J.C. (2019, July 12). Facebook to be fined $5bn for Cambridge Analytica privacy violations – reports. *The Guardian*. Retrieved from https://www.theguardian.com/technology/2019/jul/12/facebook-fine-ftc-privacy-violations.

CHAPTER 4

Sex, gender, and cultural considerations in social media

It wasn't their words, it's that I started to believe them.

—Tran (2018; August 21)

I remember watching the first *Star Wars* film (Kurtz & Lucas, 1977) at the movie theater as if it were yesterday. As a kindergartener, it was my first movie and I saw it with my two BFFs (and our mothers). The three of us—newly minted Star Wars fans—left the theater quoting our new-found hero, Princess Leia, portrayed brilliantly by the late (and great) Carrie Fisher. However, as I grew older, I began to reflect on the lack of gender and ethnic diversity of the Star Wars universe, and I realized that my friends and I loved Princess Leia because of her beauty, brilliance, and moxie, and because she was the only prominent female character in a fictional universe with a large oversupply of men.

Fast forward a generation and I had the pleasure of taking my children to see the latest series of Star Wars films featuring a young woman named Rey as the new hero. This updated Star Wars universe was more diverse, featuring far more women and much more variation in the ethnicity of the humanoid characters. To me, this was fantastic—a much-needed update to reflect the diverse contemporary world we currently live in. Actress Kelly Marie Tran, a young woman born in the United States to Vietnamese refugees, played one such character named Rose Tico in Episodes 8 and 9 of Star Wars. Also reflective of the increased diversity in the updated Star Wars universe was a character named Finn was portrayed by British actor, John Boyega, who was born in London to parents of Nigerian descent.

Boyega and Tran share one thing in common other than costarring in these films: both were bombarded with racist insults from Internet trolls in the wake of their performances, as the increased diversity in the updated Star Wars universe was not well received by a vocal minority (Shoard, 2018; June 11; When racists tried to strike Star Wars, 2015; October 20). Tran reacted to this by deleting her social media account

Psychological Processes in Social Media
DOI: https://doi.org/10.1016/B978-0-12-811320-2.00004-6

stating: "Their words seemed to confirm what growing up as a woman and a person of color already taught me: that I belonged in margins and spaces, valid only as a minor character in their lives and stories." (Tran, 2018; August 21). Boyega, on the other hand, chose to stay on social media stating: "Through social media, we get to engage, we get to have fun... I don't know, for me anyway, when I see that [backlash], I'm like, well, that's actually not true. But no, it is actually not true. So, it's kind of like [*shrugs*] it is what it is. But to engage, to connect with the fans who otherwise wouldn't get a day to day experience, especially during things like the press tour, and behind the scenes stuff, is always good." (Vary, 2019; December 11).

Despite their similar positions, Tran withdrew from social media while Boyega decided to ignore the racist trolls and instead focus on the positive interactions with fans that were also facilitated by the affordances of social media. While there are myriad reasons why these two actors made different choices in their response to online harassment, this chapter focuses on two key differences that distinguish them: their gender and their culture. Much like personality, gender and culture are two core individual differences that drive much of our behavior, both online and offline. Gender, sex, and culture are dimensions that vary between people and also impact their social media use. This chapter reviews similarities and differences in the way men and women across cultures use social media. As with personality (covered in Chapter 3), gender and culture also affect the psychological processes observed on social media.

Understanding sex versus gender

People often use the terms gender and sex interchangeably. However, social scientists and other scholars differentiate between the two words such that sex refers to the biological aspect of being male or female (i.e., based on the presence of sex organs, sex-specific hormones, and X or Y chromosomes). Based on this definition of sex, most people in the world are either biologically male or female (Lips, 2017)[1]. Gender, on the other hand, refers to stereotypical beliefs and cultural expectations for people based on their biological sex. For instance, in the United States (US), there has long been a cultural expectation that women are more *communal*

[1] While it is exceptionally rare, some people are born with chromosomal abnormalities making them intersex, people who have both male and female biological markers.

than men and will therefore be more nurturing, self-effacing, sensitive to the needs of others, kind, and comfortable expressing emotions (Eagly, Wood, & Diekman, 2000). Conversely, in the US, cultural expectations for men focus on agency. Men are expected to be more *agentic* than women and this can be seen in societal expectations that men ought to be independent, self-aggrandizing, task-focused, and physically and mentally strong. Empirical evidence suggests that these socially constructed expectations guide people in understanding what is typical for others based on their gender. This does not mean that every single man is more agentic than every single woman nor is every single woman more communal than every single man. Indeed, evidence suggests that there are more differences within the sexes than between them (Lips, 2017). Instead, gender-based expectations for behavior reflects the idea that people are generally aware of societal expectations and they generally attempt to conform to them.

An important aspect of discerning the difference between sex and gender is to understand that not everyone's biological sex matches their gender as some people do not identify with a particular gender and others identify with the gender that does not correspond to their biological sex. While individuals in the former category refer to themselves as nonbinary and people in the latter category call themselves transgender or trans in short. Some transgender individuals choose to transition through hormone treatments and/or surgery to change their physical appearance to match their gender identities (Lips, 2017). While the number of people who do not fit into "the gender binary" is growing, research on these individuals is still in its nascence. When possible, research examining social media use among nonbinary and transgender samples will be reviewed throughout this text. However, much of the existing research on social media uses the more traditional binary conceptualization of gender and only examines people who are either male and identify as a man or female and identify as a woman. Finally, it is important to point out that people's gender identity is unrelated to their sexual orientation.

Understanding culture

Culture refers to the common attitudes, norms, traditions, behaviors, and dialects that unify people residing in a set location and within a specific timeframe (Triandis, 2011). Different cultural groups may be narrowly defined—for instance, specific college campuses have their own unique cultures with some more focused on academic achievements and others on collegiate sports, Greek life, or balancing working full time with attending school—or broadly defined such as the country people reside in. Regardless of a culture's breadth, different cultures vary in many ways, especially with respect to the types of behaviors that are considered normative or socially acceptable. While there are several commonly accepted models of culture, the principal distinction utilized in this book primarily differentiates cultures broadly based on their location on the individualism collectivism continuum. On the one end of the spectrum, individualistic cultures emphasize the goals and achievements of individual people and place the needs of an individual above that of the group. On the other end, collectivistic cultures emphasize the goals, achievements, and needs of the group as more important than those of the individual (Hofstede, 1983). Generally, the United States, Canada, and Western Europe are considered individualistic cultures, while countries in Asia, Eastern Europe, and Central and South America are considered more collectivistic in nature. Thus, because of the abovementioned geographic locations associated with different types of cultures, researchers often use the term *Western* to refer to individualistic cultures and *Eastern* to refer to collectivistic cultures. Finally, as reviewed in Chapter 1, people from Eastern and Western cultures tend to use different social media platforms, largely because of censorship of the US-created social media applications in China. As a result, the literature is not always clear on whether psychological processes observed in people's social media use are due to differences between cultures or differences in the design and features of the particular social media application.

Gender, culture, and social media use

Throughout the history of the Internet, marked differences have been documented in people's Internet use based on geographic location, socioeconomic status, personality, and other demographic factors. With respect to gender, this research has shown that in the United States, men use the Internet more for seeking information, while women use it more for maintaining social relationships (Fallows, 2005). The same general pattern has been documented in the social media use of men and women. Specifically, men and women generally use social media at similar rates, yet the types of social media platforms men and women tend to use and the activities they engage in while using social media differ in ways that make sense when considering gender role expectat. For instance, research suggests that US women have a stronger preference for using social media relative to US men largely due to the ease of using social media to communicate with friends and family (Kimbrough, Guadagno, Muscanell, & Dill, 2013; Muscanell & Guadagno, 2012). Other research has established that in the Western world, women use more image-focused social media platforms such as Pinterest, Tumblr, and Instagram (Gazit, Aharony, & Amichai-Hamburger, 2019) as well, while men are more heavily invested in using news aggregators and discussion-focused social media such as Twitter/X and Reddit (Demographics of Social Media Users & Adoption in the United States, 2020; June 5). Another distinction between men and women concerns the type of activities they engage in while using social media and this distinction also maps onto social role expectations as described earlier. Thus women tend to use social media in a way that maintains existing social relationships while men tend to use social media more to seek out information, develop new relationships, and find job opportunities (Krämer, Neubaum, & Eimler, 2017; Muscanell & Guadagno, 2012).

In collectivistic cultures, the research on gender differences in social media is still emerging. However, based on demographic differences in general use, it is an open question as to whether the gender differences in social media use described earlier generalize outside of Western, individualistic cultures. For instance, unlike the United States, in China, men are the majority of Internet users (Thomala, 2020; May 05) with their gender accounting for 12.8−4% more Internet use than women across time. Similar results have also been reported in Central and South America (Gray, Gainous, & Wagner, 2017). With respect to social media specifically, the evidence suggests that women use social media more than men do primarily in individualistic cultures, while the opposite is the case in many collectivistic cultures, particularly those in Africa and southwestern Asia (Garcia et al., 2018).

Finally, while there is growing evidence that social media use (and Internet use more broadly defined) has been instrumental in connecting people whose gender identity does not match their biological sex (Darwin, 2017; McKenna & Bargh, 1998), it is unclear whether people who identify as nonbinary or trans—those whose gender identity is fluid, does not fit in a category, or does not match their biological sex—use social media at rates similar to others in their culture. There is, however, a new but growing body of literature examining how people's gender identity affects how they use social media. Throughout this chapter and this book, research on this demographic will also be examined.

Psychological processes differentiated by gender and culture on social media

Given the importance of gender and culture in driving human social behavior, these key individual differences also often impact the psychological processes inherent in people's social media use. Furthermore, gender and culture sometimes interact to produce different psychological outcomes. For instance, as reviewed earlier, men use social media more than women do in collectivistic cultures, while in the United States—an individualistic culture, women are the more numerous social media users. Thus the remainder of this chapter will review select examples of research demonstrating the influence of gender and culture on psychological outcomes in the scholarship on people's use of social media. Next, I examine some of the psychological processes introduced in previous chapters and discuss how the findings change when you take gender and culture into consideration. Note that there is significantly more research on gender differences in social media use compared to the studies on differences across cultures. Furthermore, throughout the rest of the book, I include relevant discussions of the impact that people's gender and cultur have on their social media use.

Language use

As already demonstrated, people's social media words and actions—their digital footprints—are often associated with psychologically meaningful information about them. This begs the question of whether this is the case for gender and culture. The emerging evidence suggests that this is indeed the case. For instance, an examination of the language used by 15,000 men and women in their Facebook posts indicated that, relative to men, women's language included the expression of more positive emotions, the use of more adverbs for emphasis, and more discussion of their interpersonal relationships. Whereas men, relative to women, spent more time discussing politics, competitive sports, and masculine stereotyped activities (e.g., guns and video games). Consistent with gender role expectations, women also expressed more warmth, sociability, and humility than men did (Park et al., 2016). Similar findings were reported in a related study which also showed these gender differences in both the expressions used and topics discussed by men and women (Schwartz et al., 2013). See Fig. 4.1 for word clouds that display the gender differences in social media content from this latter study.

There is minimal research on the role of culture in language use on social media. However, the extant research supports the notion that, similar to gender, people's language use is reflective of their cultural backgrounds (e.g., DeAndrea, Shaw, & Levine, 2010). Overall, the emerging

Figure 4.1 Gender differences in language use on social media (Schwartz et al., 2013).

evidence suggests that people's language use on social media is reflective of cultural expectations for behavior such that women express more communal characteristics and men gravitate toward more agentic means of expression.

Social comparison

In Chapter 2, I introduced the concept of social comparison, defined as the psychological process in which people compare themselves to others based on social standing, skills, abilities, and other characteristics. While most of that section focused on the ways in which social media use has been associated with amplified social comparison processes, the work of Haferkamp and Krämer (2011) also made it clear that men and women compare themselves to others via social media using different domains with men more focused on achievements at work and school and women more focused on their appearance. In support of this, Haferkamp, Eimler, Papadakis, and Kruck (2012) examined gender differences in motivations for social media use among German students, reporting that women generally engaged in more social comparison than men did, reporting that they spent more time comparing themselves to others' profiles.

While this is understandable given the different societal expectations for men and women, it also suggests different psychological implications for men and women who use social media. For women, their social media use increases their exposure to idealized and curated images of similar others and may lead to the formation of inaccurate ideas about the typical physical appearance of other women. Without realizing the extent to which such are images staged or edited, this type of constant upward social comparison may be psychologically harmful to many women. Evidence for this possibility was provided by a study that examined whether social comparison processes on social media affect women more than comparable exposure to more traditional forms of media (Fardouly, Diedrichs, Vartanian, & Halliwell, 2015). To examine this, women sampled from a university in the United Kingdom were randomly assigned to spend 10 minutes browsing one of the following: their Facebook accounts, a women's fashion magazine website (Cosmopolitan), or a nonappearance-related website on home crafting. Results revealed that, compared to women who browsed the fashion magazine or home crafting website, women who spent 10 minutes browsing their Facebook accounts reported more negative moods. This is consistent with other research demonstrating that relative to men, women engage in more upward and downward social comparison based on others' pictures on Facebook (Fox & Vendemia, 2016). Furthermore, other research has illustrated that time spent on Pinterest fitness boards is associated with risky dieting activities (Lewallen & Behm-Morawitz, 2016).

In light of these findings, it is unsurprising that other work has found that there are differential risks associated with social media use for men versus women. For instance, a meta-analysis on problematic Facebook use—defined by the authors as "a problematic behavior which creates problems and impairments in different domains of one's life, such as school, work, friendships, and romantic relationships (Lee, Cheung, & Thadani, 2012) (p. 263)"—revealed that women show higher rates of problematic use relative to men (Marino, Gini, Vieno, & Spada, 2018). This meta-analysis included 56 samples from studies of social media use conducted all over the globe. Taken together, the research on social comparison on social media illustrates that women engage in more social comparison than men do and this tendency may be psychologically harmful to women. Furthermore, the evidence also suggests that this gender difference may be universal rather than culture-specific.

Self-presentation

Defined in Chapter 2 as the process people use to attempt to control the impressions others form of them, self-presentation is also referred to as *impression management*. Generally, the literature on self-presentation indicates that because of different gender role expectations for men and women, there are gender differences both in the ways in which men and women attempt to make a good impression on others and the way these efforts are perceived (Guadagno & Cialdini, 2007). This gender difference is observable on social media particularly where pictures are involved. For instance, research has demonstrated how US women put more effort into their appearance-based self-presentation on social media. Specifically, this research revealed that women generally report that they are more likely to edit their photos prior to posting them on social media and are also more likely to post photos on social media relative to men (Fox & Vendemia, 2016). This emphasis on editing photos of oneself prior to posting to social media is not unique to the United States and has been documented in other cultures such as South Korea (Lyu, 2016). This tendency was also documented among a sample of German social media users. However, in this case, men were more likely to edit their profile photographs (Haferkamp et al., 2012).

Other evidence suggests that people do engage in Goffman-esque self-presentational performances in their social media interactions. For instance, Kuo, Tseng, Tseng, and Lin (2013) examined the extent to which Taiwanese students reported engaging in self-presentational behaviors on Facebook (e.g., using Facebook to post images or status updates). The authors hypothesized that three types of self-presentational factors affect the extent to which people engage in self-presentation on social media: (1) expressive control, defined as people's perceived ability to regulate their actions (e.g., posting on or liking other people's comments and posting their own messages); (2) privacy control, defined as people's perception that they can control the information they share on Facebook through the use of private chatrooms and privacy settings; and (3) image control, defined as the perception that we can control our images on social media. In an examination of the impact of these factors on people's Facebook use, the authors found that all three dimensions predicted self-presentation attempts but the results differed for men and women. Specifically, they found that perceived expressive control was more predictive of self-presentation behaviors for men, while privacy and image control were higher for women.

Privacy preferences

Another way in which men and women differ in their social media activities pertains to their privacy preferences. Overall, the research in this area suggests that women are more concerned about maintaining their privacy. For instance, the study of Taiwanese undergraduate students' social media described earlier also revealed that women reported a greater interest in setting privacy controls and controlling the impressions others formed from the content of their profiles, while men were more interested in their ability to use social media features that communicate information (Kuo, et al., 2013). Consistent with these findings, a recent meta-analysis found that relative to men, women were more likely to utilize their social media privacy settings, untag themselves in photographs, and show caution in disclosing identifying information such as their home addresses (Tifferet, 2019). Participants in this meta-analysis were primarily sampled from the United States but also included samples from across the globe—just not enough to facilitate a cross-cultural comparison of studies.

This gender difference is unsurprising given that women are generally aware that, relative to men, they will be more heavily evaluated by women on their physical appearance—a phenomenon called objectification (Fredrickson & Roberts, 1997). Combined with the literature on social comparison and self-presentation described earlier, it makes sense that women would be more oriented toward controlling their social media presence.

Social support

One of the best aspects of Social Media is that it allows people to connect with others who may be geographically distant but similar in their experiences, worldviews, social dynamics, or group membership. As a result of this, combined with the relative anonymity afforded by many social media applications, people have increasingly been turning to their screens to seek out social support. Social support is a term used to describe the extent to which a person receives support from others in their social environments and has been linked to people's psychological well-being (Taylor, 1989). Research suggests that online social support is important for people's psychological well-being, especially when they have fewer options for in-person social support (Cole, Nick, Zelkowitz, Roeder, & Spinelli, 2017).

While the question of whether social media use is good for people's well-being is a current controversy in the literature, we will discuss it in greater detail in Chapter 9 (Social Media and Well-Being). Nonetheless, research on gender differences in social support has established that, compared to men, women both give and receive more social support on social media. This has been demonstrated meta-analytically (Tifferet, 2020) and in studies examining gender differences in motivations for social media use (Ferenczi, Marshall, & Bejanyan, 2017).

The role of social media as a pathway for social support has been well documented among the transgender community too. For instance, interviews with the US-based members of this community have demonstrated the important role of social media in connecting with other members of their community and providing them with normative guidelines and social support when dealing with difficult situations such as coming out (Fox & Ralston, 2016). The affordances of social media—the visual anonymity and the opportunity to connect with similar others in geographically disparate locations helped facilitate this valuable learning experience. Other research documents the importance of social media in connecting transgender youth with both similar others and role models as sources of social and emotional support (Selkie, Adkins, Masters, Bajpai, & Shumer, 2020). One such study also illustrated that for this group of young adults, social support from online connections is often considered superior to offline sources (Ybarra, Mitchell, Palmer, & Reisner, 2015). This is of huge importance to this community given that relative to cisgender young adults, trans youth are at high risk for experiencing negative mental health outcomes such as anxiety, depression, and suicidal ideation (Haas et al., 2010). These findings are not unique to Western samples and have been documented among the trans community in China as well (Han, Han, Qu, Li, & Zhu, 2019).

Summary

Returning to the opening story, when Mark Hamill—the *Star Wars* actor famous for portraying Jedi Knight Luke Skywalker—commented on the online harassment that his costar received, he supported Ms. Tran by calling out her harassers and expressing his admiration for via Twitter (see Fig. 4.2). While his support did not bring her back to social media, it illustrates the importance of public social support and highlights the idea that for some famous people, especially those from certain gender and cultural groups, the sheer volume of online harassment may drown out any positive benefits of social media use. In summary, this chapter sets the groundwork for understanding how people's gender identity and cultural background can influence their social media use. As the literature reviewed in this chapter reveals, gender and culture should be considered when attempting to understand the psychological factors that drive people's social media use. As a result, throughout the rest of the book, as I review the scholarship relevant to each chapter, I will identify the culture from which the sample was obtained and will also describe any reported gender differences because these factors matter when examining psychological processes in social media.

Figure 4.2 Luke Skywalker actor Mark Hamill tweets in support of his costar Kelly Maria Tran (Hamill, 2018; June 6).

References

BBC Trending. (2015, October 20). When racists tried to strike Star Wars. *BBC News*. <https://www.bbc.com/news/blogs-trending-34583416> Retrieved 01.08.20.

Cole, D. A., Nick, E. A., Zelkowitz, R. L., Roeder, K. M., & Spinelli, T. (2017). Online social support for young people: Does it recapitulate in-person social support; can it help? *Computers in Human Behavior*, *68*, 456–464.

Darwin, H. (2017). Doing gender beyond the binary: A virtual ethnography. *Symbolic Interaction*, *40*(3), 317–334.

DeAndrea, D. C., Shaw, A. S., & Levine, T. R. (2010). Online language: The role of culture in self-expression and self-construal on Facebook. *Journal of Language and Social Psychology*, *29*(4), 425–442.

Eagly, A. H., Wood, W., & Diekman, A. B. (2000). *Social role theory of sex differences and similarities: A current appraisal*, . *The Developmental Social Psychology of Gender* (vol 12, p. 174). Mahwah, New Jersey: Erlbaum.

Fallows, D. (2005). How women and men use the Internet. *Pew Internet & American Life Project*, *28*, 1–45.

Fardouly, J., Diedrichs, P. C., Vartanian, L. R., & Halliwell, E. (2015). Social comparisons on social media: The impact of Facebook on young women's body image concerns and mood. *Body Image*, *13*, 38–45.

Ferenczi, N., Marshall, T. C., & Bejanyan, K. (2017). Are sex differences in antisocial and prosocial Facebook use explained by narcissism and relational self-construal? *Computers in Human Behavior*, *77*, 25–31.

Fox, J., & Ralston, R. (2016). Queer identity online: Informal learning and teaching experiences of LGBTQ individuals on social media. *Computers in Human Behavior*, *65*, 635–642. Available from https://doi.org/10.1016/j.chb.2016.06.009.

Fox, J., & Vendemia, M. A. (2016). Selective self-presentation and social comparison through photographs on social networking sites. *Cyberpsychology, Behavior, and Social Networking*, *19*(10), 593–600.

Fredrickson, B. L., & Roberts, T. A. (1997). Objectification theory: Toward understanding women's lived experiences and mental health risks. *Psychology of Women Quarterly*, *21*(2), 173–206.

Garcia, D., Kassa, Y. M., Cuevas, A., Cebrian, M., Moro, E., Rahwan, I., & Cuevas, R. (2018). Analyzing gender inequality through large-scale Facebook advertising data. *Proceedings of the National Academy of Sciences*, *115*(27), 6958–6963.

Gazit, T., Aharony, N., & Amichai-Hamburger, Y. (2019). Tell me who you are and I will tell you which SNS you use: SNSs participation. *Online Information Review*, *44*, 139–161.

Gray, T. J., Gainous, J., & Wagner, K. M. (2017). Gender and the digital divide in Latin America. *Social Science Quarterly*, *98*(1), 326–340.

Guadagno, R. E., & Cialdini, R. B. (2007). Gender differences in impression management in organizations: a qualitative review. *Sex Roles*, *56*(7–8), 483–494.

Haas, A. P., Eliason, M., Mays, V. M., Mathy, R. M., Cochran, S. D., D'Augelli, A. R., ... Clayton, P. J. (2010). Suicide and suicide risk in lesbian, gay, bisexual, and transgender populations: Review and recommendations. *Journal of Homosexuality*, *58*(1), 10–51.

Haferkamp, N., & Krämer, N. C. (2011). Social comparison 2.0: Examining the effects of online profiles on social-networking sites. *Cyberpsychology, Behavior, and Social Networking*, *14*(5), 309–314.

Haferkamp, N., Eimler, S. C., Papadakis, A. M., & Kruck, J. V. (2012). Men are from Mars, women are from Venus? Examining gender differences in self-presentation on social networking sites. *Cyberpsychology, Behavior, and Social Networking*, *15*(2), 91–98.

Hamill, M. [@HamillHimself]. *What's not to love?* [Tweet]. Twitter. (2018, June 6) <https://twitter.com/HamillHimself/status/1004482255295692802?s = 2>.

Han, X., Han, W., Qu, J., Li, B., & Zhu, Q. (2019). What happens online stays online?——Social media dependency, online support behavior and offline effects for LGBT. *Computers in Human Behavior, 93*, 91–98. Available from https://doi.org/10.1016/j.chb.2018.12.011.

Hofstede, G. (1983). The cultural relativity of organizational practices and theories. *Journal of International Business Studies, 14*(2), 75–89.

Kimbrough, A. M., Guadagno, R. E., Muscanell, N. L., & Dill, J. (2013). Gender differences in mediated communication: Women connect more than do men. *Computers in Human Behavior, 29*(3), 896–900.

Krämer, N. C., Neubaum, G., & Eimler, S. C. (2017). *A brief history of (social) Cyberspace. Cyberemotion. Understanding complex systems* (pp. 11–35). Springer Nature.

Kuo, F. Y., Tseng, C. Y., Tseng, F. C., & Lin, C. S. (2013). A study of social information control affordances and gender difference in Facebook self-presentation. *Cyberpsychology, Behavior, and Social Networking, 16*(9), 635–644.

Kurtz, G., & Lucas, G. (1977). Star Wars: Episode IV - A new hope *[Motion picture]*. United States: 20th Century Fox.

Lee, Z.W., Cheung, C.M., & Thadani, D.R. (2012, January). An investigation into the problematic use of Facebook. In 2012 45th Hawaii international conference on system sciences (pp. 1768–1776). IEEE.

Lewallen, J., & Behm-Morawitz, E. (2016). Pinterest or thinterest?: Social comparison and body image on social media. *Social Media + Society, 2*(1), 2056305116640559.

Lips, H. M. (2017). *Sex and gender: An introduction*. Waveland Press.

Lyu, S. O. (2016). Travel selfies on social media as objectified self-presentation. *Tourism Management, 54*, 185–195.

Marino, C., Gini, G., Vieno, A., & Spada, M. M. (2018). A comprehensive meta-analysis on problematic Facebook use. *Computers in Human Behavior, 83*, 262–277, http:/doi.org/10.1016/j.chb.2018.02.009.

McKenna, K. Y., & Bargh, J. A. (1998). Coming out in the age of the Internet: Identity "demarginalization" through virtual group participation. *Journal of Personality and Social Psychology, 75*(3), 681.

Muscanell, N. L., & Guadagno, R. E. (2012). Make new friends or keep the old: Gender and personality differences in social networking use. *Computers in Human Behavior, 28*(1), 107–112.

Park, G., Yaden, D. B., Schwartz, H. A., Kern, M. L., Eichstaedt, J. C., Kosinski, M., et al. (2016). Women are warmer but no less assertive than men: Gender and language on Facebook. *PLoS One, 11*(5), e0155885. Available from https://doi.org/10.1371/journal.pone.0155885.

Pew Research Center. *Demographics of social media users and adoption in the United States*. (2020, June 05). <https://www.pewresearch.org/internet/fact-sheet/social-media/>, Retrieved 28.09.20.

Schwartz, H. A., Eichstaedt, J. C., Kern, M. L., Dziurzynski, L., Ramones, S. M., Agrawal, M., . . . Ungar, L. H. (2013). Personality, gender, and age in the language of social media: The open-vocabulary approach. *PLoS One, 8*(9), e73791.

Selkie, E., Adkins, V., Masters, E., Bajpai, A., & Shumer, D. (2020). Transgender adolescents' uses of social media for social support. *Journal of Adolescent Health, 66*(3), 275–280. Available from https://doi.org/10.1016/j.jadohealth.2019.08.011.

Shoard, C. (2018, June 11). Pro-'straight white male hero' group behind Star Wars actor's abuse. *The Guardian*. <https://www.theguardian.com/film/2018/jun/11/anti-disney-group-harassment-star-wars-female-actors-daisy-ridley-kelly-marie-tran>.

Taylor, S. E. (1989). *Positive illusions: Creative self-deception and the healthy mind.* Basic Books/Hachette Book Group.

Thomala, L. China: Distribution of internet users by gender 2020. (2020, May 05). <https://www.statista.com/statistics/265148/percentage-of-internet-users-in-china-by-gender/> Retrieved 28.09.20.

Tifferet, S. (2019). Gender differences in privacy tendencies on social network sites: a meta-analysis. *Computers in Human Behavior, 93*, 1–12.

Tifferet, S. (2020). Gender Differences in Social Support on Social Network Sites: A Meta-Analysis. *Cyberpsychology, Behavior, and Social Networking, 23*(4), 199–209.

Tran, K.M. (2018, August 21). I won't be marginalized by online harassment. *The New York Times.* <https://www.nytimes.com/2018/08/21/movies/kelly-marie-tran.html?searchResultPosition = 1> Retrieved 01.08.20.

Triandis, H. C. (2011). Culture and self-deception: A theoretical perspective. *Social Behavior and Personality: An International Journal, 39*(1), 3–13.

Vary, A.B. (2019, December 11). John Boyega: 'Star wars' fandom conflict is 'the most stupid thing in the world.' *Variety.* <https://variety.com/2019/film/features/john-boyega-star-wars-fandom-conflict-1203433706/>.

Ybarra, M. L., Mitchell, K. J., Palmer, N. A., & Reisner, S. L. (2015). Online social support as a buffer against online and offline peer and sexual victimization among US LGBT and non-LGBT youth. *Child Abuse & Neglect, 39*, 123–136.

CHAPTER 5

Social influence processes in social media

Power is in tearing human minds to pieces and putting them together again in new shapes of your own choosing.

—Orwell, 1949

I will never forget the 2016 US presidential election. The night before the election, I could not sleep, instead staying up all night filled with anxiety and dread. Despite polls indicating that the United States was about to elect former Secretary of State Hillary Rodman Clinton as its first woman President (Latest Election Polls 2016, 2016 November 8), I was convinced the polls were wrong and she was going to lose to Donald Trump, considered by the majority of American voters as completely unsuited and unqualified to serve as President (Ferner, 2016; September 15; The New York Times Editorial Board, 2016, September 26). Why was I so worried? Because my social media was broken. Not in terms of the technical functionality of the software but in terms of the social interaction I observed on my Facebook news feed. My friends were attacking each other, expressing scorn in response to legitimate news stories and denouncing them as false, linking as evidence news articles that were highly contradictory and from obscure, dubious, or fringe sources. At the time, I did not understand what was going on—I just observed a change in conduct among my social media friends and wondered why all this odd behavior on my Facebook news feed was occurring. For example, some of my male friends laughed at and mocked factual news coverage establishing that Secretary Clinton was the more honest Presidential candidate (Abramson, 2016; March 28) and in response, I ended up unfriending them. I even had a family member emailed me to insist that I should vote for Donald Trump because my family member

Psychological Processes in Social Media
DOI: https://doi.org/10.1016/B978-0-12-811320-2.00006-X

believed an entirely false and totally preposterous idea that Secretary Clinton was part of a pedophilia ring run out of a pizza parlor.[1]

These are just a few examples of the ways in which my technology-mediated interactions became weird in the months leading up to the 2016 US presidential election. While watching the election results the following night, I was crushed that Secretary Clinton lost the election as her opponent won the electoral college—the anachronistic system through which the US presidents are selected. While Secretary Clinton won the popular vote by a substantial margin (2,868,686 million votes; Leamon & Bucelato, 2017; December), in the months following the election, it slowly became clear that much of the weirdness in social interactions that I had observed on Facebook was due to an unprecedented amount of election interference, primarily from the efforts of the Russian government–funded Internet Research Agency (IRA; DiResta et al., 2018; Howard, Ganesh, Liotsiou, Kelly, & François, 2018; Mueller, 2019; March). This inference was not limited to Facebook but spread across other social media platforms and occurred in concert with the targeted advertising campaign launched by Cambridge Analytica described in Chapter 3, with both efforts benefitting Donald Trump. Specifically, the IRA interfered in the US election using, among other things, social media's targeted advertising aimed to pit Americans against each other through the spread of disinformation. While the impact of these activities on the election is thus far unknown, there are compelling arguments that the IRA's effort did affect voting behavior (Jamieson, 2018). While the social media companies may have more information on this, thus far, they have not been entirely forthcoming in sharing data (e.g., such as people's comments in response to the IRA efforts) that could more directly address this question (DiResta et al., 2018).

Furthermore, this election interference did impact people's perceptions of the truth and disrupted their relationships with friends and family members. One such study found that over one-quarter of American social

[1] This false claim spread wide and is now known as the conspiracy theory #pizzagate. Started by alt-right conspiracy theorist Alex Jones infamous for attacking the victims and survivors of the Sandy Hook Elementary School Mass shooting, this theory falsely claimed that Hillary Clinton was running a child sex trafficking ring from the basement of a pizza parlor. One of Jones' followers believed him and showed up armed with multiple guns including an AR-15 assault rifle, terrorizing the restaurant's employees and customers rather than freeing the nonexistent captives from the restaurant's nonexistent basement (for more details, see Guadagno & Guttieri, 2019).

media users randomly sampled shortly after the 2016 US presidential election reported perceived such disruptions but did not link them to Russia or propaganda (Guadagno, Oilvieri, & Kimbrough, 2024; June). How do we understand the ways in which these influence operations deployed by the IRA over social media influence people's attitudes, beliefs, and potential behavior? This chapter will examine the literature on social influence and persuasion—defined as a change in a person's beliefs or behavior as a result of real or imagined input from other individuals (Cialdini, 2009)—and address the question of how these psychological processes changed in technology-mediated environments such as social media. Specifically, I review the literature on social influence on social media and integrate it with what is now known about the IRA's efforts to influence the outcome of the 2016 US presidential election in favor of President Donald Trump.

Fake news and information warfare

What people have labeled "fake news" refers to information passed off as credible, factual news but is in fact untrue and often intentionally intended to deceive. While fake news is not new—indeed, instances of fake news have been recorded throughout human history (Burkhardt, 2017), nor is concern about new technologies and the spread of fake news (e.g., Allcott & Gentzkow, 2017). What is new is the ability of the Internet and social media to spread such information widely and rapidly owing to a combination of the ways in which social media interconnects people, allows for the transmission of one-to-many messaging, and the viral nature in which information spreads online (note Chapter 6 will delve deeply into the psychological impact of virality on social media). This term has been applied to a wide variety of news ranging from rumors, conspiracy theories, inaccurate reporting, parodies, and factual information that people do not agree with (Weedon, Nuland, & Stamos, 2017; April 27).

The IRA's efforts have been labeled "fake news" but that is a mono-mer. The IRA launched a series of coordinated activities to influence American beliefs and behavior. Over a 2-year period, starting in 2014, these activities ranged from creating accounts and groups impersonating the US citizens, launching thousands of bot accounts all pushing the same message, to purchasing thousands of targeted advertisements that sowed chaos and discord through the dissemination of disinformation (Mueller, 2019; March). These Russian "trolls" (employees of the IRA masquerading as real

Americans) also set up events in the United States that pitted groups of people on different sides of a political issue against each other by organizing competing protests at the same time and the same place throughout the United States (discussed in detail in Chapter 6). Mainstream media outlets quoted some of these accounts, spreading disinformation by presenting the IRA's troll words as those of actual American citizens (Mueller, 2019; March). Some of these troll accounts (e.g., Jenna Abrams—discussed in detail next) obtained thousands of social media followers. See Table 5.1 for definitions and examples of fake news, misinformation, and disinformation, all of which have been associated with information operations, influence operations, or information warfare, referring to attempts by foreign adversaries to selectively spread information intended to affect the psychological functioning of their enemy by sowing chaos, disrupting interpersonal relationships, and affecting the emotions, beliefs, motivations, and behaviors of their targets (Lin & Kerr, 2017).

The IRA's information operations reflected a sophisticated understanding of the affordances of the different social media applications. Thus activities on Facebook were different from activities on Twitter. Furthermore, once the IRA realized that their activities were being discovered and reported on in the news media, their efforts shifted to other social media platforms such as Instagram (DiResta et al., 2018). The IRA's primary motivation in these efforts has been to sow discord and distrust among Americans by amplifying preexisting ideological and ethical divides and undermining people's faith in humanity and in the American federal authority (Kirk, 2019; April 9).

Real-world consequences of influence operations

Data from Silverman (2016) suggests that the majority of Americans (62%) turn to social media for news. This is unfortunate because this same analysis also revealed that, compared to the most popular factual news stories, the most popular fake news stories were shared more broadly on Facebook and were focused on supporting Donald Trump's candidacy—either by disparaging negative coverage, falsifying positive coverage, or denigrating his opponents. As a result, people unwittingly spread misinformation and disinformation, thereby amplifying its impact. Research has also shown that in the United States, most adults who use social media see this misinformation and that older individuals, people from lower income brackets, and those less educated are most likely to share

Table 5.1 Definitions and examples of the ways in which inaccurate information appears on social media.

Term	Definition	Example
Fake news	Information passed off as credible, factual news but is in fact untrue and often intentionally intended to deceive. This includes rumors, conspiracy theories, propaganda, and inaccurately reported news.	• Pizza Gate (there was no pedophilia run by Democrats in the restaurant's nonexistent basement) • Seth Rich conspiracy theory that he was murdered by the Clintons (he was not) • Pope Francis endorsed Donald Trump for President (he did not)
Misinformation	Inaccurate information, not necessary created and spread with the intent to deceive.	• Misquoting people and/or quoting them out of context • Inaccurate statistics • Inaccurate details of an event • Quoting Russian trolls believing them to be real Americans
Disinformation	English translation of Russian term "dezinformatsiya" and refers to the intentional spread of false information with the intent to sow chaos and discord or intimidate an opponent. Also referred to as *information warfare*.	• The IRA's targeted advertising campaign • ISIS's use of Twitter to intimidate Iraqi soldiers into fleeing from Mosul • Messages spread on social media telling certain voter blocks that their polling location had changed • Falsely claiming that Special Counsel Robert Mueller is politically biased, a closet Democrat, or a sexual predator

misinformation (Allcott & Gentzkow, 2017; Glenski, Weniger, & Volokova, 2018). This also describes the groups of individuals who are likely to have the lowest levels of media literacy, defined as people's capacity to obtain, understand, assess, and produce media (Kimbrough & Guadagno, 2019).

Based on that information that's been released by the social media companies to the United States Congress has illustrated that in the months leading up to the 2016 US presidential election, the IRA's influence operations reached 126 million Facebook users, 20 million Instagram users, and 1.4 million Twitter users and uploaded more than 1000 videos on YouTube (DiResta et al., 2018). Furthermore, as the news media started reporting on the IRA's influence operations on Facebook and Twitter, the IRA changed gears to instead disseminate misinformation on Instagram, eventually disseminating nearly twice as much content on Instagram relative to Facebook. Thus not only did the IRA understand the affordances of each social media platform, but they also recognized when their efforts were detected and shifted course accordingly.

With respect to the ads and posts placed on Facebook by the IRA, not all were equally effective. Instead, they ranged both in success and cost and data indicates that the most successful ads and posts were viewed by nearly 359,345 Americans, 24,838 of whom clicked on the ad. This broad reach cost the IRA a little more than $1000 US dollars. On the more outrageous yet less popular end of the spectrum of ads, see Fig. 5.1, which displays an image associating Secretary Clinton with Satan, was seen by a small number of people, and cost the IRA just over $1 (see the detailed metadata in Fig. 5.2). Fig. 5.3 details the amount of disinformation placed on Facebook, Twitter, and Instagram from 2015 to 2017—the volume is large and the trend over time suggests that these efforts are stopping. Overall, the IRA's budget for this influence operation is estimated to have totaled $25 million (DiResta et al., 2018).

Furthermore, these activities were coordinated such that key events in the 2016 US presidential election (e.g., debates) corresponded with increases in IRA activity (Howard et al., 2018). Thus the efforts by the IRA and others to misinform the American public were broadly seen and shared and were also relatively inexpensive. In the following sections, I describe how these efforts served to amplify existing divisions among Americans by employing tactics that map onto key psychological characteristics that have been shown by to be effective in influencing people to change their attitudes and behaviors.

Figure 5.1 Example of Russian-placed social media ad linking Hillary Clinton to Satan.

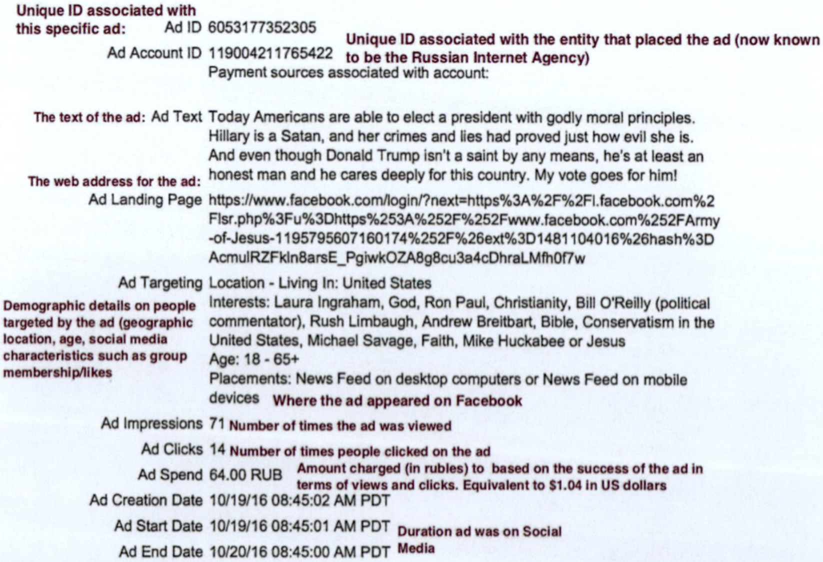

Unique ID associated with this specific ad: Ad ID 6053177352305

Ad Account ID 119004211765422 — Unique ID associated with the entity that placed the ad (now known to be the Russian Internet Agency)

Payment sources associated with account:

The text of the ad: Ad Text Today Americans are able to elect a president with godly moral principles. Hillary is a Satan, and her crimes and lies had proved just how evil she is. And even though Donald Trump isn't a saint by any means, he's at least an honest man and he cares deeply for this country. My vote goes for him!

The web address for the ad: Ad Landing Page https://www.facebook.com/login/?next=https%3A%2F%2Fl.facebook.com%2Flsr.php%3Fu%3Dhttps%253A%252F%252Fwww.facebook.com%252FArmy-of-Jesus-1195795607160174%252F%26ext%3D1481104016%26hash%3DAcmulRZFkln8arsE_PgiwkOZA8g8cu3a4cDhraLMfh0f7w

Ad Targeting Location - Living In: United States

Demographic details on people targeted by the ad (geographic location, age, social media characteristics such as group membership/likes

Interests: Laura Ingraham, God, Ron Paul, Christianity, Bill O'Reilly (political commentator), Rush Limbaugh, Andrew Breitbart, Bible, Conservatism in the United States, Michael Savage, Faith, Mike Huckabee or Jesus

Age: 18 - 65+

Placements: News Feed on desktop computers or News Feed on mobile devices — Where the ad appeared on Facebook

Ad Impressions 71 — Number of times the ad was viewed

Ad Clicks 14 — Number of times people clicked on the ad

Ad Spend 64.00 RUB — Amount charged (in rubles) to based on the success of the ad in terms of views and clicks. Equivalent to $1.04 in US dollars

Ad Creation Date 10/19/16 08:45:02 AM PDT

Ad Start Date 10/19/16 08:45:01 AM PDT

Ad End Date 10/20/16 08:45:00 AM PDT — Duration ad was on Social Media

Figure 5.2 Metadata accompanying the social media ad linking Hillary Clinton to Satan edited to explain the different labels. In red text, I annotated the metadata to provide guidance on deciphering the text.

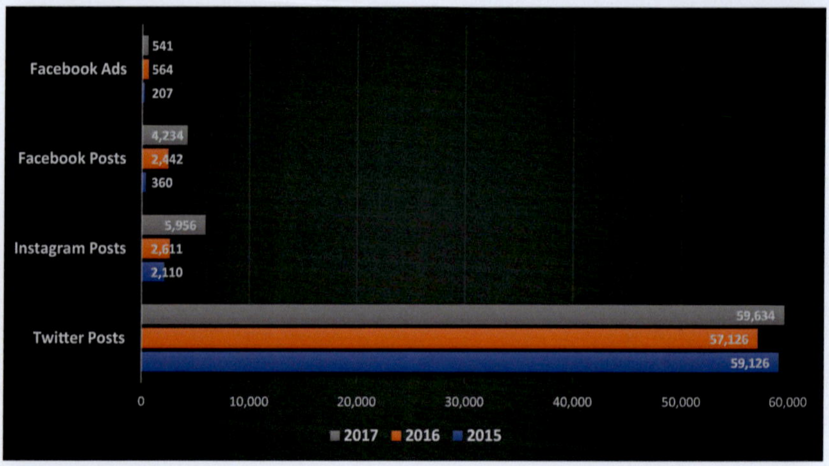

Figure 5.3 Data on the increasing amount of IRA activity on Facebook, Twitter, and Instagram from 2015 to 2017 drawn from Howard et al. (2018).

Social media and social influence processes

> *Doublethink means the power of holding two contradictory beliefs in one's mind simultaneously, and accepting both of them.*
>
> ***—Orwell, 1949***

What reason do we have to believe that these kinds of campaigns are effective in changing people's beliefs and behavior? The literature on social influence and persuasion can help explain this. People generally do not think deeply about issues (Cialdini, 2009). In social psychology, we call this *heuristic processing*. People tend to believe that other people are honest; people tend to believe information as factual; people tend to accept information as true information (Gilbert, Tafarodi, & Malone, 1993; Levine, 2014). It takes mental effort to erase such information from our minds and/or to disbelieve and as the literature reviewed next indicates, this does not often happen while people are interacting with others and evaluating information shared within their social media networks.

In the social influence and persuasion literature, the elaboration likelihood model (Petty & Brinol, 2012; Petty & Cacioppo, 1984) establishes the conditions under which people vary in the amount of cognitive effort they put into processing persuasive appeals. In thousands of studies conducted over many years, this body of literature indicates that people tend to process this information in *centrally* or *peripherally*. In the case of central processing, people focus on the content of a message (e.g., the quality of the arguments), and are influenced by these factors. People are more likely to process persuasive appeals through the central route of persuasion if the topic is important to them, they have the attentional resources available to process the message, they know something about the topic, and the arguments are written. When people process persuasive appeals peripherally, they use decision cues or cognitive heuristics to evaluate the merits of the persuasive appeal. As a result, people processing via the peripheral route may be more influenced by the quantity rather than the quality of arguments or be swayed by the perceived creditability associated with the persuasive appeal rather than the veracity of its claims. People are most likely to engage in this type of message processing when the topic is of little relevance to them, they are experiencing information overload, and they know very little about the topic.

Consuming information through a device such as a computer or smart phone increases people's tendency to process information heuristically (Guadagno, Muscanell, Sundie, Hardison, & Cialdini, 2013; Lee, Lindsey,

& Kim, 2017; Rodriguez, Gummadi, & Schoelkopf, 2014; May). This makes people vulnerable to social influence resulting from information warfare campaigns. Thus, while using social media, people do not typically process information centrally for a number of reasons. For instance, owing to the design of many social media platforms and online news websites, people often experiencing information overload while using these technologies (Holton, Chyi, 2012), thereby making them more susceptible to persuasion via the peripheral route. One of my own studies illustrated this when we found that people, especially those without domain-relevant expertise, were more influenced by a persuasive appeal presented on a computer relative to comparable communications presented via paper (Guadagno et al., 2013). We hypothesized that this was because information presented through technology was perceived as more credible because of the technological sophistication of the communication mode. In Internet parlance, I reference the following meme: "if the internet says it, it must be true."

Given that evidence suggests that for much of the time, people's online interactions largely take place via the peripheral route of persuasion, what other types of decision cues or cognitive heuristics could influence people in this context and thereby be used in information operations? Cialdini's (2009) model of social influence and persuasion proposes that there are six primary principles of influence that function as heuristics that help guide people's behavior and influence their responses. These principles are as follows: scarcity, reciprocity, commitment/consistency, authority, social validation (covered in Chapter 6), and liking/similarity. While the different principles have varying underlying mechanisms (to be discussed in detail next), they all work best under situations in which an influence target uses heuristics rather than deep thought to guide decision-making. This framework has been widely embraced by social influence researchers and is one that I have employed in my own research on social influence and persuasion (e.g., Guadagno, & Cialdini, 2002, 2005, 2007; Guadagno, 2017; Guadagno, Okdie, & Muscanell, 2013). It's also been applied to frame and examine social engineering online (Goel, Williams, & Dincelli, 2017; Muscanell, Guadagno, & Murphy, 2014; Parsons, Butavicius, Delfabbro, & Lillie, 2019).

For the remainder of this chapter, I review the conceptual overlap between Cialdini's (2009) principles of influence, how these principles have been shown to function on social media, and how I think they manifest in influence operations. I contend that many of the influence operations have been successfully worked because they leverage one or more of these decision heuristics that have been long-demonstrated to influence people's attitudes and behavior. Furthermore, I maintain that this is in part because social media itself has been designed to do—not to explore people to influence operations but to influence them to engage with the application longer.

Scarcity

When something is scarce, people desire it more (Cialdini, 2009). The scarcity heuristic states: "If it is rare, then it must be good." Time pressure magnifies the effect, particularly in conditions of risk and uncertainty, the treat of loss—referred to as *loss aversion* (Tversky & Kahneman, 1991). The power of the principle is derived from two main points: (1) things that are difficult to attain are typically perceived as more valuable, so the availability of an item can serve as a shortcut cue to its quality and (2) according to psychological reactance theory (Brehm, 1966), we respond to the loss of freedoms by wanting the freedom more than before. This is often illustrated by censorship—by denying people's access to a product or information that was once freely available, demand for the product or service increases (Cialdini, 2009). Under conditions of scarcity, information, goods, and services are considered valuable because they are rare. In a marketing context, this can increase the price/value of items (e.g., limited edition cars). This may be due to a limited availability or limited time or may be due to the exclusivity and/or secrecy of information.

Given the ubiquity of information online, it may seem odd to consider the impact of this influence principle on people's attitudes and behaviors. Thus, to understand this, instead it makes sense to consider the impact that scarce information such as hacked or leaked information and scare opportunities owing to time limits has on what people pay attention to in their social media lives. More relevant to information operations, other research has examined the role of scarcity in social engineering attempts, finding that scarcity can be effective in phishing schemes through messages indicating that a person does not click on a link in set, short timeframe, they will lose the opportunity (e.g., Taib, Yu, Berkovsky, Wiggins, & Bayl-Smith, 2019; September).

While the research on scarcity in online environments, there are reasons to suspect that scarcity may be effective in drawing people's attention and influencing their behavior. For instance, anyone who has found themselves spending too much money to purchase a desired item in an online auction has experienced the influence of scarcity (Dunn, 2002; Reynolds, Gilkeson, & Niedrich, 2009). Other research has examined scarcity in the context of Internet scams in which viruses are messages that frame different products and services as hard to find/obtain or limited in availability, people have been scammed by social engineers (Muscanell et al., 2014).

Wikileaks describes itself as a site that "... specializes in the analysis and publication of large datasets of censored or otherwise restricted official materials involving war, spying and corruption (Wikileaks, 2015; November 3)." By its very definition, the site evokes scarcity and signals that the information available on the site is rare, exclusive, and worth attending to. This certainly played out in the months leading up to the 2016 US presidential election. For instance, one case study chronicled the release of one of several election-related troves of hacked emails (Proferes & Summers, 2019) indicating that this repository of stolen emails was released in batches during the last month of the election. By releasing them in batches, Wikileaks helped keep this scarce, exclusive information in the news. Similarly, Wikileaks leaks also amped up the scarcity of the information by falsely accusing Twitter of censoring the information dumps. Given the importance of free speech in American culture, the notion of censorship as abhorrent, people's interest in accessing these leaked, stolen materials was piqued. Thus scarcity is one reason I assert that the Wikileaks email releases spread so widely and were perceived as credible and therefore harmful to Clinton's campaign as evidenced by declining poll numbers in the final month prior to the election (Murray, 2017; August 23). Scarcity was also a theme in many of the IRA's expressing antiimmigrant sentiment. Fig. 5.4 provides an example of one such ad which makes the argument that immigration will cause a loss of American culture as well as economic losses. Thus, because it provides access to scarce, exclusive, and private information, people attend to this information more.

Reciprocity

Reciprocity is an influence principle, often referred to as the reciprocity norm or Golden Rule, in which people feel an obligation to give to those who have given to them (Gouldner, 1960). Traditionally, social influence researchers have documented the effectiveness of reciprocity in the give and take of negotiations (Mislin, Boumgarden, Jang, & Bottom, 2015), the effectiveness of free gifts increasing the likelihood of a purchase (Cialdini, 2009), effectiveness of reciprocity (writing "thank you" on the

Ad image

Ad text

The Census Bureau published the new data in its International Data Base, which contains population estimates and projections up to the year 2050.The figure from the Census Bureau is a calculation of net migration—meaning the total number of immigrants who will arrive in the United States in 2015 would actually be larger than 1.24 million.

Of course, the United States is the country of immigrants. But if America had huge undeveloped lands and needed workers at the earliest stage, today there is a jobs deficit. Today the government must restrict immigration that is a reason of interethnic tensions in the United States. High unemployment rate fuels intolerance toward immigrants that are ready to work illegally for low wages. So, besides social problem, immigrants threaten the U.S. economy. Those who work illegaly (*sic*) don't pay taxes that are an important part of state budget. Working illegaly (*sic*), they break the law. Lack of immigration restrictions increases crime rates.

Moreover, more and more immigrants cannot speak English. One-fifth of people in the United States speak a foreign language at home, according to a report of the Center for Immigration Studies.

You see, increasing amount of immigrants in the United States creates social and economic problems. However, we have a risk not only to worsen the U.S. economy, but also to lose our culture. America can't be the Tower of Babel, we cannot allow everybody to live here if immigration threatens us. We don't hate foreigners, we are glad to see tourists from every corner of the world, but we cannot allow them to stay here.

It's the bathos (*sic*) of stupidity to stimulate immigration when it creates enormous problems for the nation.

Figure 5.4 Example of Facebook ad placed by the IRA and is intended to stir up antiimmigrant sentiment through scarcity. The orange text highlights the ad's loss framing.

check) to increase a server's tip (Rind & Strohmetz, 1999), and in the context of reciprocating concessions (Cialdini et al., 1975). In the largely text-based world of the Internet, reciprocity in the length of messages sent and received has been documented (Feeley, Anker, & Aloe, 2012; Stocks, Mirghassemi, & Oceja, 2018) as has the effectiveness of reciprocal concessions in a virtual gaming environment (Eastwick & Gardner, 2009).

On social media, reciprocity manifests in multiple ways. For instance, the affordances of social media facilitate reciprocal interactions between people as well as between business and individuals. One study of Chinese mircrobloggers found that anticipated reciprocal communication in the form of feedback on and responses to their posts contributed to their enjoyment of and motivations for engaging in microblogging (Liu, Min, & Han, 2019). In my research, I have found that people are more likely to patronize companies who interact with them on Twitter by replying to or retweeting their messages (Guadagno, Sardos, & Kimbrough, 2024, April). In two studies, we examined people's intentions to patronize a restaurant as a function of whether the restaurant's corporate Twitter account engaged with a hypothetical customer by replying to them. Compared to no response or simply retweeting the customer, we found that this interaction increased intentions to patronize but only among women.

Other research on the influence of reciprocity in social media indicates that reciprocity in online communities works to the extent that it is accepted as a norm within the group as indicated by whether members feel indebted to help other members in the group (Feng & Ye, 2016). This was documented in a discussion forum for Chinese students discussing the GRE and other standardized tests. Thus reciprocity can be effective in influencing people on social media, but it has not been widely studied.

Applied to the question of influence operations, I suggest that one of the underlying mechanisms behind virality (to be covered extensively in Chapter 6) and social media connections is reciprocity. For instance, on social media platforms that allow for one-way connections (e.g., Twitter, Reddit), it may be that when someone follows another person, they experience pressure to reciprocate by following back. While there is no empirical evidence on this point to date, these types of social media platforms are rife with messages in people's profiles indicating that there is no guarantee that the user will follow someone in exchange for being followed. People would not feel the need to post such messages if they did not feel the pressure to reciprocate. Furthermore, when someone likes or shares another person's post, they may feel pressure to reciprocate as well. Thus, by reciprocating in this manner, influence operators may be able to target key social media figures and gradually shape their perceptions through the strategic use of the reciprocity norm.

Commitment and consistency

People need to be consistent with their thoughts and behaviors (Cialdini, 2009). According to the consistency heuristic: "It worked for me before, so I can just relax and trust that it will work for me again." Commitment drives consistency as myriad studies have shown that to the extent that a commitment is public and voluntary, we are more likely to consistently keep this commitment. Small, incremental commitments have been shown to shift people's actions and attitudes across time (Freedman & Fraser, 1966). Furthermore, consistency in behavior leads people to infer self-relevant characteristics (Bem, 1967). For instance, if a post on social media convinces me to donate money for hurricane relief, I may infer that I am a helpful person.

When people interact with others online, they are more self-focused owing to visual anonymity (Guadagno & Cialdini, 2005). Because consistency is an internal process (i.e., it works because people expect themselves to be consistent with prior actions), it is widely effective online in gaming contexts (Eastwick & Gardner, 2009) and while chatting or emailing (Markey, Wells, & Markey, 2001; Study 3; Petrova, Cialdini, & Sills, 2007). On social media, examples of commitment and consistency—related behaviors include liking[2] or sharing someone's post (Lane & Dal Cin, 2018), clicking through links (Guadagno, Muscanell, Rice, & Roberts, 2013; in review, Study 2), and watching YouTube on autoplay while consuming increasingly extreme content (Nicas, 2018; February 7; Ribeiro, Ottoni, West, Almeida, & Meira, 2019). Thus commitment and consistency are important to understate the role of people's media consumption on their behavior and beliefs.

In addition, inconstancies between people's behavior and attitudes have been shown to cause discomfort in individuals, causing them to shift their behavior to align with their attitudes or their attitudes to align with their beliefs (Festinger, 1957; Greenwald & Ronis, 1978). This process is referred to as cognitive dissonance and has been demonstrated in a wide variety of contexts. One early study examined whether people would change their beliefs after agreeing to exaggerate the pleasantness of the experimental task to another research participant under one of three conditions (Festinger & Carlsmith, 1959). In one condition, participants were paid sufficient money to justify their fib; participants in the second condition were not paid enough money to justify lying about their experience; and participants in the control condition were not asked to lie. After telling this lie, participants in both conditions were asked how much they enjoyed the experimental task. Participants who were poorly compensated for lying rated the task as significantly more enjoyable than beforehand and when compared to the other two conditions. More relevant to social media, other research has demonstrated dissonance in the context of writing. Compared to participants assigned a perspective, participants allowed to choose whether to write about a controversial issue from their perspective or take the counterview were more likely to shift their beliefs toward the opposing position.

When considering the vast amount of information on the Internet, the research reviewed earlier suggests that people likely search for and attend to people and news sources that are consistent with their established

[2] Note that while this action may pressure the poster to reciprocate the like, the actor may infer from that like that they have traits or preferences associated with the post (i.e., after liking a post that offers to donate money to aid an animal shelter for each like, I may infer that I am an animal rights activist).

beliefs. Furthermore, they may stubbornly cling to this consistent, yet false information even when they know it to be false. People have a preference for seeking and interpreting new information in ways that are consistent with their prior beliefs and decisions, and avoiding inconsistent information, a phenomenon known as *confirmation bias* (Nickerson, 1998). The confirmation bias has been shown to be associated with echo chambers online and has been linked to the success of bot networks in influencing people's perceptions that their opinion is one that is commonly held by many others (e.g., examined in the context of Brexit and the 2016 US presidential election; Gorodnichenko, Pham, & Talavera, 2018). The effectiveness of the confirmation bias on Internet content has also been shown with respect to edited images (Shen et al., 2019), with more tech-savvy people showing less susceptibility to such images. Furthermore, one study illustrated the conformation bias by demonstrating that people are more likely to believe misinformation that more closely aligns to their preexisting beliefs (Allcott & Gentzkow, 2017). Thus commitment and consistency processes can not only affect our self-perception and our behavior, it can also alter the way in which we process new information.

As much of the literature reviewed indicates, commitment and consistency—based social influence appeals are influential largely owing to self-persuasion (Bem, 1967; Cialdini, 2009). Furthermore, the mere act of liking such a group or a social media post is in itself a commitment and consistency manipulation. For instance, many of the Facebook groups designed to appeal to different demographic groups, inviting them to real-world events that pitted them against people on an opposing side of an issue (e.g., the Black vs Blue Lives Matters fictitious Facebook groups). Not only did people targeted with this disinformation show commitment and constancy when they initially clicked on the content, but also those who signed up to attend a Facebook event increased their commitment to the cause by the mere act of RSVPing. This led to multiple rallies for two opposing groups set in at the same date, time, and location. For instance, in 2016 alone, there were at least eight such rallies (Guadagno & Guttieri, 2019), and, in some cases, violence between the groups (Allbright, 2017; November 1).

Authority

Traditionally, authority comes from many different sources, including clothing (e.g., suits, uniforms), cars, degrees, occupations, and celebrity status (Cialdini, 2009). People attend to the words and actions of authorities owing to the authority heuristic which states that "If an expert says it's so, then it must be true." Thus authorities are effective at influencing people because people tend to believe that an authority provides accurate information and excellent advice (Cialdini, 2009). As a result, people will sometimes ignore their own moral compass and follow the commands of an authority even when it may harm another person (e.g., Milgram, 1974).

In order to be effective online, an authority needs to convey their status. Online, this information is conveyed by a person's email signature, the appearance and content of a person's or organization's website or social media profile, or the amount of social media followers. For people to be influenced by an authority, they need to attend to the text or other information that conveys authority. For instance, research has shown that phishing attempts in which the message comes from a purported authority are quite effective in influencing people to click on a suspect link (Taib et al., 2019; September). Furthermore, one such study demonstrated that people who merely claim expertise online are treated as if they possess that expertise (Van Der Heide & Walther, 2009). Similarly, research has shown that people are more influenced by expert film reviews when there is little additional existing information (i.e., aggregated user reviews; Flanagin, 2017).

There are other forms of authority unique to social media (e.g., follower count). People with large follower counts may be seen as an authority despite having zero domain-relevant expertise. Thus it may be that people equate being "social media famous" (e.g., successful YouTubers and social media influencers with high follower counts) with authority and expertise. Sometimes this is founded, as genuine authorities (e.g., law enforcement, world leaders, and world-renowned experts) do tend to have high follower counts; however, it is sometimes difficult to distinguish between genuine authorities and people famous for their physical appearance or having a high follower count. Furthermore, in the social media environment, having a high follower count is a very effective means of establishing authority, even if the individual has no domain-relevant expertise. For instance, after releasing an update that implemented a change in the social media app's design, Snapchat lost an estimated 1.3 billion dollars in value because a reality television star—Kylie Jenner, part of the Kardashian family—tweeted a disparaging remark expressing a lack of interest in using the updated version of the Snapchat application (see Fig. 5.5). This tweet influenced her fans to create an online petition signed by 1.2 million people asking Snap to roll back the Snapchat design

Figure 5.5 The Tweet that experts believe cost Snapchat $1.3 billion in value illustrates the power of authority even when the authority figure has no domain-relevant expertise.

change (https://www.change.org/p/snap-inc-remove-the-new-snapchat-update), reflected general user disappointment, and cost Snap, Inc 8% in value on the stock market (Hills, 2018; February 23; Ahmed, 2018; February 23). Thus the power of an authority figure on social media is tremendous because the size of their social media network allows them to send one message to millions of followers who will then reply and/or share it with their network. While this process often happens organically, this can also be manipulated by bot networks and fake followers.

While fake followers serve one basic service: to increase the social media profile of the person they follow, bot networks are more complex and more dangerous. Especially, bot networks can be programmed in a number of ways that amplify and spread the message and create a sense of false consensus. For instance, they can target a specific individual such as a world leader and then share a consistent piece of disinformation about this leader, thereby changing their beliefs (e.g., see Farb, 2019; September 15, for a fascinating analysis of the influence of fake followers on Donald Trump). This may have both online and offline consequences as the leader may change their policies to align with the disinformation and they may also share it with their millions of followers, thereby participating in its spread. They can also work in concert with an authority and broadly distribute the message throughout social media.

For instance, Broniatowski et al. (2018) analyzed nearly 2 million tweets and found that compared to real tweet users, Russian bot and troll accounts were more likely to tweet about vaccination and spread antivaccination misinformation that supported people on both sizes of this issue.

The Centers for Disease Control and Prevention (2019, April 25) reports that the incidence of measles in the United States is at a 25-year high, which is particularly concerning for three reasons: (1) it suggests that the IRA's efforts may be increasing the extent to which Americans feel polarized on this issue; (2) other countries are also experiencing increasing numbers of measles diagnoses (e.g, Mezzofiore, 2018; August 7) and this has also been linked to social media (Aquino et al., 2017); and (3) there is no scientific evidence supporting a relationship between autism and vaccination. Instead, the first study on the topic and the only one to report this link was later found to be fraudulent, retracted from publication, and the researcher lost his medical license (Belluz, 2019; March 5; Wakefield et al., 1998), while innumerable population-based studies have found any relationship (e.g., Hviid, Hansen, Frisch, & Melbye, 2019; Jain et al., 2015). Thus one false piece of information has caused a debate that should not exist, and it is jeopardizing the lives of all people—vaccinated or not.

Health information and advice online is another subject in which both the advice given and the source expertise are sometimes questionable. Searching for health information is quite common; doctors tell patients to stop looking up their symptoms on Google. People joke about checking "Dr. Google" for medical information. Indeed, data suggests that the vast majority—an estimated 80% of adults in the United States—search online for medication information (Weaver, 2019; July 16). Given the high variability in the quality and accuracy of health information posted online (Chumber, Huber, & Ghezzi, 2015), it begs the question of what information people find most convincing. Walther, Jang, and Hanna Edwards (2018) examined this in a study that looked at crowdsourced knowledge gathering services (e.g., Quora, Yahoo Answers) and found that when conflicting information is provided, consensus outranks self-professed expertise. Furthermore, their results also found that when the advice provided was poor in quality, it was significantly less persuasive. This study suggests both limitations to the effectiveness of online expertise and questionable wisdom of the crowd that may override the advice of someone with domain-relevant expertise. Furthermore, given the discussion of antivaccination beliefs and Russian disinformation attempts, these results suggest that people should carefully check the source of medication information on social media to ensure that it comes from an authoritative source such as the Centers for Disease Control and Prevention in the United States.

Organizations can serve as authorities too. For instance, in the pre–social media age, mainstream news media served this purpose. Perhaps recognizing this, one of the key themes in the IRA's influence operations against the United States was to erode trust in the media (DiResta et al., 2018). They used two approaches to achieve this: (1) promote new "niche community media, which was positioned in opposition to unrepresentative (across a myriad of axes) mainstream media" (p. 66) and (2) "actively undermine trust in journalism" (p. 66) by spreading memes that portrayed the mainstream media as dishonest purveyors of propaganda. Also, the IRA attacked our trust in election integrity by spreading rumors of mass voter fraud (see Fig. 5.6). Similarly, many of the sources of disinformation work in part because the design of their website, social media pages, and news postings appear to be credible by mirroring the appearance of credible news sources.

Liking

What makes us like others? We like people who are physically attractive, friendly, similar to us, flatter us, and cooperate with us (Cialdini, 2009). The liking heuristic states that "if a friend or someone else in your group asks for a favor, it pays to say yes". Thus liking implies a social bond. And, people are influenced by others whom they find likable and see as similar to them (Cialdini, 2009). This principle of influence explains why celebrities are often used to sell produce and services—because we like and admire them, want them to be our friends, and find them physically attractive. People do not tend to consider whether celebrities have any actual expertise relevant to the product—their fame gives them the same credibility as people who are not famous but have legitimate domain expertise. Similarly, mere exposure to a person or idea increases our liking for it because of increased familiarity. Relevant to the question of disinformation, research has shown that mere exposure to fake news on social media increases ratings of accuracy, even if one exposure increased people's beliefs that the fake news headline was true, subsequent exposure deepened people's beliefs. This was the case even when the news was not consistent with participants' preexisting beliefs, persisted across time (in this study, 1 week), and was flagged as a disputed informational claim (Pennycook, Cannon, & Rand, 2018).

The IRA attempted to interfere with the liking on a broad, wide-scale fashion through their attempts to amplify the many political, ideological, and ethnic divides that distinguish Americans from their friends (DiResta et al., 2018). For instance, the various secessionist campaigns popular in California and Texas were amplified by the IRA and these actions pitted

Figure 5.6 A Facebook ad placed by the IRA in August 2016 that falsely accused Hillary Clinton of voter fraud in an attempt to undermine American adults' trust in election outcomes. This was viewed by 4733 people and cost the IRA approximately $7.57 US Dollars.

friends and family against each other (see Fig. 5.7). Disrupting these relationships makes everyone weaker and more isolated and has left many friends and family groups fractured. Thus, in this case, the IRA attempted

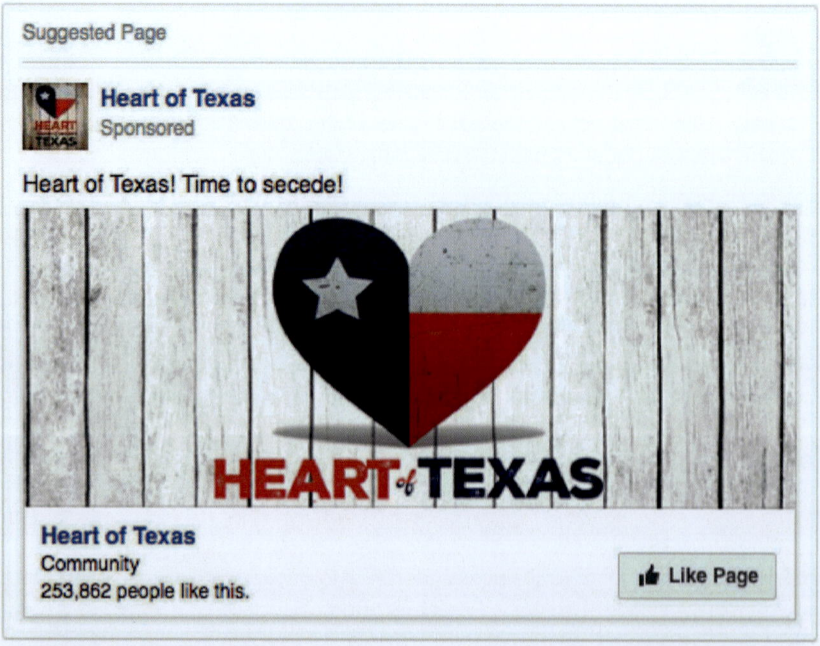

Figure 5.7 Example of ad placed on social media by the IRA encouraging Texas to secede from the United States. This ad was seen by 12,334 Americans and cost the IRA a little over $120 US Dollars.

to disrupt the power that liking brings. In the following sections, I review the literature on physical attractiveness, friendship, and similar avenues of social influence and persuasion on social media as a means to highlight the importance of liking social relationships broadly.

Physical attractiveness

It should come as no surprise to any reader that people gravitate toward beautiful people (Eagly, Ashmore, Makhijani, & Longo, 1991). This is why celebrity endorsements of products and services are an effective and time-honored advertising technique (Cialdini, 2009), why the cosmetic surgery industry is thriving (American Society of Plastic Surgeons, 2019; March 11), and on social media, why beautiful people—consider Essena O'Neill from Chapter 2—can become "social media famous" and/or a social media influencer even if they were not previously well known. Indeed, research on celebrity endorsements on social media supports this and suggests that there are also situational factors that influence the effectiveness of the endorsement. For instance, Russell and Rasolofoarison

(2017) examined the extent to which celebrity endorsements affected purchase intentions and found that naturally occurring associations (e.g., candid pictures of a celebrity carrying a product) were more influential than staged photographs. Similarly, other research has shown that the effectiveness of celebrity varies as a function of product type and the type of product. Specifically, this research revealed that people shared celebrity endorsements on a Chinese microblogging platform differently as a function of product type (utilitarian—shampoo, toothpaste, vs hedonistic—chocolate) and whether the endorsements were self-deprecating (most influential with utilitarian products) or self-enhancing (most influential with hedonic products; Minxue, Shunyu, & Maohong, 2018). One limitation to celebrity influence is whether people are aware that the celebrity is attempting to influence them. Research has shown that social media influencers are less effective at getting their followers to purchase the products they promote when there is more open/explicit knowledge of their intentions to market-sponsored products (Stubb & Colliander, 2019).

Applied to the question of information warfare, the use of young, attractive, politically conservative White women as the façade of many troll and bot accounts represents an attempt to influence people—especially conservatives to adopt more divisive and extreme views using liking and similarity. For instance, DiResta et al. (2018) further report that many of these trolls created personas, some 3841 different person accounts, resulting in over 72 million engagements—that purported to represent different positions among the American electorate (e.g., Black Lives Matter, Left wing, and Right wing). Many of these troll accounts used photographs of real people. For instance, at its height, the Twitter account of Jenna Abrams, revealed as one of the many Russian troll accounts—had more than 70,000 followers, engaged in Twitter debates with celebrities, and this fake account's tweets were both spread broadly on social media and picked up by the mainstream media (Collins & Cox, 2017; November 3; Guadagno & Guttieri, 2019). I will have more to say on the role of bots and trolls in the norm setting in Chapter 6 (Virality).

Friendship

It should come as no surprise that people like their friends. As a result, people's friends can be a strong source of influence. Before the age of social media, people often looked to their friends and family for recommendations on products and services. Online, this referred to as e-word of mouth (e-wom), in this environment, the dynamic has changed such that people will accept recommendations from strangers given the right circumstances (Flanagin, 2017). Social media allows people to express themselves to a far wider audience and once messages spread throughout social media, people may find themselves being influenced by friends of friends or even people whose posts their friends like and shared regardless of the presence of any actual relationship.

Despite this, other evidence indicates that even on social media, friendship status still carries weight. For instance, one commonly used social engineering scam documented by Muscanell et al. (2014) relies on this by sending a Facebook friend request to the target. This request appears to come from an old friend but once accepted, the scammer impersonating the old friend initiates a conversation intended to get the target person to click on a link so that the scammer can steal their identifiable information. People targeted by this scam have reported that they clicked the link because it came from their friends. Other research also validates the power of friendship on social media by demonstrating that people consider more carefully movie evaluations from their friends (Lee, Hosanagar, & Tan, 2015). When their friends' evaluations were unavailable, only then did participants consider the feedback of strangers along with the film's overall popularity. Other evidence indicates that, among other things, people are more likely to join Facebook groups when they receive an invitation to join from more than one friend (Kwon, Stefanone, & Barnett, 2014). Related to the Influence Campaign that interfered with the outcome of the 2016 US presidential election, many IRA's social media ads were specifically targeted not only people but also their friends who liked the official page for the legitimate activist group Black Lives Matters.

Similarity

Similarity can manifest on a number of dimensions: attitudes, background, experiences, or appearance. More broadly, research has shown that perceived similarity between people and corporate blogs can increase brand loyalty (Zhang, Barnes, Zhao, & Zhang, 2018), people are more influenceable online when the person is trying to persuade them that he/she is similar to them (Guadagno & Cialdini, 2007); and similarity was the main dimension employed to test the effectiveness of some of IRA's techniques during the 2017 Alabama special election that resulted in the election of Democrat Doug Jones by presenting republications with messages from similar others as a means to decrease their support of alleged pedophile, Roy Moore (Shane & Blinder, 2018; December 19).

Defense against illicit influence attempts

Reality exists in the human mind, and nowhere else.

—Orwell, 1949

While it was far beyond the scope of this chapter to document all the different types of disinformation that have been disseminated through social media, suffice it to say that the IRA and the alt-right are not the only actors to spread fake news and disinformation nor is the United States the only target of such information operations. Indeed, one report documented evidence of disinformation campaigns targeting elections in 16 countries (Angola, Armenia, Colombia, Ecuador, France, Gambia, Germany, Indonesia, Italy, Kenya, Rwanda, South Korea, Turkey, and the United Kingdom; Freedom of the Net, 2018). A second report documented such efforts targeting 24 countries and found that while most (72%) of these campaigns were launched by Russia, China, Iran, and Saudi Arabia accounted for the remaining attempts to spread disinformation in the populace of other countries (Martin & Shapiro, 2019). What be done to reduce the flow of disinformation on social media? As I review next, preliminary research has pointed to some potential remedies in the form of fact-checking, forewarning, and priming.

Fact-checking

Fact-checking verifies the accuracy of information presented as factual. Online, there are several websites that fact-check such as Snopes and PolitiFact. However, typically people have to make an effort to search these websites to verify whether a particular piece of information posted on social media as factual news is actually true. Empirical evidence has found that fact-checking can help dispel false beliefs. For instance, Hameleers & van der Meer (2020) found evidence that fact-checking can be successful in reducing the effectiveness of misinformation that is consistent with people's preexisting political beliefs. This was the case regardless of whether fact-checking was an affordance of the system or an option that participants were free to select. These results suggest that adding fact-checking to social media news is one potential way that technology companies could reduce the impact of misinformation on people. Other research indicates that people are nearly twice as likely to accept fact-checking on Twitter when the source of the fact-check is a friend—operationally defined as someone who follows and is followed by the research participant (Margolin, Hannak, & Weber, 2018). It should be noted that Facebook has started integrating fact-checking into its platform for certain types of posts (Ortutay, 2019; September 25), but the remaining social media applications are far behind in this endeavor.

Forewarning

Inoculation theory (McGuire, 1961) is one of the most widely accepted theories of resistance to persuasion. It proposes that people's resistance to a social influence attempt can be increased by exposing them to a weak version of persuasive arguments prior to a persuasion attempt actually occurring. It is called inoculation theory because it instills resistance to persuasion psychologically much in the same way the vaccinations help our immune systems fight disease by exposing people to a weaker version of the virus. Inoculation theory has been shown over time to be widely effective in facilitating resistance to persuasion (Banas & Rains, 2010). The effectiveness of inoculation theory has been examined in the combatting misinformation on social media.

One such study created a video game intervention in which participants were assigned to play the part of someone who makes money by generating and disseminating fake news (Roozenbeek & van der Linden, 2019). The goal of the game was to attract as many followers as possible while maintaining as high of credibility as they could by employing six commonly used misinformation tactics, many of which have been described earlier in this chapter: discrediting people and information, spreading conspiracy theories, trolling others, polarizing group opinions, impersonating others, and manipulating people's emotional reactions (e.g., fear, outrage, and empathy). To examine this, participants were recruited to play a fake news game through a university press release that promised to inoculate people by teaching them propaganda tactics. People who followed the link to the game were invited to participate in the scientific study of the game's effectiveness after they played for a few minutes. Nearly one-third of people attracted to the game agreed to participate, resulting in a sample of nearly 15,000 people. Results revealed that playing this game significantly increases people's ability to recognize misinformation, especially those found at pretest to be more susceptible to fake news. Thus these results suggest that inoculating people by teaching them the tactics used by creators of misinformation can be effective in helping people resist its influence.

Priming

Other research has shown that priming (unconsciously making an idea or concept salient in someone's mind) people for critical thinking or accuracy helps them resist misinformation. For instance, Lutzke, Drummond, Slovic, and Árvai (2019) sampled more than 2500 participants who were primed for critical thinking by reading through a list of recommendations for appraising the veracity of news spread online. Compared to a control group who did not receive such training, participants primed for critical thinking were less likely to like, share, or trust misinformation on climate change. Most importantly, this manipulation had no impact on participants' evaluations of legitimate news on climate change. Similarly, Brashier, Eliseev, and Marsh (2020) found that people focusing on accuracy produced similar effects but only among those who had domain-relevant knowledge on the topic.

Thus, while preliminary research suggests that there are many techniques that can help people resist the influence of misinformation on social media, more research works need to be conducted, especially with respect to whether these different techniques can work additively together to instill resistance to misinformation in people. However, fundamentally, this is not an issue that can be solved solely by individuals. There are far too many social media users, too much information on the Internet, and information spreads too quickly for any one person to fully protect themselves from disinformation. At the government level, social media needs to be regulated. At the corporate level, I urge social media companies to reframe their business models such that people are the customer, not the data point (Guadagno, 2019; August 28). One thing is certain, now that the Russian social media influence operation playbook is out there, other actors—both foreign and domestic—are now using it.

Summary

Social influence surrounds us—it always does. Social media has just made it more ubiquitous, obvious, and easier for one person to influence many. In this chapter, the running example of misinformation and influence operations presents an extreme and nefarious example of online social

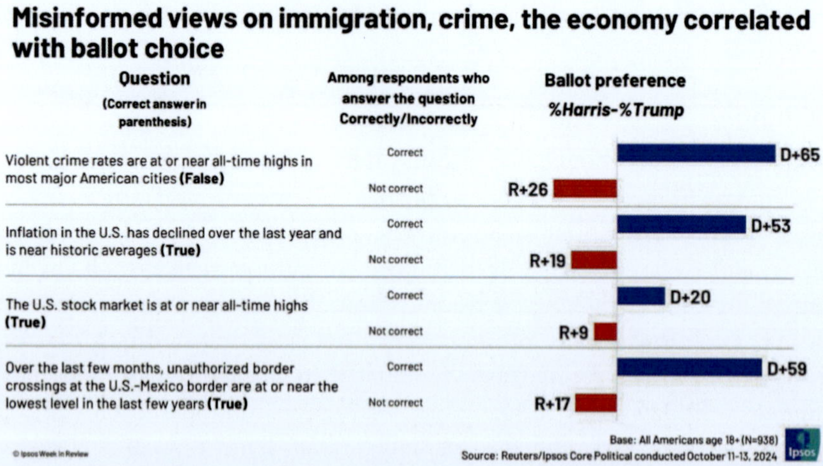

Figure 5.8 Polling data collected a month before the 2024 US presidential election shows that likely Trump voters beleived misinformation. *Young, C., Feldman, S., Mendez, B. (2024, October 18). The link between media consumption and public opinion. Report available online at: https://www.ipsos.com/en-us/link-between-media-consumption-and-public-opinion.*

influence, and it also highlights that all humans are influenced by the behavior of others and the content that spreads online (as we will examine in Chapter 6 on virality). The governments and individuals intentionally created social media content intended to confuse, mislead, sow chaos, and harm the credibility of legitimate authorities and institutions have become very good at misleading people to believe false information (Jamieson, 2018). This has disrupted people's lives and has led to a tremendous amount of global political turmoil, including potentially the election of an illegitimate president in the United States, both in 2016 and again in 2024 (see Fig. 5.8). The future of democratic societies—those that encourage open public discourse—is at stake. Thus I urge my readers to think carefully when evaluating information and to evaluate the credibility of sources, look for corroborating evidence, and fact-check before believing or repeating news and other information presented on social media. I hope that reviewing the literature on social influence and persuasion on social media through the lens of misinformation will inoculate each and every one of my readers to resist misinformation attempts. Stay mindful and vigilant and remember that not everything presented as factual on the Internet is true.

References

Abramson, J. (2016, March 28). This may shock you: Hillary Clinton is fundamentally honest. *The Guardian*. Retrieved from: <https://www.theguardian.com/commentisfree/2016/mar/28/hillary-clinton-honest-transparency-jill-abramson>.

Ahmed, T. (2018, February 23). Is Snapchat over? Kylie Jenner possibly caused $1.3 billion loss in value, but it's not dead yet, expert says. *Newsweek*. Retrieved from: <https://www.newsweek.com/snapchat-over-kylie-jenner-possibly-caused-13-billion-loss-value-its-not-dead-817849>.

Allbright, C. A Russian Facebook page organized a protest in Texas. *A different Russian page launched the counterprotest*. (2017, November 1). The Texas Tribune website: <https://www.texastribune.org/2017/11/01/russian-facebook-page-organized-protest-texas-different-russian-page-l/>. Retrieved 22.05.18

Allcott, H., & Gentzkow, M. (2017). Social media and fake news in the 2016 election. *Journal of Economic Perspectives*, *31*(2), 211–236.

American Society of Plastic Surgeons. (2019, March 11). *New plastic surgery statistics reveal trends toward body enhancement*. [press release]. Retrieved from: <https://www.plasticsurgery.org/news/press-releases/new-plastic-surgery-statistics-reveal-trends-toward-body-enhancement>

Aquino, F., Donzelli, G., De Franco, E., Privitera, G., Lopalco, P. L., & Carducci, A. (2017). The web and public confidence in MMR vaccination in Italy. *Vaccine*, *35*(35), 4494–4498.

Banas, J. A., & Rains, S. A. (2010). A meta-analysis of research on inoculation theory. *Communication Monographs*, 77(3), 281–311.

Belluz, J. (2019, March 5). Research fraud catalyzed the anti-vaccination movement. Let's not repeat history. *Vox*. Retrieved from: <https://www.vox.com/2018/2/27/17057990/andrew-wakefield-vaccines-autism-study>.

Bem, D. J. (1967). Self-perception: An alternative interpretation of cognitive dissonance phenomena. *Psychological Review*, *74*, 183–200.

Brashier, N. M., Eliseev, E. D., & Marsh, E. J. (2020). An initial accuracy focus prevents illusory truth. (in press) *Cognition*, *194*.

Brehm, J. W. (1966). *A theory of psychological reactance*. Oxford, England: Academic Press.

Broniatowski, D. A., Jamison, A. M., Qi, S., AlKulaib, L., Chen, T., Benton, A., ... Dredze, M. (2018). Weaponized health communication: Twitter bots and Russian trolls amplify the vaccine debate. *American Journal of Public Health*, *108*(10), 1378–1384.

Burkhardt, J. M. (2017). History of fake news. *Library Technology Reports*, *53*(8), 5–9.

Centers for Disease Control and Prevention. (2019, April 25). *CDC Media Statement: Measles cases in the U.S. are highest since measles was eliminated in 2000* [press release]. Retrieved from: <https://www.cdc.gov/media/releases/2019/s0424-highest-measles-cases-since-elimination.html>.

Chumber, S., Huber, J., & Ghezzi, P. (2015). A methodology to analyze the quality of health information on the internet: The example of diabetic neuropathy. *The Diabetes Educator*, *41*(1), 95–105. Available from https://doi.org/10.1177/0145721714560772, http://doi.org.stanford.idm.oclc.org/.

Cialdini, R. B. (2009). *Influence: Science and Practice* (5th ed.). Boston: Allyn & Bacon.

Cialdini, R. B., Vincent, J. E., Lewis, S. K., Catalan, J., Wheeler, D., & Darby, B. L. (1975). Reciprocal concessions procedure for inducing compliance: The door-in-the-face technique. *Journal of Personality and Social Psychology*, *31*, 206.

Collins, B., & Cox, J. (2017, November 3). Jenna Abrams, Russia's clown troll princess, duped the mainstream media and the world. *The Daily Beast*.Retrieved from: <https://www.thedailybeast.com/jenna-abrams-russias-clown-troll-princess-duped-the-mainstream-media-and-the-world>.

DiResta, R., Shaffer, D. K., Ruppel, B., Matney, R., Fox, R., Albright, D. J., ... Research, C. (2018). The Tactics & Tropes of the Internet Research Agency. US Senate Documents.

Dunn, J. (2002). Political obligation in its historical context: essays in political theory. Cambridge University Press.

Eagly, A. H., Ashmore, R. D., Makhijani, M. G., & Longo, L. C. (1991). What is beautiful is good, but ...: A meta-analytic review of research on the physical attractiveness stereotype. *Psychological Bulletin*, *110*, 109–128.

Eastwick, P. W., & Gardner, W. L. (2009). Is it a game? Evidence for social influence in the virtual world. *Social Influence*, *4*, 18–32.

Farb, M. (2019, September 15). *Trump's Twitter bots*. Retrieved from: <https://www.unhackthevote.com/trumps-twitter-bots/>.

Feeley, T. H., Anker, A. E., & Aloe, A. M. (2012). The door-in-the-face persuasive message strategy: A meta-analysis of the first 35 years. *Communication Monographs*, *79*(3), 316–343. Available from https://doi.org/10.1080/03637751.2012.697631, http://doi.org.stanford.idm.oclc.org/.

Feng, Y., & Ye, H. (2016). Why do you return the favor in online knowledge communities? A study of the motivations of reciprocity. *Computers in Human Behavior*, *63*, 342–349. Available from https://doi.org/10.1016/j.chb.2016.05.007, http://doi.org.stanford.idm.oclc.org/.

Ferner, M. (2016, September 15). Donald Trump is unqualified to be President, majority of Americans say. *HuffPost*. Retrieved from: <https://www.huffpost.com/entry/donald-trump-unqualified-poll_n_57dad724e4b04a1497b2f7da>.

Festinger, L. (1957). *A theory of cognitive dissonance* (Vol. 2). Stanford University Press.

Festinger, L., & Carlsmith, J. M. (1959). Cognitive consequences of forced compliance. *The Journal of Abnormal and Social Psychology*, *58*(2), 203.

Flanagin, A. J. (2017). Online social influence and the convergence of mass and interpersonal communication. *Human Communication Research*, *43*(4), 450–463. Available from https://doi.org/10.1111/hcre.12116.

Freedman, J. L., & Fraser, S. C. (1966). Compliance without pressure: the foot-in-the-door technique. *Journal of Personality and Social Psychology*, *4*(2), 195.

Freedom of the Net (2018). The Rise of Digital Authoritarianism. Retrieved from: <https://freedomhouse.org/report/freedom-net/freedom-net-2018>.

Gilbert, D. T., Tafarodi, R. W., & Malone, P. S. (1993). You can't not believe everything you read. *Journal of Personality and Social Psychology*, *65*(2), 221.

Goel, S., Williams, K., & Dincelli, E. (2017). Got phished? internet security and human vulnerability. *Journal of the Association for Information Systems*, *18*(1), 22–44.

Gorodnichenko, Y., Pham, T., & Talavera, O. (2018). Social media, sentiment and public opinions: Evidence from# Brexit and# USElection *(No. w24631)*. National Bureau of Economic Research.

Gouldner, A. W. (1960). The norm of reciprocity: A preliminary statement. *American Sociological Review*, 161–178.

Greenwald, A. G., & Ronis, D. L. (1978). Twenty years of cognitive dissonance: Case study of the evolution of a theory. *Psychological Review*, *85*(1), 53.

Guadagno, R. E., Sardos, A., & Kimbrough, A. M. (2024). PERSUASIVE: International Conference on Persuasive Technology. In Proceedings of the 19th International Conference on BCSS 2024. Conference conducted in Wollongong, Australia, 10–12 April 2024.

Guadagno, R. E., Oilvieri, A. F., & Kimbrough, A. M. (2024). Social Media in the aftermath of the 2016 US presidential election: Disruption at the cost of connection. *Proceedings of the 23rd European Conference on Cyber Warfare and Security,* Jyväskylä,

Finland, 26-28 June 2024. https://papers.academic-conferences.org/index.php/eccws/article/download/2471/2119.

Guadagno, R. E. (2017). Compliance: A contemporary review. In S. Harkins, K. Williams, & J. Burger (Eds.), *The oxford handbook of social influence* (pp. 107–128). New York: Oxford University Press.

Guadagno, R. E. (2019, August 28). *People as commodity: Black Mirror's "Smithereens"*. Peer Review, Sloan Science & Film. Retrieved from: <http://www.scienceandfilm.org/articles/3246/people-as-commodity-black-mirrors-smithereens>.

Guadagno, R. E., & Cialdini, R. B. (2002). Online persuasion: An examination of gender differences in computer-mediated interpersonal influence. *Group Dynamics: Theory Research and Practice, 6*, 38–51.

Guadagno, R. E., & Cialdini, R. B. (2005). Online persuasion and compliance: Social influence on the Internet and beyond. In Y. Amichai-Hamburger (Ed.), *The social net: The social psychology of the Internet* (pp. 91–113). New York: Oxford University Press.

Guadagno, R. E., & Cialdini, R. B. (2007). Persuade him by email, but see her in person: Online persuasion revisited. *Computers in Human Behavior, 23*, 999–1015.

Guadagno, R. E., & Guttieri, K. (2019). Fake News and Information Warfare: An Examination of the Political and Psychological Processes from the Digital Sphere to the Real World. In I. Chiluwa, & S. A. Samoilenko (Eds.), *Handbook of research on deception, fake news, and misinformation online* (pp. 167–191). IGI Global.

Guadagno, R. E., Muscanell, N. L., Rice, L. M., & Roberts, N. (2013). Social influence online: The impact of social validation and likability on compliance. *Psychology of Popular Media Culture, 2*, 51–60. Available from https://doi.org/10.1037/a0030592.

Guadagno, R. E., Muscanell, N. L., Sundie, J. M., Hardison, T. A., & Cialdini, R. B. (2013). The opinion changing power of computer-based multi media presentations. *Psychology of Popular Media Culture, 2*, 110–116.

Guadagno, R. E., Okdie, B. M., & Muscanell, N. L. (2013). Have we all just become 'Robo-sapiens'? Reflections on social influence processes in the Internet Age. *Psychological Inquiry, 24*, 1–9.

Hills, M. C. (2018, February 23). Snapchat's $1.3 billion drop in value is linked to a Kardashian. *Forbes*. Retrieved from: <https://www.forbes.com/sites/meganhills1/2018/02/23/snapchat-stock-value/#34287986e457>.

Hameleers, M., & van der Meer, T. G. L. A. (2020). Misinformation and polarization in a high- choice media environment: How effective are political fact-checkers? *Communication Research, 47*(2), 227–250. Available from https://doi.org/10.1177/0093650218819671.

Holton, A. E., & Chyi, H. I. (2012). News and the overloaded consumer: Factors influencing information overload among news consumers. *Cyberpsychology, Behavior, and Social Networking, 15*(11), 619–624.

Howard, P. N., Ganesh, B., Liotsiou, D., Kelly, J., & François, C. (2018). The IRA, Social Media and Political Polarization in the United States, 2012–2018. University of Oxford.

Hviid, A., Hansen, J. V., Frisch, M., & Melbye, M. (2019). Measles, mumps, rubella vaccination and autism: A nationwide cohort study. *Annals of Internal Medicine, 170*(8), 513–520.

Jamieson, K. H. (2018). Cyberwar: How Russian *hackers and trolls helped elect a president what we don't, can't, and do kn*ow. Oxford University Press.

Jain, A., Marshall, J., Buikema, A., Bancroft, T., Kelly, J. P., & Newschaffer, C. J. (2015). Autism occurrence by MMR vaccine status among US children with older siblings with and without autism. *JAMA: the Journal of the American Medical Association, 313* (15), 1534–1540.

Kirk, K. (2019, April 9). How Russia sows confusion in the U.S. Vaccine Debate. *Foreign Policy*. Retrieved from: <https://foreignpolicy.com/2019/04/09/in-the-united-states-russian-trolls-are-peddling-measles-disinformation-on-twitter/>.

Kimbrough, A. M., & Guadagno, R. E. (2019). Social media use as media literacy. In R. Hobbs, & P. Mihailidis (Eds.), The International Encyclopedia of Media Literacy (pp. 1–7). Hoboken, New Jersey: Wiley. Available from https://doi.org/10.1002/9781118978238.ieml0224.

Kwon, K. H., Stefanone, M. A., & Barnett, G. A. (2014). Social network influence on online behavioral choices exploring group formation on social network sites. *American Behavioral Scientist*, *58*, 1345–1360.

Lane, D. S., & Dal Cin, S. (2018). Sharing beyond Slacktivism: the effect of socially observable prosocial media sharing on subsequent offline helping behavior. *Information. Communication & Society*, *21*(11), 1523–1540.

Leamon, E.J., & Bucelato, J. (2017, December). *Federal Elections* 2016. Election Results for the U.S. President, the U.S. Senate and the U.S. House of Representatives. (Federal Election Commission). Washington, D.C. Retrieved from: <https://transition.fec.gov/pubrec/fe2016/federalelections2016.pdf>.

Lee, S. K., Lindsey, N. J., & Kim, K. S. (2017). The effects of news consumption via social media and news information overload on perceptions of journalistic norms and practices. *Computers in Human Behavior*, *75*, 254–263.

Lee, Y. J., Hosanagar, K., & Tan, Y. (2015). Do I follow my friends or the crowd? Information cascades in online movie ratings. *Management Science*, *61*, 2241–2258.

Lin, H. S., & Kerr, J. (2017). *On cyber-enabled information/influence warfare and manipulation*. Retrieved from: <https://www.americanbar.org/content/dam/aba/administrative/law_national_security/Herbert%20Lin%20Cyber-Enabled%20Info%20Influence%20Warfare%20and%20Manipulation.authcheckdam.pdf>.

Levine, T. R. (2014). Truth-default theory (TDT) a theory of human deception and deception detection. *Journal of Language and Social Psychology*, *33*(4), 378–392.

Liu, X., Min, Q., & Han, S. (2019). Understanding users' continuous content contribution behaviours on microblogs: An integrated perspective of uses and gratification theory and social influence theory. *Behaviour & Information Technology*. Available from https://doi.org/10.1080/0144929X.2019.1603326, http://doi.org.stanford.idm.oclc.org/.

Lutzke, L., Drummond, C., Slovic, P., & Árvai, J. (2019). Priming critical thinking: Simple interventions limit the influence of fake news about climate change on Facebook. *Global Environmental Change*, *58*, 101964.

Margolin, D. B., Hannak, A., & Weber, I. (2018). Political fact-checking on Twitter: When do corrections have an effect? *Political Communication*, *35*(2), 196–219.

Markey, P. M., Wells, S. M., & Markey, C. N. (2001). Personality and social psychology in the culture of cyberspace. In S. P. Shohov (Ed.), *Advances in psychology research* (Vol. 9, pp. 103–124). Huntington, NY: Nova Science Publishers, Inc.

Martin, D. A., & Shapiro, J. N. (2019). Trends in online foreign influence efforts. Princeton Univiversity.

McGuire, W. J. (1961). Resistance to persuasion conferred by active and passive prior refutation of same and alternative counterarguments. *Journal of Abnormal Psychology*, *63*, 326–332.

Mezzofiore, G. (2018, August 7). Why Italy's U-turn on mandatory vaccination shocks the scientific community. *CNN*. Retrieved from: <https://edition.cnn.com/2018/08/07/health/italy-anti-vaccine-law-measles-intl/index.html>.

Milgram, S. (1974). The dilemma of obedience. *The Phi Delta Kappan*, *55*(9), 603–606.

Minxue, H., Shunyu, Y., & Maohong, L. (2018). Self-enhancing or self-deprecating: How can celebrity endorsement enhance the marketing effectiveness of advertisements in social media. *Acta Psychologica Sinica*, *50*(8), 907–919. Available from https://doi.org/10.3724/SP.J.1041.2018.00907.

Mislin, A. A., Boumgarden, P. A., Jang, D., & Bottom, W. P. (2015). Accounting for reciprocity in negotiation and social exchange. *Judgment and Decision Making, 10*(6), 571–589. Available from https://search-proquest-com.stanford.idm.oclc.org/docview/1789764352?accountid = 14026.

Murray, M. (2017, August 23). 12 days that stunned a nation: How Hillary Clinton lost. *NBC News*. Retrieved from: <https://www.nbcnews.com/politics/elections/12-days-stunned-nation-how-hillary-clinton-lost-n794131>.

Muscanell, N. L., Guadagno, R. E., & Murphy, S. (2014). Weapons of influence misused: A social influence analysis of why people fall prey to internet scams. *Social and Personality Psychology Compass, 8*(7), 388–396.

Mueller, R. S. (2019, March). Report on the investigation into Russian Interference in the 2016 Presidential Election *(Vol. 1 & 2)*. U.S. Department of Justice. Retrieved from: <https://www.justice.gov/storage/report.pdf>

Nicas, J. (2018). How YouTube drives people to the Internet's darkest corners, February 7*The Wall Street Journal*, Retrieved from. Available from https://www.wsj.com/articles/how-youtube-drives-viewers-to-the-internets-darkest-corners-1518020478.

Nickerson, R. S. (1998). Confirmation bias: A ubiquitous phenomenon in many guises. *Review of General Psychology, 2*(2), 175–220.

Ortutay B. (2019, September 25). Facebook says it isn't fact checking politicians on the social platform. *Time*. Retrieved from: <https://time.com/5686621/facebook-fact-checking-politicians/>.

Orwell, G. (1949). *Nineteen Eighty-Four*. London: Secker and Warburg.

Parsons, K., Butavicius, M., Delfabbro, P., & Lillie, M. (2019). Predicting susceptibility to social influence in phishing emails. *International Journal of Human-Computer Studies, 128*, 17–26.

Pennycook, G., Cannon, T. D., & Rand, D. G. (2018). Prior exposure increases perceived accuracy of fake news. *Journal of Experimental Psychology. General, 147*(12), 1865.

Petrova, P. K., Cialdini, R. B., & Sills, S. J. (2007). Consistency-based Compliance across Cultures. *Journal of Experimental Social Psychology, 43*, 104–111.

Petty, R. E., & Brinol, P. (2012). A multiprocess approach to social influence. *Six degrees of social influence: Science, application, and the psychology of Robert Cialdini*, 49–58.

Petty, R. E., & Cacioppo, J. T. (1984). The effects of involvement on responses to argument quantity and quality: Central and peripheral approaches to persuasion. *Journal of Personality and Social Psychology, 46*, 69–81.

Proferes, N., & Summers, E. (2019). Algorithms and agenda-setting in Wikileaks'# Podestaemails release. *Information, Communication & Society*, 1–16. Available from https://doi.org/10.1080/1369118X.2019.1626469.

Reynolds, K. E., Gilkeson, J. H., & Niedrich, R. W. (2009). The influence of seller strategy on the winning price in online auctions: A moderated mediation model. *Journal of Business Research, 62*(1), 22–30.

Ribeiro, M. H., Ottoni, R., West, R., Almeida, V. A., & Meira, W. (2019). *Auditing Radicalization Pathways on YouTube. arXiv preprint arXiv, 1908*, 08313.

Rind, B., & Strohmetz, D. (1999). Effect on restaurant tipping of a helpful message written on the back of customer's checks. *Journal of Applied Social Psychology, 29*(1), 139–144. Available from https://doi.org/10.1111/j.1559-1816.1999.tb01378.x, http://doi.org.stanford.idm.oclc.org/.

Rodriguez, M. G., Gummadi, K., & Schoelkopf, B. (2014, May). Quantifying information overload in social media and its impact on social contagions. In *Eighth International AAAI Conference on Weblogs and Social Media*.

Roozenbeek, J., & van der Linden, S. (2019). Fake news game confers psychological resistance against online misinformation. *Palgrave Communications, 5*(1), 12.

Russell, C. A., & Rasolofoarison, D. (2017). Uncovering the power of natural endorsements: A comparison with celebrity-endorsed advertising and product placements.

International Journal of Advertising: The Review of Marketing Communications, 36(5), 761–778. Available from https://doi.org/10.1080/02650487.2017.1348033.

Shane, S., & Blinder, A. (2018, December 19). Secret experiment in Alabama senate race imitated Russian tactics. *The New York Times*. Retrieved from: <https://www.nytimes.com/2018/12/19/us/alabama-senate-roy-jones-russia.html>.

Shen, C., Kasra, M., Pan, W., Bassett, G. A., Malloch, Y., & O'Brien, J. F. (2019). Fake images: The effects of source, intermediary, and digital media literacy on contextual assessment of image credibility online. *New Media & Society, 21*(2), 438–463.

Silverman, C. (2016). *This Analysis Shows How Viral Fake Election News Stories Outperformed Real News On Facebook*. Buzzfeed News. Retrieved July 14, 2019, from https://www.buzzfeednews.com/article/craigsilverman/viral-fake-election-news-outperformed-real-news-on-facebook.

Stocks, E. L., Mirghassemi, F., & Oceja, L. V. (2018). How is your day going? reciprocity norm in everyday communication. *International Journal of Psychology, 53*(3), 167–175. Available from https://doi.org/10.1002/ijop.12369, http://doi.org.stanford.idm.oclc.org/.

Stubb, C., & Colliander, J. (2019). This is not sponsored content"—The effects of impartiality disclosure and e-commerce landing pages on consumer responses to social media influencer posts. *Computers in Human Behavior, 98*, 210–222. Available from https://doi.org/10.1016/j.chb.2019.04.024.

Taib, R., Yu, K., Berkovsky, S., Wiggins, M., & Bayl-Smith, P. (2019). *Social engineering and organisational dependencies in phishing attacks. IFIP Conference on Human-Computer Interaction* (pp. 564–584). Cham: Springer, September.

The New York Times. (2016 November 8). Latest Election Polls 2016. Retrieved from: <https://www.nytimes.com/interactive/2016/us/elections/polls.html>.

The New York Times Editorial Board. (2016, September 26). Why Donald Trump should not be president. *The New York Times*. Retrieved from: <https://www.nytimes.com/2016/09/26/opinion/why-donald-trump-should-not-be-president.html>.

Tversky, A., & Kahneman, D. (1991). Loss aversion in riskless choice: A reference-dependent model. *The Quarterly Journal of Economics, 106*(4), 1039–1061.

Van Der Heide, B., & Walther, J. B. (2009, May). *Computer-mediated communication and persuasion: Testing a social information processing/heuristic-systematic synthesis*. Paper presented at the annual meeting of the International Communication Association, Chicago, IL.

Wakefield, A. J., et al. (1998). RETRACTED: Ileal-lymphoid-nodular hyperplasia, non-specific colitis, and pervasive developmental disorder in children. *The Lancet, 351*, 637–641.

Walther, J. B., Jang, J., & Hanna Edwards, A. A. (2018). Evaluating health advice in a web 2.0 environment: The impact of multiple user-generated factors on HIV advice perceptions. *Health Communication, 33*(1), 57–67. Available from https://doi.org/10.1080/10410236.2016.1242036.

Weaver, J. (2019, July 16). More people search for health online. *MSNBC News*. Retrieved from: <http://www.nbcnews.com/id/3077086/t/more-people-search-health-online/#.XZp-1C2ZMWo>.

Weedon, J., Nuland, W., & Stamos, A. (2017). *Information operations and Facebook*. Retrieved from Facebook: <https://fbnewsroomus.files.wordpress.com/2017/04/facebook-and-information-operations-v1.pdf>.

Wikileaks (2015, November 3). *What is WikiLeaks*? Retrieved from: <https://wikileaks.org/What-is-WikiLeaks.html>.

Zhang, K. Z. K., Barnes, S. J., Zhao, S. J., & Zhang, H. (2018). Can consumers be persuaded on brand microblogs? an empirical study. *Information & Management, 55*(1), 1–15. Available from https://doi.org/10.1016/j.im.2017.03.005.

CHAPTER 6

Virality, social validation, and emotional contagion on social media

It's very easy to make a viral video, but longevity and consistency, that's hard.

—Michelle Phan, Make Up Artist Turned Social Media Influencer (Bowles, 2014; October 27)

As Ms. Phan stated above, in the current social media environment, virality is the coin of the realm—this is how social media platforms and other Internet technology firms make their money. Viral content ranges widely; from inflammatory rants, dancing babies, silly and adorable children and pets, perceptual illusions illustrated by dresses and audio recordings, live-streamed violence such as mass shootings and the murder of unarmed Black men by American police, a seemingly endless stream of videos capturing racist "Karens[1]," a term for American women known for calling the police on people of color without cause, political violence such as the January 6, 2021 storming of the US capital by Trump supporters, and videos of kind, caring people saving wild animals from certain death. Social media companies utilize algorithms—computer programs that perform a specific predetermined set of actions—which track what content engages individual people and then prioritizes what these people see on their social media feeds. User engagement allows for the collection of data on individual users while they are using the app. So, the longer users are engaged (i.e., using social media), the better the algorithms are at predicting content that will keep people using the app.

I have studied the viral spread of content through social media for well over a decade and have often been asked to describe the "formula" for virality. It boils down to this: if the content is interesting, it evokes a

[1] Apologies to any readers named Karen. I have friends named Karen and think it is unfortunate that their name has been co-opted by the Internet to signify a racist White woman. While there are many instances in which women such as those have had their bad behavior filmed and spread online, the long-term repercussions in terms of ostracism, harassment, and job loss may be significantly worse than the bad behavior filmed.

Psychological Processes in Social Media
DOI: https://doi.org/10.1016/B978-0-12-811320-2.00005-8

strong emotional response—especially a negative one—and is seen by enough people and/or shared by someone with a huge social media following, the content will likely spread rapidly and "go viral." Although understudied, the timing of a message effects its likely virality as well. This chapter delves deeply into the psychological processes related to the spread of viral content on social media by reviewing the effect of people's emotions or affect on the ways in which people are susceptible as a social influence and persuasion. Specifically, from a psychological perspective, it is a combination of Cialdini's (2009) principle of social validation—people do what others do, especially when social norms are unclear—and the ways in which people's emotional reactions to provocative content combine to facilitate the viral spread of such content.

In Chapter 5, I reviewed research focusing on how social influence and persuasion on social media generally affects people's thoughts, behaviors, and beliefs. This chapter further examines this question by examining how people's emotional responses and perceptions of other's behavior influence their own behavior when using social media. After reviewing the core psychological principles necessary to understand this process, I will review the ways in which social media is uniquely designed to influence people to spread content far and wide by reviewing the relevant literature on psychology and virality and presenting notable examples of successful intentional and unintended viral spread. This chapter concludes with a discussion on the implications of virality on people's attitudes, beliefs, and perceptions of reality/truth (Fig. 6.1).

Figure 6.1 Viral social media content spread (Loewald, 2023a).

Virality and memes defined

The term "going viral" is colloquially understood to describe any photo, video, tweet, or other mediated message that spreads rapidly across the Internet. While the viral spread of information is nothing new—rumors, gossip, and (mis)information have long been a part of the human experience. The widespread adoption of social media has vastly increased the breadth and frequency of viral content. Indeed, the spread of viral content such as videos, images, and news stories has become so commonplace that the phrase "going viral" or "virality" has become a commonly used phrase. See Fig. 6.2 for an example of a tweet from Sesame Street's Cookie Monster that went viral.

The term "Internet meme" has also emerged as a widely used phrase to describe the video, audio recording, photograph, or other content that starts to go viral online, particularly when the content shifts as it spreads, often becoming a caricature of the original content and referencing inside jokes and popular culture content that some, but not all, perceivers will understand. See Fig. 6.3 for a creative visualization of people spreading information virally.

The term "meme" stems from Dawkins (2016) notion of the ways in which individual bits of cultural information propagates from person to person while undergoing variation, selection, and retention. These memes spread due to social learning and social validation (Guadagno, Cialdini, & Evron, 2010), essentially indicating that memes spread largely because people see others spreading them and respond in kind. Although these terms have become a regular part of our everyday language, the psychological processes

Figure 6.2 Uplifting viral tweet from the Cookie Monster (CookieMonster, 2022, November 22).

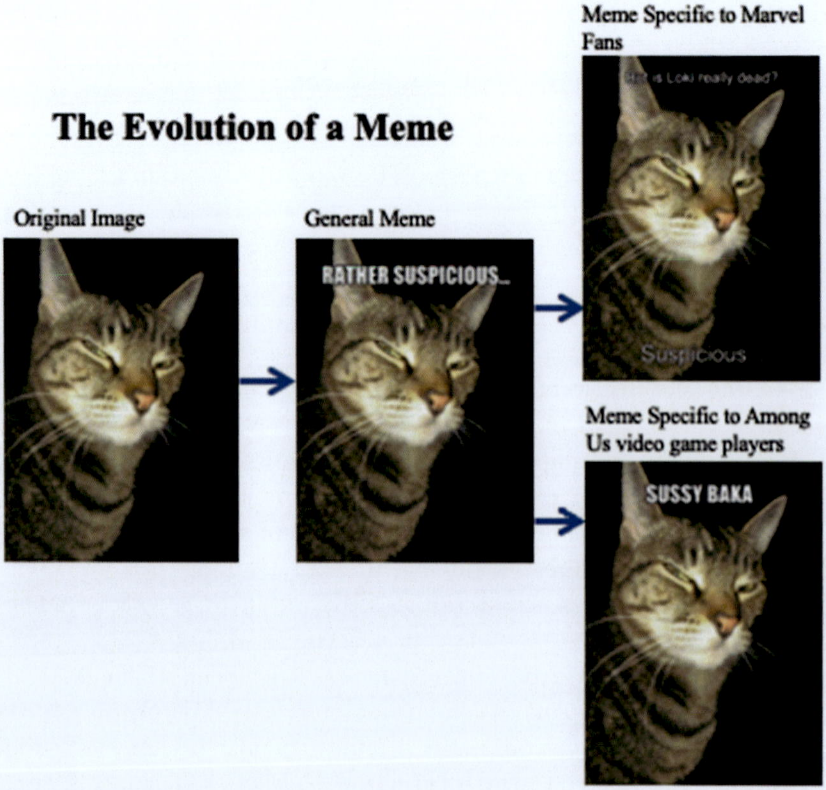

Figure 6.3 Different types of memes (Loewald, 2023b).

that determine what images, audio recordings, or videos will "go viral" is a question that has been only recently examined in the social science literature. Generally, as stated earlier, content that evokes a strong emotional response, is spread by influential people and/or by many people, tends to go viral. However, the scholarship also reveals that culture, timing, and veracity of the content also affect the extent to which it spreads virally. In the following sections, I review in detail the psychological processes involved in many of these contributing factors.

Social validation

Social validation or social proof is one of Cialdini's (2009) six principles of persuasion and refers to the influence that the people have on our behavior. As with the other principles, this is a heuristic process. In this case, the more people engage in the same behavior such as spreading Internet content, the more others will follow suit. This process is more likely to occur when the other people are similar or if the context has weaker explicit norms. It is under these circumstances that people are most likely to be influenced by the actions of others.

In one of my early studies (Guadagno, Muscanell, Rice, & Roberts, 2013), my students and I examined the role of social validation on compliance with a prosocial request on social media. Undergraduate research participants were asked to read a fictitious blog post and respond to a request to volunteer help with an upcoming food drive. Social validation information was provided by the number of fictitious students who responded positively or negatively to the request. In one condition, participants were given social validation information that the normative response was to agree to volunteer and in the other, they were given similar information suggesting that most other students refused (refusal of social validation information). There was also a control condition in which no social validation information was provided to assess baseline compliance with the request. The results of the study demonstrated the effect on social validation such that students who thought other students volunteered were significantly more likely to also volunteer and when the other, fictitious students refused, participants in that condition followed suit. These results demonstrate the power of other people in digital environments.

Other research supports the finding that the behavior of others on social media is influential. For instance, Nesi, Rothenberg, Hussong, and Jackson (2017) examined the role of social media and peer influence on drinking behaviors. To assess this, high school students were asked about the extent to which they posted alcohol-related content on social networking sites. Participants also reported the extent to which their friends engaged in the same behaviors and were asked about their own alcohol consumption. Results indicated that even after controlling for demographics and risk factors, the extent to which participants' friends posted about alcohol predicted their own alcohol consumption one year later. Additional results indicated that this relationship was driven by perceived norms relating to alcohol use. The role of social validation has also been shown to predict the applications people install from social media—if their friends use it, they are more likely to as well. Finally, anecdotal evidence from an interview with a former employee for the Russian Internet Research Agency (IRA) also highlights the importance of peers. In this case, the former

On what it was like to work for the Internet Research Agency:

"I arrived there, and I immediately felt like a character in the book "1984" by George Orwell — a place where you have to write that white is black and black is white. Your first feeling, when you ended up there, was that you were in some kind of factory that turned lying, telling untruths, into an industrial assembly line. The volumes were colossal — there were huge numbers of people, 300 to 400, and they were all writing absolute untruths. It was like being in Orwell's world."

On how this paid Russian troll was instructed to behave online:

"You got a list of topics to write about. Every piece of news was taken care of by three trolls each, and the three of us would make up an act. We had to make it look like we were not trolls but real people. One of the three trolls would write something negative about the news, the other two would respond, "You are wrong," and post links and such. And the negative one would eventually act convinced. Those are the kinds of plays we had to act out."

Figure 6.4 Excerpt from an interview with a Russian troll on the role of social validation in their disinformation campaign against the United States in the months leading up to the 2016 US presidential election (Troianovski, 2018; February 17).

troll for hire reported that they created narratives showing a multiperson social media exchange that resulted in a change in political views for the fictitious target (Troianovski, 2018; February 17). See Fig. 6.4 to read what an IRA employee or paid troll had to say about their tactics.

Indeed, the power of social validation has also been faked in various social engineering and disinformation campaigns in which bots—simple computer programs masquerading as real people—like or share content that the bot owner/operator wants to promote (Muscanell, Guadagno, & Murphy, 2014). There is also an open question as to whether fictitious social validation played a role in the various election outcomes of the last decade. Several studies have explored the role of bots in political discussions and their effects on virality (e.g., Shao, Ciampaglia, & Varol, 2018). These studies have found that the use of bots can lead to increased polarization, spread of misinformation, and the manipulation of public opinion. Bots can create an illusion of widespread support for a particular political viewpoint by generating many messages, likes, and/or retweets, thereby influencing the overall perception of a topic or candidate. The presence of bots can distort the public discourse and undermine the authenticity of political conversations. This can have negative consequences for the vitality of politics by eroding trust, increasing polarization, and impeding genuine engagement between citizens and political actors.

Other research makes it clear that there are distinct norms on social media and violating them is risky (Muscanell, Ewell, & Wingate, 2016).

Given this, it is unsurprising that one of the key ways in which the IRA influence operations ran was through the use of bots and trolls to convey the impression that many others believed as disinformation they were spreading. See Fig. 6.4 for an example. Specifically, DiResta et al. (2018) argues that one of the ways in which the IRA's campaigns attempted to influence Americans was by attempting to shift perceptions to normalize that accepting foreign-provided discrediting information on a political opponent is socially acceptable (it's not), and attacking distinguished public servants such as former FBI Director James Comey and former Special Counsel Robert Mueller as "corrupt Democratic Party shills" rather than the staunch Republicans that they are.

In summary, this section makes it clear that one of the psychological processes underlying the spread of viral information is the belief that other people like us spread such information. Next, I explore the role of affect in this process.

Affect

"Affect" and "emotion" are often used interchangeably in everyday language, but in psychology, they are distinct concepts with unique meanings (Forgas & Smith, 2007; Wetherell, 2012). Affect refers to people's emotional states, which is often a response to a stimulus that can be internal or external. Affect is considered a primary psychological process that's largely unconscious and can be described along dimensions of valence (from negative to positive) and arousal (from calm to excited). It is more foundational, immediate, and raw compared to emotions. Affect is often described as the raw, automatic, or instinctual response that one has to things. Examples of affect can include feeling happy after receiving good news, feeling nervous before a big speech, feeling startled when you hear a loud noise, or feeling outraged by a provocative video on YouTube.

Emotions, on the other hand, are complex and involve several components: physiological arousal, cognitive processes (such as the appraisal or interpretation of the situation), expressive behaviors, and conscious experiential feelings. Emotions are generally thought of as more specific, acute, and intense than affect, and they are usually directed toward a specific object or event. They also typically involve a more complex and sophisticated cognitive appraisal process, often involving concepts such as goals, beliefs, or values. Examples of emotions include feeling guilty because you believe you did something wrong, and feeling proud because you value.

Emotional contagion

Not only people's affective and emotional experiences are impacted by internal psychological processes and situational context, but these feelings can also be spread to others through a process called emotional contagion. Scholars define emotional contagion as "the tendency to automatically mimic and synchronize expressions, vocalizations, postures, and movements with those of another person's and, consequently, to converge emotionally" (Hatfield, Cacioppo, & Rapson, 1994). Thus it is an automatic, nonconscious, and fundamental part of emotional exchange that allows people to understand and respond empathetically to the feelings of others. Across a myriad of academic disciplines, there is ample evidence that people catch emotions from others—both offline and online (Hatfield & Rapson, 2010). Research on emotional contagion provides insights into how people synchronize their emotions in various social settings and can be applied to understanding phenomena such as crowd behavior, adapting healthy lifestyle choices (e.g., increase fitness or stop smoking), cultural attitudes, and workplace dynamics. Indeed, the infamous study mentioned at the opening of this book provided one such early example of emotional contagion occurring as part of people's social media use.

Recall that in Chapter 1, I discussed how Kramer, Guillory, and Hancock (2014) conducted a study that edited the newsfeeds of approximately 700,000 Facebook users so that, depending on condition, these Facebook users read posts with more negative emotion words, positive emotion words, or fewer words generally (control condition). Their results showed an effect of emotional contagion such that people exposed to more negative emotion words in posts included more negative emotion words in their posts relative to users in the control condition. Facebook users exposed to the news feed edited to show more positive emotion words responded similarly except that their posts conveyed more positive emotions. These effects were also found to last several days.

Putting it all together: virality on social media

As the abovementioned research suggests, the main factors contributing to the virality of social media content are a combination of people's perception of social norms—they tend to do what other people, especially similar others do—and the affective responses individuals have to social media content. Heath, Bell, and Sternberg (2001) published one of the first studies illustrating the role of affect in the spread of viral content online by examining urban legends. In this case, their results indicated that urban legends that evoked negative affect such as the emotions of disgust, anger, or fear were the most likely to spread virally. Similarly, Berger and Milkman (2010) and Berger and Milkman (2012) examined the affective content of 7000 articles from the New York Times to understand the characteristics related to each article's viral spread. They controlled factors such as location on the newspaper's website and author's prominence and reported that articles that evoked positive affect (e.g., awe and interest) or negative affect such as anger and anxiety were the most likely to be shared via email. Furthermore, these affective responses were likely to be highly physiologically arousing. Articles that evoked low-arousal emotions such as sadness were less likely to go viral. The authors speculated that the heightened physiological arousal associated with the more viral content was reflective of the belief that the content was more worth sharing.

Along with some of my former students, I conducted two studies designed to obtain a better understanding of what makes YouTube videos go viral by examining emotion evoked by the video and whether there was an impact of the source—the group membership of the person who sent it—of the viral content impacts the likelihood that people will involve themselves in the spread of this content (Guadagno, Rempala, Murphy, & Okdie, 2013). Our research team investigated this question by assessing the role that people's emotional responses to viral content played on participants' intentions to spread the Internet meme. In an additional, follow-up study, we replicated and expanded upon our first study by investigating whether receiving the video from an ingroup member (a fellow university student, someone seen as being in the same group as participants—their ingroup) or an outgroup member (a student from the rival university, someone seen as being in a different group than participants—their outgroup) of the Internet meme would affect whether people would contribute to the spread of the content online.

Across both studies, we found that people were more likely to spread Internet memes when they had strong emotional responses to the content (Guadagno et al., 2013). When there was no source of the video as in Study 1, videos that evoked positive affect were the ones that participants were more likely to intend to spread. To put it simply, participants were more likely to intend to spread funny and cute videos such as "Charlie Bit My Finger" (Royer, 2009; April 7), while memes that evoked negative affect such as anger or disgust such as "Don't Tase me Bro" (Dubs, 2009; January 15) were less likely to spread. When we examined the source of the video in Study 2—the person who shared it with them—we found that people were more likely to spread Internet memes that made people angry but only when the video came from a student from another university (or in Social Psychologist lingo, an *outgroup* member). Once again, we found that positive affect evoking videos were more likely to be spread overall. However, there was also an effect for source such that participants were more likely to intend to spread anger-evoking videos when they were shared by a fictitious outgroup member. A mediation analysis revealed that this result was due to participants' finding anger-inducing videos more interesting if they were sent by an outgroup member. This points to the importance of perceived group membership in virality.

When virality and politics collide: moral outrage

The role of affect in the spread of viral content has been investigated widely and generally supports the notion that strong emotions—in some case positive and in other cases negative—underlie the spread of viral content. Work by Professor Jay Van Bavel and colleagues has further explored this issue and linked it to moral outrage, which is heavily linked to people's beliefs about what is right and what is wrong (Van Bavel, Robertson, del Rosario, Rasmussen, & Rathje, 2023). Specifically, with his many collaborators, Professor Van Bavel has conducted numerous studies on moral outrage and social media and generally found that online platforms can amplify the expression of moral outrage, a strong feeling of anger or disgust in response to perceived moral transgressions (Brady, Crockett, & Van Bavel, 2020; Van Bavel et al., 2023). This research points to the role of social media in shaping, triggering, and amplifying moral emotions due to the design of the platforms and the nature of online interactions.

In their MAD Model of Moral Contagion, Van Bavel and colleagues report that expressions of moral outrage are more prevalent in digital environments than in face-to-face interactions because a combination of the affordances of social media that underlies virality reviewed earlier (the transparency, reach, and speed of messages) and the relative anonymity of the social media environment (Brady et al. 2020). Especially, the authors suggest that social media platforms provide a low-cost, high-reward avenue for expressing outrage, which can then be amplified by likes, shares, and retweets, leading to a cycle that can sometimes escalate. They argue that the rewarding aspects of social media (such as receiving likes and shares) can lead to a kind of "outrage feedback loop," where users are incentivized to express more outrage over time. This is because outrage can signal moral virtue, attract social attention, and lead to greater engagement; hence, it's often amplified in online contexts (Van Bavel et al., 2023).

One such study examined the extent to which negative affect toward a political outgroup drives viral spread on social media (Rathje, Van Bavel, & Van Der Linden, 2021). To examine this, Facebook and Twitter posts from news media and the US congress members (totaling 2,730,215 messages) were analyzed for affect and viral spread, operationalized as likes and shares. Their findings indicate that social media content concerning the opposing political group was shared or retweeted almost double the rate of posts about one's own political group. Each word related to the opposing political group—Republications or Democrats—increased the chances of a post being shared by 67%. Language targeting the opposition consistently proved to be the most powerful factor in determining shares and retweets. On average, the impact of such language was approximately 4.8 times stronger than language expressing negative emotions and about 6.7 times more potent than moral-emotional language—both of which are known as the drivers of social media activity. Posts with language about the opposition frequently received "angry" reactions (the dominant reaction across all datasets), while those about one's own group were more likely to get "love" reactions, highlighting a bias for one's own group and against the opposing one. Notably, this trend was consistent regardless of political stance or the social media platform used. However, the effect was more pronounced among political leaders compared to news media outlets. Overall, language targeting the opposition stands out as the most significant factor affecting social media engagement, implying that social media could be incentivizing content that showcases hostility toward opposing groups.

Thus, consistent with the findings of my earlier study (Guadagno et al., 2013), this research highlights how social media can polarize communities, given that outrage tends to spread more within in-groups (defined in this case as people who share the same moral or ideological views), which can reinforce existing beliefs and divide communities (Brady *et al.* 2020; Van Bavel et al., 2023). Overall, Van Bavel and his colleagues' work has provided critical insights into how social media platforms can fuel moral outrage, the implications for societal polarization, and how these platforms might be redesigned to foster healthier public discourse.

Real-world impact of virality

As the earlier sections illustrate, there is ample evidence demonstrating that people's psychological states spread along with viral content on social media. This begs the question, "do these psychological states also spread offline?" Overall, the limited evidence suggests the answer is yes. In 2010, I published an observational study on Russia's first attempt to sow discord online by targeting Estonia (Guadagno et al., 2010). Estonia is unique in that it is one of the most digital countries which is progressive but also increases its vulnerability to cybersecurity threats. Incensed by a perceived slight from the Estonian government—the government moved the statue that was built to honor the fallen World War II Soviet soldier from the capital city center to a cemetery outside of the city—Russian actors launched a series of direct denial of service (DDoS; the continuous flow of data to a particular website is so intense that it either shuts down the targeted site or makes accessing it excessively challenging) attacks against Estonian cyberinfrastructure. Relevant to this chapter, there were two unique aspects of this cyberattack: (1) Russian trolls spread messages on Russian-language social media spurring moral outrage due to the perceived insult to the ingroup (ethnic Russians living in Russia and Estonia) with simple instructions to join the DDoS attack and (2) the moral outrage spread offline and Estonians of Russian descent started rioting.

A similar spread was also observed in the months leading up to the 2016 US Presidential election. Specifically, Russian trolls used Facebook to organize protests and counterprotests such as pro- and anti-Islamic groups at the same time and in the same place (Bertrand, 2017; November 1). For example, on May 21, 2016, a group orchestrated by Russians, called Heart of Texas, organized a rally against the "Islamization of Texas" at an Islamic center in Houston via social media. Simultaneously, another Russian-operated Facebook group named United Muslims of America set up an event titled "Save Islamic Knowledge." These groups aimed their advertisements at distinct subsets of Facebook users, leading to actual individuals assembling with conflicting intentions. When these two groups encountered each other, tensions rose, leading to verbal confrontations, though not physical altercations

(Allbright, 2017; November 1). In this way, the Russians managed to create division at a cost of around $200.

The above mentioned examples are descriptive in nature. That is, researchers can say that the events are related, and the real-world discord occurred after the social media messages spread. As a result, we cannot conclude that the social media messages caused the subsequent violence. To date, there is one experiment that demonstrated a causal connection between moral outrage on social media and real-world violence (Mooijman, Hoover, Lin, Ji, & Dehghani, 2018). To examine this, the authors first collected data from Twitter illustrating that in 2015 during the Baltimore protests in response to the police killing of an African American man named Freddie Gray (Lopez, 2016; July 27), there were more moral tweets. Next, the authors conducted three experiments examining the perception of the August 2017 White Supremacist protest in Charlottesville, Virginia, United States (Elliott, 2022; August 12). The evidence from these three studies demonstrated that engaging in violence during a protest was seen as acceptable when observers perceived the issue to be related to moral values, there was highly perceived moral cohesion (i.e., participants believed others shared their moral convictions), and they were certain of their attitudes on the matter. Thus, while more research works need to be conducted on this issue, the extant literature suggests that viral outrage can spread offline.

Cultural differences in virality

The research reviewed earlier was conducted primarily in the United States, an individualistic culture (described in Chapter 4). As a result, we cannot conclude that the results generalize to a collectivistic culture. A series of experiments conducted by Hsu et al. (2021) addressed this question. Specially, the authors examined the affect associated with viral content in the United States and Japan, a collectivistic culture, predicting that culture would differentiate the type of tweets that influenced people. To examine this, Twitter data was collected from the US and Japanese users and analyzed using sentiment analysis (described in Chapter 1) to assess arousal level, affect, and emotional contagion in a sample of 1888 users from the United States. (55,867 tweets) and 1825 users from Japan (63,863 tweets). Results revealed a significantly different pattern of tweet content and social influence such that users from the United States posted more high-arousal positive content than Japanese users. Consistent with the above mentioned sections, users from the United States were more influenced by high-arousal negative content while Japanese users were more influenced by high-arousal positive content. Furthermore, across samples, users were more influenced by content that violated their cultural affective values. These results support the idea that there are likely significant cultural differences in the psychological underpinnings of virality. However, more research is needed to thoroughly address the question of culture's role in virality.

Summary

Going viral isn't born, it is made

—Jonah Berger

In summary, in the world of social media, negative emotions rule, at least in the Western world. While viral content is an important part of the business models of social media companies, this financial decision impacts users' psychological states and spreads across them. This begs the question of the ethics involved in using algorithms to prioritize content that keeps people engaged on social media posting and clicking away. While it is the case that social media companies are increasingly willing to stop violent and extremist content from being shared, a lot still spread. There is also a heavy psychological toll taken on the gatekeepers—the content moderators who have an extremely high burn-out rate (Barrett, 2020; Elliott, 2023).

Consider also, the Russian IRA placed advertisements and posts described in this and the previous chapter. While some spread more than others, all were seen by target users in the United States. The effect of this viral spread of disinformation on real world behavior is understudied. While moral outrage and other negative affect induced by viral content may have long-lasting effects on the people targeted by the rage of others (e.g., the aforementioned Karens), there is much in this area that still needs to be understood. My advice is to think before you share or like content and ask yourself, "is this an emotional experience you really want others to share?"

References

Allbright, C. (2017). A *Russian facebook page organized a protest in Texas. A different Russian page launched the counterprotest.* The Texas Tribune. <https://www.texastribune.org/2017/11/01/russian-facebook-page-organized-protest-texas-different-russian-page-l/>.

Cialdini, R. B. (2009). *Influence: Science and practice* (5th ed.). Boston: Allyn & Bacon.

Berger, J., & Milkman, K. (2010). Social transmission, emotion, and the virality of online content. Wharton research paper, 106, 1–52.

Barrett, P. M. (2020). *Who moderates the social media giants*. Center for Business. Available from https://bhr.stern.nyu.edu/wp-content/uploads/2024/02/NYUContentModerationReport_FINALVERSION.pdf.

Berger, J., & Milkman, K. L. (2012). What makes online content viral? *Journal of Marketing Research*, *49*(2), 192–205.

Bertrand, N. (2017). Russia organized 2 sides of a Texas protest and encouraged "both sides to battle in the streets." *Business Insider*. <http://www.businessinsider.com/russia-trolls-senate-intelligence-committee-hearing-2017-11>.

Bowles, N. (2014). Michelle Phan: From YouTube star to $84 million startup founder. *Vox*. <https://www.vox.com/2014/10/27/11632302/michelle-phan-youtube-star-to-startup-founder>.

Brady, W. J., Crockett, M. J., & Van Bavel, J. J. (2020). The MAD model of moral contagion: The role of motivation, attention, and design in the spread of moralized content online. *Perspectives on. Psychological Science*, *15*(4), 978–1010.

CookieMonster, (@MeCookieMonster). (2022). *When something is important, it mean a whole lot. Make sure your friends know how important dey (sic) are to you, just like beautiful cookie*. <https://twitter.com/MeCookieMonster/status/1597620394756014080?lang = en>

Dawkins, R. (2016). The selfish gene. Oxford University Press.

DiResta, R., Shaffer, K., Ruppel, B., Sullivan, D., Matney, R., Fox, R., … & Johnson, B. (2018). The tactics and tropes of the Internet Research Agency. *New Knowledge*.

Dubs, J. (2009). *Don't Tase Me Bro!* Know Your Meme. <https://knowyourmeme.com/memes/dont-tase-me-bro>.

Elliott, D. (2022). *The charlottesville rally 5 years later: "it's what you're still trying to forget."* NPR. <https://www.npr.org/2022/08/12/1116942725/the-charlottesville-rally-5-years-later-its-what-youre-still-trying-to-forget>.

Elliott, V. (2023). *Meta's gruesome content broke him. now he wants it to pay*. Wired. <https://www.wired.com/story/meta-kenya-lawsuit-outsourcing-content-moderation/>.

Forgas, J. P., & Smith, C. A. (2007). *Affect and emotion. The Sage handbook of social psychology* (pp. 146–175). Sage Publications.

Guadagno, R. E., Cialdini, R. B., & Evron, G. (2010). What about Estonia? A social psychological analysis of the first Internet war. *CyberPsychology, Behavior, & Social Networking*, *13*, 447–453.

Guadagno, R. E., Muscanell, N. L., Rice, L. M., & Roberts, N. (2013). Social influence online: The impact of social validation and likability on compliance. *Psychology of Popular Media Culture (Canadian Ethnology Society)*, *2*(1), 51.

Guadagno, R. E., Rempala, D. M., Murphy, S., & Okdie, B. M. (2013). What makes a video go viral? An analysis of emotional contagion and Internet memes. *Computers in Human Behavior*, *29*(6), 2312–2319.

Hatfield, E., Cacioppo, J., & Rapson, R. L. (1994). *Emotional contagion*. New York: Cambridge University Press.

Hatfield, E., & Rapson, R. L. (2010). Emotional contagion. In I. B. Weiner, & W. E. Craighead (Eds.), *Encyclopedia of psychology* (4th Edition). Hoboken, NJ: John Wiley and Sons.

Heath, C., Bell, C., & Sternberg, E. (2001). Emotional selection in memes: The case of urban legends. *Journal of Personality and Social Psychology*, *81*(6), 1028–1041. Available from https://doi.org/10.1037/0022-3514.81.6.1028.

Hsu, T. W., Niiya, Y., Thelwall, M., Ko, M., Knutson, B., & Tsai, J. L. (2021). Social media users produce more affect that supports cultural values, but are more influenced by affect that violates cultural values. *Journal of Personality and Social Psychology, 121*(5), 969.

Kramer, A. D., Guillory, J. E., & Hancock, J. T. (2014). Experimental evidence of massive-scale emotional contagion through social networks. *Proceedings of the National Academy of Sciences, 111*(24), 8788–8790.

Loewald, R.J. (2023a). *Viral social media content spread.*

Loewald, R.J. (2023b). *Different types of memes.*

Lopez, G. (2016). *The Baltimore protests over Freddie Gray's death, explained.* Vox. <https://www.vox.com/2016/7/27/18089352/freddie-gray-baltimore-riots-police-violence>.

Mooijman, M., Hoover, J., Lin, Y., Ji, H., & Dehghani, M. (2018). Moralization in social networks and the emergence of violence during protests. *Nature Human Behaviour, 2* (6), 389–396.

Muscanell, N. L., Ewell, P. J., & Wingate, V. (2016). "S/He posted that?!" Perceptions of topic appropriateness and reactions to status updates on social networking sites. *Translational Issues in Psychological Science, 2*(3), 216.

Muscanell, N. L., Guadagno, R. E., & Murphy, S. (2014). Weapons of influence misused: A social influence analysis of why people fall prey to internet scams. *Social and Personality Psychology Compass, 8*(7), 388–396.

Nesi, J., Rothenberg, W. A., Hussong, A. M., & Jackson, K. M. (2017). Friends' alcohol-related social networking site activity predicts escalations in adolescent drinking: mediation by peer norms. *Journal of Adolescent Health, 60*(6), 641–647.

Rathje, S., Van Bavel, J. J., & Van Der Linden, S. (2021). Out-group animosity drives engagement on social media. *Proceedings of the National Academy of Sciences, 118*(26), e2024292118.

Royer, T. (2009). *Charlie Bit my finger.* Know Your Meme. <https://knowyourmeme.com/memes/charlie-bit-my-finger>.

Shao, C., Ciampaglia, G. L., Varol, O., et al. (2018). The spread of low-credibility content by social bots. *Nat Commun, 9*, 4787. Available from https://doi.org/10.1038/s41467-018-06930-7.

Troianovski, A. (2018). A former Russian troll speaks: "it was like being in Orwell's world." *The Washington Post.* <https://www.washingtonpost.com/news/worldviews/wp/2018/02/17/a-former-russian-troll-speaks-it-was-like-being-in-orwells-world/>.

Van Bavel, J. J., Robertson, C., del Rosario, K., Rasmussen, J., & Rathje, S. (2023). Social Media and Morality. *Annual Review of Psychology.*

Wetherell, M. (2012). *Affect and emotion. Affect and emotion.* Sage.

CHAPTER 7

Romantic relationships on social media

Today, if you own a smartphone, you're carrying a 24–7 singles bar in your pocket.
(Anzari, 2015).

Breakups are painful for everyone. In the world of social media, breakups are often quite public, especially when one or both members of the couple are social media savvy celebrities. Sometimes a celebrity breakup becomes a public spectacle. Take the case of actress Megan Fox, well-known for starring in the Transformers and the Teenage Mutant Ninja Turtles film franchises. At the start of 2023, she was dating a singer named Machine Gun Kelly (MGK). Her Instagram was filled with selfies and photos of her dates with MGK. Then on February 12, Fox's Instagram page changed dramatically—all photos of MGK were gone and the lyrics from Beyonce's song Lemonade appeared: "You can taste the dishonesty, it's all over your breath" (Lutkin, 2023; February 12). She also unfollowed him. Several hours later Fox deleted her entire Instagram account (Rice, 2023; February 12). These changes led people to assume that MGK had cheated on Fox and that they had broken up. However, a little over two months later, Fox's Instagram account reopened, featuring sultry pictures of the actress (Small, 2023; May 22). While MGK has yet to reappear on her Instagram page, the couple has been photographed out on dates. The truth behind the couple's relationship drama should be a private matter. However, owing to the public nature of their professions combined with the public nature of social media, their relationship problems spread virally.

This chapter will examine the influence of social media use on the formation, maintenance, and dissolution of romantic relationships. Specifically, I review how the affordances of social media and our perceptions of potential romantic partners affect romantic relationships across their life cycles. The literature on social media's role in relational conflict and romantic jealousy will also be reviewed. Research suggests that much of people's social media time is spent forming and maintaining romantic relationships. This change in dating has also produced a series of new slang terms such as

Psychological Processes in Social Media
DOI: https://doi.org/10.1016/B978-0-12-811320-2.00008-3

"sliding into his/her DMs" or making a relationship "Facebook official" or describing a "soft launch breakup." This change in societal technology use has also affected how the dissolution of a romantic relationship is reflected on social media. Specifically, this chapter will cover the affordances of social media, how social media affects relationship formation, relationship maintenance, relationship conflict, relationship dissolution, gender, and cultural differences.

Social media affordances related to romantic relationships

The affordances or features of social media have altered both the ways in which people find romantic partners and the way they disclose information about their relationships. In particular, while using social media, there is an increased visibility of information on romantic relationships built into many social media applications. For instance, on Facebook, people can state their relationship status (e.g., single, in an open relationship, in a committed relationship, in a civil union, in a domestic partnership, engaged, married) and they can also link to their partner's social media profiles. Research suggests that approximately 70% of people share their romantic relationship status on Facebook (Krueger & Forest, 2020).

On other social media platforms, people will often add a link to their romantic partner on their profiles. As a result, people's social media connections can find out more details of a romantic relationship than they would have prior to the advent of social media (Fox, 2015). This increased visibility not only influences the impressions formed by friends and family but also affects relationship commitment. Illustrative of this, Lane, Piercy, and Carr (2016) surveyed social media users and found that those who were "Facebook Official" and had made their relationship status public reported greater commitment to their romantic partner compared to those who kept their relationship status private. However, this transparency in relationship status may also have its downsides as it creates a situation in which breakups are also public and may also facilitate jealousy and partner surveillance, especially after a breakup (Fox, 2015).

Overall, the transparency and longevity of information on social media have both negative and positive effects on people. Other examples include the different privacy settings that people can set on their social media content, especially their decisions to reveal or withhold certain information, can stir negative sentiments in romantic ties. The choice to display or omit relationship-centric data, like relationship status or images with one's partner, can shape both their relationship dynamics and SNS interactions. The psychological impact of these decisions will be reviewed throughout the chapter.

Stages of a romantic stages

Research on romantic relationships has documented the different ways in which relationships progress from the start of a relationship to the end. While there are many theoretical models of relationship progression, most split relationships into three general stages: the initial attraction phase, the relationship- and trust-building phase, and the relationship commitment, loyalty, and maintenance phase (Gottman & Gottman, 2017; Levinger, 1980). Of course, this work has also illustrated that, for romantic relationships that dissolve before the death of a partner, there is also the relationship deterioration phase before the end of a relationship. These relationship stages parallel theoretical perspectives on falling in love and have generally been found to be a global, cross-cultural phenomenon (Sorokowski et al., 2021). Social media use affects romantic relationships across their lifespan as it affects the way people find romantic partners, jealousy, and relationship commitment, and plays a role in relationship dissolutions. The sections below will review each.

The initial attraction phase

Finding partners on social media

The first time I incorporated social media into my undergraduate social psychology course—maybe in 2009 or 2010—I decided to start the lecture by asking my students what they primarily used Facebook for. I naively expected my students to describe how Facebook enriched their relationships with friends, family, and romantic partners. But no. The class of 200 students said in unison "To stalk people." And then we all burst into laughter, possibly for different reasons. People of my generation—I am Generation X, comprising of people born from 1965 to 1980; the last generation that grew up without access to personal computing devices—we did not have email let alone social media to help us keep in touch with people, form new relationships, check out the profiles of people we were interested in, or to keep track of ex-partners. So, I was surprised to learn that my students admitted that they primarily used Facebook for surveillance and social comparison (see Chapter 2) purposes. It led to a terrific class discussion and taught me a lot about the way younger adults see social media.

This illustrates one of the paradoxes of social media. Due to the connectedness afforded by this technology, people have access to significantly more romantic partners than ever before. However, changes in relationship status—engagements, marriages, and breakups—also play out in public. In the social media age, the adage about romantic relationships: "there are plenty of fish in the sea" has never been truer. People's use of social media and online dating to find romantic partners has never been higher. For instance, a recent Pew Internet survey revealed that 30% of Americans over 18 have tried online dating (Vogels & McCain, 2023; February 2). Furthermore, when examining the data by age, over 53% of young adults (18–29) have tried online dating. People from the LGBTQ community also use online dating more than cisgender individuals (51% vs. 28%). See Fig. 7.1.

Gender differences in mate preferences and online dating. While times have changed the ways in which people search for romantic partners, there are general trends about the characteristics men and

Figure 7.1 Online Dating (Loewald, 2023).

women search for in a romantic partner that have not changed. For instance, research has long demonstrated that men tend to look for younger partners, while women tend to look for older partners. This finding is consistent and stable across time, culture, and communication modality and has been reported in samples ranging from hunter-gatherer tribes, archival US marriage data, dating advertisements in print media, and online dating preferences. So, the same trend is found in primitive cultures, old-school personal ads, and analyses of data from online dating sites such as OK Cupid (Kenrick & Keefe, 1992; Wade, 2015; July 3).

When it comes to desired traits in potential romantic partners, men and women are similar in seeking romantic partners who are kind, reliable, outgoing, and intelligent (Botwin, Buss, & Shackelford, 1997). However, significant gender differences exist in the way that men and women approach the search for romantic partners. Due to differing parental investment between men and women (i.e., women bear a greater burden when it comes to reproduction and child-rearing), human mate selection is primarily driven by female choice (Darwin, 1871). This is evident in the disparity between men and women in being approached through online dating profiles. Men tend to approach women more often on these platforms. For example, one study found that 57% of men versus 23% of women never received a single email from a prospective date (Hitsch, Hortaçsu, & Ariely, 2009).

Furthermore, the likelihood of being contacted by potential dates varied according to the content of participants' profiles, aligning with the evolutionary psychological framework on mate selection (Buss, 1989; Kenrick, Sadalla, Groth, & Trost, 1990). Hitsch et al. (2009) reported that for men, income—indicative of status—was the strongest predictor of being approached by potential dates, with higher earners receiving more messages. For women, physical appearance—indicative of fertility—attracted the most messages. Short men and overweight women were the least likely to receive messages through the dating site. These findings align with the deceptive self-presentation practices of men and women previously reviewed (Toma, Hancock, & Ellison, 2008) and have been replicated in more recent findings (Cox, 2023; February 9). Individuals searching for a mate are aware of what traits are considered attractive and tend to alter their profiles to reflect these desirable characteristics.

Guadagno, Okdie, and Kruse (2012) explored how different modes of communication and the expectation of meeting influenced the level of deceptive self-presentation in online dating. Participants completed personality assessments under one of four conditions: anticipating a face-to-face meeting with a date, an email meeting with a date, no meeting with a data, or a control condition with no mention of online dating. The findings revealed that, compared to baseline measures, male participants enhanced their self-presentation when anticipating a future interaction with a prospective date. Notably, male participants highlighted their positive traits more when the potential date was less immediate (e.g., email meeting) than in more immediate scenarios (e.g., face-to-face meeting) or control conditions. This study illustrates an important difference between online dating and meeting romantic partners in offline contexts: people are more likely to misrepresent themselves (also see Toma & Hancock, 2012).

Other research on online dating has shown that the design of online dating applications impacts people's perceived control over the selection of potential romantic partners (Tong, Hancock, & Slatcher, 2016). Specially, this research demonstrated that, compared to dating sites that used algorithms to select matches, people felt like they had more control over dating applications that allowed them to search profiles themselves. This increased sense of control also resulted in greater satisfaction with online dating. While online dating and social media provide new ways for potential romantic partners to meet, research suggests that consent is important, especially as these relationships turn sexual. For instance, some men believe that sending a picture of their genitals (called a "dick pic") will be an effective way to attract a romantic partner. Unfortunately, research suggests that while this practice is quite common, it is not well-received as the majority women find this practice off-putting rather than titillating (Marcotte, Gesselman, Fisher, & Garcia, 2021). Finally, empirical evidence has shown that the act of scrolling through people's online dating profiles can cause cognitive load, limiting people's ability to think deeply when considering options, and leads to the selection of less-than-ideal romantic partners (Wu & Chiou, 2009).

Most of the research reviewed in this section relates to heterosexual, cisgender relationships, there is also the question of how romantic relationships form when the partners are GLBTQ. There is minimal but mounting evidence that online dating offers members of the GLBTQ community opportunities to find potential romantic partners more safely and privately (Benotsch et al., 2016; Lucero, 2017). Unfortunately, the psychological science on this community is limited at this time so little else is known about how this population differs from their cisgender peers. As a result, unless explicitly stated, the research reviewed in the rest of this chapter will be based on research examining heterosexual, cisgender individuals.

The relationship- and trust-building phase

Problems in established romantic relationships

While the abovementioned section focuses on the search for a romantic partner, this section covers the intersection between social media and problems in established relationships. This includes infidelity, partner surveillance, jealousy, and relationship contentment. This section will also discuss how gender and personality affect romantic relationships. Research has shown that social media use can have a significant effect on the ways in which people engage in maintenance of romantic relationships (Kwok & Wescott, 2020).

The ease of cheating

Because society disapproves of infidelity, it is difficult to get an accurate estimate of its prevalence, as not everyone who cheats on their romantic partner is willing to admit to it. Self-report data suggest that among married partners, 20%–25% admit to cheating. These numbers become higher as the relationship commitment is lower, ranging from 33% to 50% of partners admit to infidelity (Luo, Cartun, & Snider, 2010; Wiederman, 1997). Anecdotally, divorce lawyers have suggested that social media facilitates cheating, and this has become a leading cause of divorce (Sexton, 2018). Just as social media provides single people with more options for potential romantic partners, the affordances of social media—in this case, the ease of finding new connections—also provides more opportunities for cheating. Indeed, research has documented the relationship between Facebook use and negative relationship outcomes such as cheating and dissolution such that heavier Facebook users have more relationship conflict, cheating, and divorce (Clayton, Nagurney, & Smith, 2013). Other research has shown that this is driven by the presentation of other potential partners which reduces commitment to existing romantic relationships (de Lenne, Wittevronghel, Vandenbosch, & Eggermont, 2019).

What constitutes cheating? Is it cheating if the people involved have never met each other? Do people have similar evaluations of virtual cheating such as sexting as they do physical sexual encounters? I studied these questions in the early days of social media (Guadagno & Sagarin, 2010).

Overall, we found that people evaluate online cheating in a similar manner as conventional, offline cheating. One notable gender difference was that women, relative to men, had somewhat stricter evaluations of actions that constituted cheating and were more likely to consider sexting as infidelity. Furthermore, the results related to infidelity suggested that, overall, people tend to experience fewer negative emotions about online infidelity compared to traditional infidelity. However, there was a significant exception: participants reported feeling notably more disgusted at the thought of their partners developing close emotional connections online. This heightened disgust could be attributed to the secrecy, anonymity, and ease with which online relationships can be formed.

Partner surveillance

Another aspect of social media is the ease with which people can view the public interactions of others. And, as the story I tell above about my wonderful students' interest in stalking others, social media allows this affordance. Not only do people look at the actions of friends, family, and former lovers, they also surveil their current or prospective romantic partners. This section reviews the impact that partner surveillance behaviors have on romantic relationships. Overall, this literature suggests that the more people engage in surveillance of their romantic partners, the greater their experience of romantic jealousy. And, the section on jealousy below will detail, romantic jealousy can be detrimental to relationship satisfaction and longevity.

An early study on the question of partner surveillance reported that active Facebook users were exposed to more information about their romantic partners and some of this information was ambiguous (e.g., a brief message from an unknown friend of the opposite sex on social media; (Muise, Christofides, & Desmarais, 2009)). The authors noted that encountering this type of content had the potential to fuel jealousy, particularly when the intention behind the message was unclear. Subsequent research examined the relationship between partner surveillance and relational outcome by asking people to imagine their partner's Facebook connection with different people: either mutual connections or unknown men or women (Muise, Christofides, & Desmarais, 2014). Their results indicated that women but not men reported more relationship jealousy when the connection was with an unknown woman. Conversely, men reported more jealousy when the connection was a mutual male connection. These results highlight the relationship between jealousy and partner surveillance and the different contexts in which men versus women feel jealousy. In a follow-up longitudinal study, the authors further documented the relationship between jealousy and partner surveillance behaviors.

Consistent with these findings, other work has found that heavier Facebook users report more frequently of checking their partner's Facebook profiles (Marshall, Bejanyan, Di Castro, & Lee, 2013). Evidence also suggests that partner surveillance can become perceived as a reciprocal behavior. Specifically, there is evidence that people who spend more time surveilling their romantic partner's social media profile and interactions, the more they perceived that their partner engaged in the same behaviors (Fox, Osborn, & Warber, 2014).

More recent research also supports these findings. Imperato, Everri, and Mancini (2023) examined partner surveillance on social media among a sample of women. They reported that participants experienced more romantic jealousy when their romantic relationship was visible and this also produced more partner surveillance behaviors. Furthermore, their results indicated that partner surveillance reduced relationship satisfaction. This tendency to "Facebook stalk" one's romantic partner is not unique to culture and has been documented across different cultures (Mushquash, Charlton, MacIsaac, & Ryan, 2022).

Jealousy

Jealousy, colloquially known as "the green-eyed monster" (see Fig. 7.2), refers to the emotion people experience when they have lost or are fearful of losing their romantic relationship. Thus jealousy encompasses feelings of anger, betrayal, loss, and insecurity (Muscanell & Guadagno, 2016).

Figure 7.2 Jealousy and Social Media (Loewald, 2023b).

This emotion is distinct from envy, which occurs as an emotional response to coveting something someone else has such as career success, their romantic partner, or their material possessions (Sagarin and Guadagno, 2004). It is jealousy, not envy that has been widely studied in the context of social media and romantic relationships and that is the focus of this section.

Data on jealousy in response to a romantic partner's social media use show that it has been reported in approximately 16% of US married couples, so it is not a common experience generally (Tandon, Dhir, & Mäntymäki, 2021). However, as the sections later demonstrate, there are situational, cultural, and individual differences that affect the extent to which people experience jealousy over their partner's social media profiles and interactions.

Illustrative of this, Muscanell, Guadagno, Rice, and Murphy (2013) studied the conditions under which people experience jealousy in response to their partner's Facebook activities. Participants read a hypothetical scenario where they encountered their partner's active Facebook profile and saw that their romantic partner was tagged in a photo with an unfamiliar person of the opposite gender. Depending on the experimental condition, the number of photos posted on Facebook featuring the participant and their partner and the privacy settings of the couple's photos varied. Results revealed that privacy settings and the presence of couple photos had a significant impact on jealousy. Specifically, women tended to report more jealousy compared to men, with women reporting the most jealousy when their partner's profile was private and there were few couple photos. Men, on the other hand, reported the greatest jealousy when the profile was private but featured many couple photos. These results highlight the contextual factors that impact the experience of romantic jealousy when viewing a partner's social media page and suggest that emphasizing one's romantic relationship can reduce the amount of jealousy experienced by romantic partners. Other research has documented that the archival nature of social media can also facilitate jealousy as people's profiles often contain images and information regarding prior relationships (Fox, 2015).

Another study reported that greater Facebook use was associated with higher levels of jealousy in response to their partner's post and a greater likelihood of intimate partner violence (Daspe, Vaillancourt-Morel, Lussier, & Sabourin, 2018). In a follow-up study, the authors also found that the extent to which romantic partners experience jealousy is dyadic, such that a couple's jealousy in response to their partner's social media behaviors is related to each other.

The various social media platforms people use have also been shown to affect jealousy in romantic relationships. For instance, compared to Facebook, people report using Snapchat more often to communicate with their romantic partners and also report higher levels of jealousy in response to their partner's interactions with others over Snapchat versus Facebook (Utz, Muscanell, & Khalid, 2015). Specific social media behaviors have also been shown to predict relationship jealousy. A recent study examined behaviors on Snapchat and found that when romantic partners posted snaps or read and commented on stories participants experienced greater jealousy.

Overall, the research reviewed highlights the negative effects that social media use can have on romantic relationships. This is driven in part by the specific features of social media platforms such as the transparency of communications and the longevity of information posted on people's social media pages. Furthermore, partner surveillance and jealousy in response to a romantic partner's social media interactions are highly related to each other. This suggests that it may be healthy for couples in romantic relationships to have an open dialog about their social media use to set clear agreed-upon expectations for social media use to best avoid these negative consequences.

Relationship commitment

Just as people's romantic relationships vary in length and satisfaction, their commitment to the relationship varies too with casual dating on the less committed end of the spectrum and marriage on the more committed side. The more committed a couple is to each other, the longer the relationship lasts and the greater their willingness to work through hardships that arise over time. Research has investigated the relationship between people's social media use and their relationship commitment, and this section will review the literature on this subject.

Research suggests that greater social media use is associated with lower commitment to romantic relationships (Abbasi, 2019). Some studies have suggested that this is because people's social media use may become problematic and their excessive social media use may disrupt the daily activities a couple engages in, decreasing the quality of their time together and decreasing relationship satisfaction and commitment (e.g., (Elphinston &

Noller, 2011)). Couples who differ in the amount of time they spend using social media may also experience more relationship conflict resulting in lower relationship commitment (Fox, 2015). This has also been shown with Twitter/X use (Clayton, 2014).

Other research has shown that highlighting a committed relationship, such as using a couple's photo as one's profile picture increases both relationship commitment and satisfaction (Ito, Yang, & Li, 2021; Papp, Danielewicz, & Cayember, 2012). Similarly, people who are more committed to their romantic relationships are also more likely to share couple photos on Facebook (Saslow, Muise, Impett, & Dubin, 2013). Overall, this research highlights that the way people post and share relationship details on social media can increase relationship happiness and satisfaction.

The end of a relationship

All romantic relationships come to an end, either by breakup or by the death of one or both of the partners[1]. This section pertains to breakups. After a breakup, social media applications have built-in affordances that allow people to remove their public connection to their former partner. Depending on the reasons behind the breakup, a former romantic couple may stay connected on social media or may end up unfollowing or blocking each other. Regardless of this, when a person emphasizes their romantic relationship on their social media profile, as in the case of Megan Fox mentioned at the start of this chapter, the end of a relationship can be quite public. Given the curated nature of many people's social media profiles (as reviewed in Chapter 2), people likely feel as if they must publicly self-present and act as if the breakup was not painful to them (Fox, 2015). Privately, however, research suggests that the end of a romantic relationship can lead to an increase in social media surveillance particularly on the part of the jilted partner (Dunn & Langlais, 2020; Tong, 2013).

A two-year longitudinal analysis of 1,027,541 Reddit posts from 6,803 Reddit users showed that people's language use was indicative of an impending breakup (Seraj, Blackburn, & Pennebaker, 2021). Specifically, people started writing more informally and personally and less analytically shortly before a breakup up and the impending dissolution could be detected up to three months before the breakup. This was shown both with divorce and the dissolution of less committed relationships. This

[1] While I realize there are also polyamorous romantic relationships, the research on this type of romantic relationship and social media is too limited to review in this chapter.

trend peaked at the point people disclosed their breakup and it took 6 months for their language use to return to baseline. Furthermore, the longer people posted about their breakup, the less well-adjusted they were one year after the breakup. Thus, while people may feel the pressure to curate their social media posts to appear as if they were unaffected by the event, the language of their posts belies this.

Individual and cultural differences

In these final sections, I review research related to the ways in which people differ in their experiences with social media and romantic relationships. Specifically, this section will cover gender differences, personality differences, and cultural differences in responses to the intersection of social media and romantic relationships. Just as the research reviewed above has shown, the different actions and choices people make with respect to their romantic relationships and social media use can affect relationship outcomes, so do these differences.

Gender differences

When it comes to falling in and out of love, there are well-known gender differences. Specifically, men fall in love faster than do women (Galperin & Haselton, 2010), yet women are more likely to end a relationship—estimates suggest that the vast majority, as much as 70% of all divorces are initiated by women (Parker, Durante, Hill, & Haselton, 2022). Women generally report more romantic jealousy than do men (Sagarin & Guadagno, 2004) and this has also been reported in the context of social media. Specifically, research has shown that women experience more jealousy when thinking of their partner receiving a message from someone they perceive as a romantic rival (Daspe et al., 2018; Fleuriet, Cole, & Guerrero, 2014).

This jealousy can be attenuated by the choices made by people's partners. For instance, Papp et al. (2012) found that women reported greater happiness when their male partners publicly declared their relationship status. Conversely, men felt more satisfied when their female partners shared couple-centric profile photos. Other research suggests that women do not perceive themselves are more jealous than their men while men expect their female partners to respond with more jealousy than they typically do (McAndrew & Shah, 2013). This research highlights a disconnect between perception and actual behavior and again points to the importance of clear and open communication between romantic partners.

Cultural differences

Research generally shows that, across cultures, there is little difference in the characteristics people want their partners. While few cultural differences have been documented in the experience of jealousy in response to a partner's social media use (Moyano, Sánchez-Fuentes, Chiriboga, & Flórez-Donado, 2017), there are differences in the dynamics between people and their social media connections as it relates to their romantic relationships. Jin and Oh (2010) compared samples of Korean and American college students and found that, while there were no cultural differences in relationship satisfaction and support from social media connections, there were differences in the level of involvement these friends and family members had in the romantic relationship. Specifically, Americans involved their social media connections in their romantic relationships more than Koreans did. While the research romantic relationships and social media has been largely examined using Western, individualistic samples, the research that exists suggests that there are minimal cultural differences in relationship dynamics. However, this is an area in which more research is needed.

Individual differences

Research has shown that certain personality traits affect the relationship between social media use and romantic relationships. This section will focus on the two most widely studied: self-esteem and attachment styles.

Self-esteem refers to the extent to which people like themselves (for review, see Chapter 2). Research generally shows that people with lower self-esteem tend to experience more jealousy over their romantic partner's Facebook and report engaging in more partner surveillance behaviors relative to people high in self-esteem (Utz & Beukeboom, 2011). This relationship has been documented with adults as well as with teenagers (Langlais, Seidman, & Bruxvoort, 2020). This pattern of results has also been shown across social media applications, including Snapchat (Utz et al., 2015).

A person's attachment style assesses the extent to which people can form healthy, stable connections with others. Attachment style is typically formed during childhood based on people's early interactions with their primary caregiver such as their mother (Hazan & Shaver, 1990). There are several different attachment styles with secure attachment being the most predictive of positive psychological outcomes. People with a secure attachment style tend to form healthy romantic relationships and are trusting, emotionally available, and comfortable with intimacy. There are three different types of insecure attachment: anxious, avoidant, and disorganized. People with an insecure attachment style have difficulty forming healthy relationships with others. Those with anxious attachment experience fear of abandonment, excessively worry over their romantic relationships and may be clingy or in need of regular reassurance. Avoidant attachment describes people who have trouble getting close to others and have a preference for independence. People with disorganized attachment often display conflicting behavior such that they both want intimacy with another but also fear it. It has been well-established that attachment style can affect the outcome of a romantic relationship (Feeney & Noller, 1990; Simpson, 1990).

With respect to social media and romantic relationships, research has documented that a person's attachment style can affect relational jealousy and partner surveillance. Fox and Warber (2013) assessed attachment style and social media behaviors and found that people with insecure attachment styles tended to engage in more partner surveillance than did people with a secure attachment style. This pattern of results has also been shown with jealousy in response to a romantic partner's social media use (Marshall, Bejanyan, Di Castro, & Lee, 2013). These results suggest that people with insecure attachment styles may use social media to search for reassurance or validation of their romantic relationships yet may also have the unintended consequence of alienating their romantic partners.

Summary

While Megan Fox and MGK continue to publicly breakup and get back together, I do not know the current status of their romantic relationship. Nor should I—it is really none of anyone's business. However, I do wish them the best. Unfortunately, the affordances of social media have broadcasted this information along with the relationship statuses of many, many others. The design of social media, especially the way we share content and personal information, makes our romantic relationships public and arguably permanent. Even when people erase or deactivate their social media accounts, people have seen their content and social media companies have archives of the deleted information. As the saying goes, nothing is ever erased from the Internet. As a result, social media presents a mixed blessing for couples. On the one hand, people can more easily find romantic partners thanks to social media. And, if used thoughtfully, social media can help strengthen a couple's commitment. Yet, at the same time, social media can also exacerbate relationship issues such as jealousy and problematic behaviors such as partner surveillance, especially among people with certain personality traits such as low self-esteem and insecure attachment style. Furthermore, there is emerging research suggesting that social media is a growing factor in relationship dissolution. Overall, the results of this chapter suggest that couples prioritize their relationships over their social media use.

References

Abbasi, I. S. (2019). Social media and committed relationships: What factors make our romantic relationship vulnerable? *Social Science Computer Review*, *37*(3), 425–434. Available from https://doi.org/10.1177/0894439318770609.

Anzari, A. (2015). Everything you thought you knew about l-o-v-e is wrong. *Time*. Available from https://time.com/aziz-ansari-modern-romance/.

Botwin, M. D., Buss, D. M., & Shackelford, T. K. (1997). Personality and mate preferences: Five factors in mate selection and marital satisfaction. *Journal of Personality*, *65* (1), 107–136.

Buss, D. M. (1989). Sex differences in human mate preferences: Evolutionary hypotheses tested in 37 cultures. *Behavior and Brain Sciences*, *12*, 1–49.

Benotsch, E. G., Zimmerman, R. S., Cathers, L., Heck, T., Mcnulty, S., Pierce, J., ... Snipes, D. J. (2016). Use of the Internet to meet sexual partners, sexual risk behavior, and mental health in transgender adults. *Archives of Sexual Behavior*, *45*(3), 597–605. Available from https://doi.org/10.1007/s10508-014-0432-x.

Clayton, R. B. (2014). The third wheel: The impact of Twitter use on relationship infidelity and divorce. *Cyberpsychology, Behavior, and Social Networking*, *17*(7), 425–430.

Clayton, R. B., Nagurney, A., & Smith, J. R. (2013). Cheating, breakup, and divorce: Is Facebook use to blame? *Cyberpsychology, Behavior, and Social Networking*, *16*(10), 717–720.

Cox, D.A. (2023, February 9). From swiping to sexting: The enduring gender divide in American dating and relationships. Findings from the January 2023 American perspectives survey. Survey Center on American Life. Downloaded from: https://www.americansurveycenter.org/research/from-swiping-to-sexting-the-enduring-gender-divide-in-american-dating-and-relationships/.

Darwin, C. (1871). *The descent of man, and selection in relation to sex*. New York: D. Appleton.

Daspe, M.-È., Vaillancourt-Morel, M.-P., Lussier, Y., & Sabourin, S. (2018). Facebook use, Facebook jealousy, and intimate partner violence perpetration. *Cyberpsychology, Behavior, and Social Networking*, *21*(9), 549–555. Available from https://doi.org/10.1089/cyber.2018.0159.

Dunn, T. R., & Langlais, M. R. (2020). "Oh, Snap!": A mixed-methods approach to analyzing the dark side of Snapchat. *The Journal of Social Media in Society*, *9*(2), Article 2.

Elphinston, R. A., & Noller, P. (2011). Time to face it! Facebook intrusion and the implications for romantic jealousy and relationship satisfaction. *Cyberpsychology, Behavior, and Social Networking*, *14*(11), 631–635.

Feeney, J. A., & Noller, P. (1990). Attachment style as a predictor of adult romantic relationships. *Journal of Personality and Social Psychology*, *2*, 281–291.

Fleuriet, C., Cole, M., & Guerrero, L. K. (2014). Exploring Facebook: Attachment style and nonverbal message characteristics as predictors of anticipated emotional reactions to Facebook postings. *Journal of Nonverbal Behavior*, *38*(4), 429–450. Available from https://doi.org/10.1007/s10919-014-0189-x.

Fox, J. (2015). 7. *The dark side of social networking sites in romantic relationships. The Psychology of Social Networking Vol.1: Personal Experience in Online Communities* (pp. 78–89). Warsaw, Poland: De Gruyter Open Poland. Available from https://doi.org/10.1515/9783110473780-009.

Fox, J., Osborn, J. L., & Warber, K. M. (2014). Relational dialectics and social networking sites: The role of Facebook in romantic relationship escalation, maintenance, conflict, and dissolution. *Computers in Human Behavior*, *35*, 527–534. Available from https://doi.org/10.1016/j.chb.2014.02.031.

Fox, J., & Warber, K. M. (2013). Romantic relationship development in the age of Facebook: An exploratory study of emerging adults' perceptions, motives, and behaviors. *Cyberpsychology, Behavior, and Social Networking*, *16*(1), 3–7.

Galperin, A., & Haselton, M. (2010). Predictors of how often and when people fall in love. *Evolutionary Psychology*, *8*(1), 147470491000800102.

Gottman, J., & Gottman, J. (2017). The natural principles of love. *Journal of Family Theory & Review*, *9*(1), 7–26.

Guadagno, R. E., Okdie, B. M., & Kruse, S. A. (2012). Dating deception: Gender, online dating, and exaggerated self-presentation. *Computers in Human Behavior*, *28*(2), 642–647.

Guadagno, R. E., & Sagarin, B. J. (2010). Sex differences in jealousy: An evolutionary perspective on online infidelity. *Journal of Applied Social Psychology*, *40*(10), 2636–2655.

Hazan, C., & Shaver, P. R. (1990). Love and work: An attachment-theoretical perspective. *Journal of Personality and Social Psychology*, *59*(2), 270.

Hitsch, G. J., Hortaçsu, A., & Ariely, D. (2009). ,. *What makes you click: An empirical analysis of online dating*. University of Chicago, Unpublished manuscript.

Imperato, C., Everri, M., & Mancini, T. (2023). Does Facebook 'threaten' romantic relationships? Online surveillance and couple visibility behaviours in romantic jealousy and couple relationship quality in a sample of Italian women. *Journal of Family Studies*, *29*(2), 792–806. Available from https://doi.org/10.1080/13229400.2021.1987295.

Ito, K., Yang, S., & Li, L. M. W. (2021). Changing facebook profile pictures to dyadic photos: Positive association with romantic partners' relationship satisfaction via perceived partner commitment. *Computers in Human Behavior*, *120*106748. Available from https://doi.org/10.1016/j.chb.2021.106748.

Jin, B., & Oh, S. (2010). Cultural differences of social network influence on romantic relationships: A comparison of the United States and South Korea. *Communication Studies*, *61*(2), 156–171.

Kenrick, D. T., & Keefe, R. C. (1992). Age preferences in mates reflect sex differences in human reproductive strategies. *Behavioral and Brain Sciences*, *15*(1), 75–91.

Kenrick, D. T., Sadalla, E. K., Groth, G., & Trost, M. R. (1990). Evolution, traits, and the stages of human courtship: Qualifying the parental investment model. *Journal of Personality*, *58*, 97–116.

Krueger, K. L., & Forest, A. L. (2020). Communicating commitment: A relationship-protection account of dyadic displays on social media. *Personality and Social Psychology Bulletin*. Available from https://doi.org/10.1177/0146167219893998.

Kwok, I., & Wescott, A. B. (2020). Cyberintimacy: a scoping review of technology-mediated romance in the digital age. *Cyberpsychology, Behavior, and Social Networking, 23*(10), 657–666.

Lane, B. L., Piercy, C. W., & Carr, C. T. (2016). Making it Facebook official: The warranting value of online relationship status disclosures on relational characteristics. *Computers in Human Behavior, 56*, 1–8.

Langlais, M. R., Seidman, G., & Bruxvoort, K. M. (2020). Adolescent romantic relationship–oriented facebook behaviors: Implications for self-esteem. *Youth & Society, 52*(4), 661–683. Available from https://doi.org/10.1177/0044118X18760647.

de Lenne, O., Wittevronghel, L., Vandenbosch, L., & Eggermont, S. (2019). Romantic relationship commitment and the threat of alternatives on social media. *Personal Relationships, 26*(4), 680–693. Available from https://doi.org/10.1111/pere.12299.

Levinger, G. (1980). Toward the analysis of close relationships. *Journal of Experimental Social Psychology, 16*, 510–544. Available from https://doi.org/10.1016/0022-1031(80)90056-6.

Lucero, L. (2017). Safe spaces in online places: Social media and LGBTQ youth. *Multicultural Education Review, 9*(2), 117–128.

Luo, S., Cartun, M. A., & Snider, A. G. (2010). Assessing extradyadic behavior: A review, a new measure, and two new models. *Personality and Individual Differences, 49*(3), 155–163.

Lutkin, A. (2023, February 12). *Megan Fox Posts About "Dishonesty" and Deletes Pics of Machine Gun Kelly On Instagram*. Elle magazine. https://www.elle.com/culture/celebrities/a42843418/megan-fox-deletes-all-pics-machine-gun-kelly-on-instagram-break-up/.

Marcotte, A. S., Gesselman, A. N., Fisher, H. E., & Garcia, J. R. (2021). Women's and men's reactions to receiving unsolicited genital images from men. *The Journal of Sex Research, 58*(4), 512–521.

Marshall, T. C., Bejanyan, K., Di Castro, G., & Lee, R. A. (2013). Attachment styles as predictors of Facebook-related jealousy and surveillance in romantic relationships. *Personal Relationships, 20*(1), 1–22.

McAndrew, F. T., & Shah, S. S. (2013). Sex differences in jealousy over Facebook activity. *Computers in Human Behavior, 29*(6), 2603–2606.

Moyano, N., Sánchez-Fuentes, M. D. M., Chiriboga, A., & Flórez-Donado, J. (2017). Factors associated with Facebook jealousy in three Spanish-Speaking countries. *Sexual and Relationship Therapy, 32*(3–4), 309–322. Available from https://doi.org/10.1080/14681994.2017.1397946.

Muise, A., Christofides, E., & Desmarais, S. (2009). More information than you ever wanted: Does Facebook bring out the green-eyed monster of jealousy? *CyberPsychology & Behavior, 12*(4), 441–444.

Muise, A. M. Y., Christofides, E., & Desmarais, S. (2014). Creeping or just information seeking? Gender differences in partner monitoring in response to jealousy on Facebook. *Personal Relationships, 21*(1), 35–50.

Muscanell, N., & Guadagno, R. (2016). Social networking and romantic relationships: A review of jealousy and related emotions. *The psychology of social networking*, 143.

Muscanell, N. L., Guadagno, R. E., Rice, L., & Murphy, S. (2013). Don't it make my brown eyes green? An analysis of Facebook use and romantic jealousy. *Cyberpsychology, Behavior, and Social Networking, 16*(4), 1–6.

Mushquash, A. R., Charlton, J. K., MacIsaac, A., & Ryan, K. (2022). Romance behind the screens: Exploring the role of technoference on intimacy. *Cyberpsychology, Behavior, and Social Networking, 25*(12), 814–820. Available from https://doi.org/10.1089/cyber.2022.0068.

Papp, L. M., Danielewicz, J., & Cayember, C. (2012). "Are we Facebook official?" Implications of dating partners' Facebook use and profiles for intimate relationship satisfaction. *Cyberpsychology, Behavior, and Social Networking, 15*(2), 85–90.

Parker, G., Durante, K. M., Hill, S. E., & Haselton, M. G. (2022). Why women choose divorce: An evolutionary perspective. *Current opinion in psychology, 43*, 300–306.

Rice, N. (2023, February 12). *Megan Fox deletes her Instagram hours after hinting at machine gun kelly split.* People magazine. https://people.com/movies/megan-fox-deletes-her-instagram-after-hinting-at-machine-gun-kelly-split/.

Sagarin, B. J., & Guadagno, R. E. (2004). Sex differences in the contexts of extreme jealousy. *Personal Relationships, 11*(3), 319–328.

Saslow, L. R., Muise, A., Impett, E. A., & Dubin, M. (2013). Can you see how happy we are? Facebook images and relationship satisfaction. *Social Psychological and Personality Science, 4*, 411–418.

Seraj, S., Blackburn, K. G., & Pennebaker, J. W. (2021). Language left behind on social media exposes the emotional and cognitive costs of a romantic breakup. *Proceedings of the National Academy of Sciences, 118*(7)e2017154118.

Sexton, J. J. (2018). *If You're in My Office, It's Already Too Late: A Divorce Lawyer's Guide to Staying Together.* Henry Holt.

Small, T. (2023, May 22). *Megan Fox finally returns to social media in sexy see-through dress.* Giant Freakin Robot. https://www.giantfreakinrobot.com/cltr/megan-fox-dresses.html.

Simpson, J. A. (1990). Influence of attachment styles on romantic relationships. *Journal of Personality and Social Psychology, 59*(5), 971–980.

Sorokowski, P., et al. (2021). Universality of the triangular theory of love: Adaptation and psychometric properties of the triangular love scale in 25 countries. *The Journal of Sex Research, 58*(1), 106–115.

Tandon, A., Dhir, A., & Mäntymäki, M. (2021). Jealousy due to social media? A systematic literature review and framework of social media-induced jealousy. *Internet Research, 31*(5), 1541–1582. Available from https://doi.org/10.1108/INTR-02-2020-0103.

Toma, C. L., & Hancock, J. T. (2012). What lies beneath: The linguistic traces of deception in online dating profiles. *Journal of Communication, 62*(1), 78–97.

Toma, C. L., Hancock, J. T., & Ellison, N. B. (2008). Separating fact from fiction: An examination of deceptive self-presentation in online dating profiles. *Personality and Social Psychology Bulletin, 34*, 1023–1036.

Tong, S. T. (2013). Facebook use during relationship termination: Uncertainty reduction and surveillance. *CyberPsychology, Behavior, & Social Networking, 16*, 1–6.

Tong, S. T., Hancock, J. T., & Slatcher, R. B. (2016). The influence of technology on romantic relationships: Understanding online dating. *Social Computing and Social Media*, 162–173. Available from https://doi.org/10.1007/978-3-319-39910-2_16.

Utz, S., & Beukeboom, C. J. (2011). The role of social network sites in romantic relationships: Effects on jealousy and relationship happiness. *Journal of Computer-Mediated Communication, 16*(11), 511–527.

Utz, S., Muscanell, N., & Khalid, C. (2015). Snapchat elicits more jealousy than Facebook: A comparison of Snapchat and Facebook use. *Cyberpsychology, Behavior, and Social Networking, 18*(3), 141–146. Available from https://doi.org/10.1089/cyber.2014.0479.

Vogels, E.A., & McCain, C. (2023, February 2). *Key findings about online dating in the U.S.* https://www.pewresearch.org/short-reads/2023/02/02/key-findings-about-online-dating-in-the-u-s/.

Wade, L. (2015, July 3). *Ok Cupid data on sex, desirability, and age.* The Society Pages. Accessed online at: https://thesocietypages.org/socimages/2015/07/03/ok-cupid-data-on-sex-desirability-and-age/.

Wiederman, M. W. (1997). Extramarital sex: Prevalence and correlates in a national survey. *Journal of Sex Research, 34*(2), 167–174.

Wu, P. L., & Chiou, W. B. (2009). More options lead to more searching and worse choices in finding partners for romantic relationships online: An experimental study. *CyberPsychology & Behavior, 12*(3), 315–318.

CHAPTER 8

Social media and aggression

Freedom of Speech doesn't justify online bullying. Words have power, be careful how you use them. (Kent, n.d.)

My kids and I are huge fans of the singer Taylor Swift. We love her music and admire her voter registration advocacy work in which 35,000 new voters registered in 2020. In 2024, this advocacy continued when, in the space of two days, over 400,000 people visited a US voter registration website mentioned in an Instagram post in which Ms. Swift endorsed the democratic US presidential candidate, Kamala Harris on September 10, 2024 (Cullen, 2024; September 12; Mier, 2023; September 20), and her overall position as a role model for girls and young women. As with most powerful women, not everyone is a fan. This became obvious when Ms. Swift started dating an American football player named Travis Kelce. While people's dating preferences are not typically a political issue, in this case, it was. Among the politically conservative media, rumors were spread about this new romantic relationship, suggesting that Ms. Swift was dating Mr. Kelce in an influence operation intended to recruit voters to the Democratic Party (Darcy & Kazybsky, 2024; January 30).

This all reached a critical point during the weekend of January 24, 2024. Over that weekend, despicable, pornographic artificial intelligence (AI)-generated images of Ms. Swift being sexually assaulted by beloved Sesame Street characters such as Oscar the Grouch started spreading on Twitter/X due to the efforts of Internet trolls. These images spread so far and wide that "Taylor Swift AI" was a trending search term for 17 hours (Devlin, 2024; January 24). One post was viewed more than 45 million times (Weatherbed, 2024; January 25). Eventually, the images were removed but the incident crossed a serious moral and ethical line in online harassment and the transmission of AI-generated images/videos called "Deep Fakes" (A technique in which AI and machine learning techniques use a person's photograph and place it into a different image/video, thereby changing the context and meaning of the content; Chesney & Citron, 2019). This incident also reflects a broader trend where celebrities,

Psychological Processes in Social Media
DOI: https://doi.org/10.1016/B978-0-12-811320-2.00009-5

particularly women, face invasive criticism and even harassment whenever their personal lives make headlines.

This example illustrates how modern technology, including AI and social media, can amplify such harassment through virality. The ability of an aggressor to hide behind their screens sets the stage for online spaces to lack accountability. The use of inappropriate images, especially ones involving beloved children's characters like Oscar the Grouch, could point to how absurd and extreme these cyberbullying tactics can become. This creates a toxic environment for public figures and everyday users alike, showing how misogyny and digital abuse often intersect.

The psychological impact of such public scrutiny of an individual resulting from online harassment can impact a target's mental health, safety, and privacy. It also opens the door to broader conversations about how female celebrities, in particular, are often held to unreasonable standards and subjected to ridicule or bullying simply for their personal choices. It is common knowledge that in mediated contexts such as social media, people will aggress against others in ways that they simply never would in a face-to-face context. The literature indicates that this is the case when people are anonymous as well as when they are identifiable.

Vogels (2021, January 13) defines online harassment as the following behaviors: intentional humiliation, insults and slurs, cyberstalking, threats of physical (IRL; in real life) violence, and repeated harassment. Cyberbullying tends to be the term used to describe these behaviors among adolescents and children, online harassment tends to be the term used for adults experiencing the same treatment. For the purpose of this chapter, cyberbullying and online harassment will be defined as the repeated use of social media to intentionally mock, insult, embarrass, intimidate, or frighten another person or group (Wingate, Minney, & Guadagno, 2013). People who harass individuals they do not know or do so because of their job are typically referred to as Internet trolls (See Fig. 8.1), while cyberbullies typically know their targets. As in the above example with Taylor Swift, trolls typically target adults, while cyberbullying tends to happen more with children and adolescents. Trolls tend to attempt to provoke outrage and chaos in addition to causing harm to their target(s), while cyberbullies are more focused on causing psychological harm to their targets. Throughout this chapter, I combine these types of online harassers because they are both forms of aggression on social media, their tactics and the psychological impact on the victims are similar.

This chapter will examine how and why people are more overtly aggressive in digitally mediated contexts such as social media. This will

Figure 8.1 An internet troll at their keyboard.

include a discussion on Internet trolling, online harassment, cyberbullying, and group-level aggression (e.g., the mob mentality as it operates online), as is often exhibited in response to a viral news story reporting an atrocious act. Specifically, this chapter covers the following topics: the prevalence of online harassment and cyberbullying, the psychology of aggression, why people are so mean on social media, the characteristics of trolls and bullies, understanding the psychological impact of being bullied and harassed online, gender and cultural differences, why people do not intervene, and recommendations preventing online harassment and cyberbullying.

Prevalence of online harassment and cyberbullying

The existing data on the prevalence of online harassment and cyberbullying establishes that it is, unfortunately, a common occurrence. For instance, in a survey of American adolescents, Schaeffer (2023, November 17) reported that 46% of their sample indicated that they had been cyberbullied. The frequency of cyberbullying was highest for older teen girls aged 15–17 and, more generally, girls reported higher rates of cyberbullying than did boys. The data also revealed that cyberbullying rates among US GLBTQ survey respondents were double that of their cisgender heterosexual peers. The data for American adults are similar with 41% reporting being harassed online (Vogels, 2021, January 13). Women are three times more likely than men to report getting targeted by sexual harassment. Among US adults identifying as GLBTQ, 70% have reported being harassed online.

Globally, the estimates for online harassment and cyberbullying are somewhat lower, with 17% of global school-aged children reporting being cyberbullied (World Health Organization, 2024, March 27). Other data indicate that the global rate of online harassment varies between 16% and 58% (Hicks, 2021). Overall, these data show that online harassment and cyberbullying are pervasive, affecting a wide cross-section of Internet users globally. However, there are clearly cultural differences in the reporting and/or prevalence of online harassment with the United States at the forefront.

Psychological underpinnings of aggression

Aggression is part of the normal human experience. Everyone experiences aggressive thoughts focused on causing harm to another. It is even normal for people to act on their aggressive thoughts. Both cyberbullying and online harassment are forms of aggression. Research in psychology indicates that aggression can be understood and described in two main ways: the type of behavior (direct/physical vs. relational/social) or the intention behind the behavior (proactive/intentional vs reactive/spontaneous). Cyberbullying and online harassment can manifest as any combination of these categories.

Direct versus relational aggression

Bullying is just one type of aggressive behavior. In the physical world, children who bully typically select targets that are younger and/or smaller, providing the bully with a physical power advantage. Because of this, verbal bullying alone is often effective because there is the threat of bodily harm implicit in the interaction. Thus, in the traditional schoolyard stereotype of bullying, a smaller child will hand over their lunch money to a larger bully because they understand that physical violence will occur if they do not comply. A behavior such as this is considered direct or overt aggression in which threats of bodily harm are used to exert control over someone else (Olweus, 1991; Pellegrini & Bartini, 2001; Smith & Boulton, 1990). This type of aggression is more commonly observed in boys and men (Goldbaum, Craig, Pepler, & Connolly, 2003; Wang, Iannotti, & Nansel, 2009; Bjorkqvist, 1994; Owens, Shute, & Slee, 2007).

On the other hand, relational aggression is characterized as a more subtle, indirect approach, often involving gossip, rumors, or nonphysical personal attacks (Bosworth, Espelage, & Simon, 1999; Underwood, Galen, & Paquette, 2001). It is relational aggression that is most frequently reported on social media, such as harassing messages, hurtful social media comments, and the sharing of compromising photos or private content (Law, Shapka, Domene, & Gagné, 2012; Smith, Mahdavi, Carvalho, & Tippett, 2006). When these types of behaviors are directed consistently as a specific person, such as the example of the trolls that targeted Taylor Swift described earlier, these behaviors would be characterized as cyberbullying and online harassment. This type of aggressive behavior is indicative of a power differential between the target and the perpetrators based on social standing instead of physical prowess. Research suggests that women and girls tend to engage in more relational aggression (Coyne, Archer, & Eslea, 2006; Wang et al., 2009) and are also more likely to be the targets and receive aggressive direct messages and social media calls.

Reactive versus proactive aggression

To understand the motivation behind cyberbullying and online harassment, it is necessary to understand the difference between reactive and proactive aggression. Reactive aggression occurs when an individual or individuals retaliate against a threat (genuine or imagined) to them, their identities, or their groups. For instance, being called names or getting swatted—when the police are contacted by a bully alleging a series but fictitious crime is taking place at an unwitting target's home—for posting a controversial political opinion would be considered reactive aggression. Sharing private conversations or publishing embarrassing photos without consent are also examples of reactive aggression (Law et al., 2012).

Conversely, proactive aggression occurs before the appearance of a threat. Instead, proactive aggression is a deliberate action intended to obtain a specific goal or resource (Crick & Dodge, 1996; Dodge & Coie, 1987). Examples of proactive aggression include mocking someone for a bully's amusement, creating a website to smear someone's reputation, creating a false identity online to "catfish" someone, or stealing personal data for financial gain (Law et al., 2012). Cyberbullying and online harassment happen because of both proactive and reactive aggression. Understanding the difference depends on understanding the motivation for aggression in the first place.

Research on cyberbullying suggest that most instances of cyberbullying and online harassment occur due to proactive aggression (Calvete, Orue, Estévez, Villardón, & Padilla, 2010). Specifically, Calvete et al. suggested the typical pattern of cyberbullying in adolescents is best described as proactive, indirect aggression. This is consistent with presocial media data on bullying in offline contexts. With indirect or relational aggression, bullies may focus on disrupting their victims' relationships to make them feel alienated from their social groups (Crick, 1995; Galen & Underwood, 1997). From this viewpoint, cyberbullying reflects key features of traditional indirect bullying (Dehue, Bolman, & Vollink, 2008), framing it as a type of relational aggression (Piazza & Bering, 2009).

Why are people so dang mean online?

In addition to the psychology of aggression briefly reviewed earlier, it is necessary to understand how communicating over text on social media changes interpersonal dynamics. When people interact through social media, communicating primarily through text, it is oftentimes more difficult to understand the intention behind another person's words. People may misperceive a joke as an insult or misread anger in a sentence when the sender had no intention to express a negative emotion. Because of the absence of social and nonverbal cues in text-based digital communication, understanding the intent of another person's words can be a challenge (Kumar & Epley, 2021). Research suggests that people sometimes misperceive neutral content as hostile and respond with hostility (e.g., Crick & Dodge, 1996; Hartman & Stage, 2000; Orobio de Castro, Veerman, Koops, Bosch, & Monshouwer, 2002), thereby unwittingly starting a cycle of cyberbullying or online harassment. The recipient of such hostility may also respond in a hostile manner that perpetuates the cycle of online aggression.

Although people's social media profiles may have their photographs and identifying information, people are still more likely to say things to another person on social media that they would never say in person (Peter, Valkenburg, & Schouten, 2005; Ward & Tracy, 2004). Research suggests that digital spaces such as social media can amplify a sense of visual anonymity (McKenna & Bargh, 2000) in which people will act in ways that is inconsistent with societal expectations for politeness because they cannot see the person or people they are communicating with. The current affordances of most forms of social media can fuel a sense of depersonalization and focus people on perceived group norms rather than their values (Postmes, Spears, & Lea, 2002) (see Fig. 8.2). The overall ease of miscommunication through text and the depersonalization experienced by people communicating via text on computers and devices facilitate group norms that can easily become toxic (Matias, 2019). Furthermore, evidence suggests that people dehumanize others when talking over text relative to voice (Schroeder & Epley, 2016). Combined these factors with the emphasis on virality and outrage that drives social media engagement (see Chapter 6), it is unsurprising that cyberbullying and online harassment are so problematic.

The combined impact of visual anonymity, the increased focus on group norms instead of individual values, and outrage that engage people's time and attention on social media, produces an environment in which the digital crowd can easily turn into an angry mob, all focused on harassing the same person. This is what happened in the case of Taylor Swift as described at the opening of the chapters. And, it has happened many times, to more vulnerable people and children who were victimized by cyberbullies and internet trolls. And, when a mob targets one person, it removes much of the individual responsibility for their actions (Canning, 1990; Wingate et al., 2013).

Figure 8.2 Depersonalization and communication via social media.

In the context of cyberbullying and online harassment, the lack of nonverbal signals from other people tends to intensify the bullying (Amichai-Hamburger & McKenna, 2006; Morton, Zettelmeyer, & Silva-Risso, 2003). The focus is heavily placed on the message since there are no visual distractions like the communicator's appearance, thereby enhancing the message's significance (Guadagno & Cialdini, 2002). Consequently, the bully is blind to the victim's immediate reactions, missing out on the emotional cues that might otherwise deter them. Studies have indicated the crucial role of such visual cues in shaping the understanding and processing of online content (Epley & Kruger, 2005). Furthermore, the cyberbully or online troll may also be unaware of the long-term negative psychological repercussions of their actions on the target of their aggression (Ronson, 2015).

One major distinction between traditional harassment and bullying versus cyberbullying and online harassment lies in the power dynamics. In cyberbullying, text-based communication via social media often diminishes the traditional power imbalances. Patchin and Hinduja (2006) shifted focus from power disparity to intent and repetition in their definition of cyberbullying, highlighting the "willful and repeated harm" inflicted through digital platforms. Notably, while 95% of cyberbullies see their actions as teasing, only 5% admit malicious intent (Law et al., 2012), contrasting with traditional bullies who often recognize their harmful intent (Erdur-Baker, 2010).

Despite the rise in cyberbullying and online harassment, accountability remains low among perpetrators. For instance, 95% of cyberbullies view their actions as harmless pranks, and only a small fraction (5%) report the intention to cause harm (Law et al., 2012). This suggests that amusement, rather than revenge, may be the primary motivator, reflecting more proactive than reactive aggression. The question remains: who are these cyberbullies, and how do they compare to traditional bullies? Chapter 3 (personality) reviews the personality traits linked to online trolls, and this research indicated that online trolls tend to be high in psychopathy (callousness and impulsivity) and machiavellianism (enjoy manipulating others). Finally, a meta-analysis examined the predictors of perpetrating in cyberbullying. Across 81 studies with 99,741 participants, the results revealed that moral disengagement, depression, perceived social norms, and propensity to bully offline were the primary predictors of cyberbullying and online harassment (Chen, Ho, & Lwin, 2017).

The psychological impact of cyberbullying and online harassment

Amanda Todd was a 15-year old girl from Canada. Before taking her life in 2012, she posted a 9-minute-long video on YouTube describing in detail her experiences of being cyberbullied and harassed by an Internet stranger for 2 years. The man used intimate photos he had taken of her at the tender age of 13 as blackmail for continued interactions. Despite enlisting the aid of her mother and changing schools, the cyberbulling and harassment persisted and became overwhelming to her as her bully followed her across multiple social media platforms. She shared her story and then took her life shortly afterward. Her harasser ended up sentenced to prison for his harassment of her and many other women and men (Kirby, 2023, December 21). This illustrates one of the worst aspects of cyberbullying and online harassment: because the Internet is omnipresent, online harassment may seem inescapable to the victims. Add to that the permanency of social media and the Internet, the effects of aggression online may persist over time and location.

Before the advent of the internet, bullying and harassment were generally restricted to offline contexts such as school and work. Because of this, victims could leave the context of bullying and get a break from the behavior. However, in the era of social media, aggressive messages are delivered to the victim at any time and place. This makes aggression on social media different from traditional, offline bullying. Research suggests that bullying offline has three distinct characteristics: (1) harm is intended by the behavior, (2) the behavior happens regularly, and (3) the bully has more power—physical, social, or financial—than their target (Solberg & Olweus, 2003). With social media, the aggression is not physical in nature as the perpetrator cannot usually physically reach their victims. Instead, the aggression is relational and can be proactive or reactive. It is the persistency and permanence of aggression online that make it so harmful to victims.

A lesser-explored aspect of cyberbullying and online harassment is the reduced sense of control victims experience. Unlike in-person bullying, where victims can mentally reconstruct events to help them cope, the narrative in cyberbullying and online harassment is largely controlled by the perpetrator, often leaving victims feeling helpless. This lack of control may explain the increased rates of depression among victims of cyberbullying (Schenk & Fremouw, 2012). More research is needed on how victims' memories of in-person versus online bullying influence their emotional health.

Bullying and harassment can have long-lasting effects on a person's mental and emotional well-being. Victims often struggle academically and socially, with heightened risks of anxiety and depression (Arseneault et al., 2006; Bacchini, Esposito, & Affuso, 2009). Conversely, habitual bullies may face social isolation and other negative outcomes as they grow older (Lochman & Wells, 2002). Other research highlights the impact of online aggression on the targets and also indicates an increase in suicidal thoughts in addition to increased depression (Ademiluyi, Li, & Park, 2022). Finally, the meta-analysis described previously also found that risky Internet technology use and being bullied in offline contexts predicted likelihood of being a victim of cyberbullying (Chen et al., 2017).

Gender differences

Historical data indicate that men tend to be more likely to engage in bullying and harassment relative to women (Forero, McLellan, Rissel, & Baum, 1999; Nansel et al., 2001; Sourander, Helstela, Helenius, & Piha, 2000). However, on social media, the literature suggests that women use this technology more than do men for purposes of communicating with others (see Chapter 1; Blair, 2003; Kimbrough, Guadagno, Muscanell, & Dill, 2012). And, as the statistics on gender and online harassment reviewed earlier in this chapter indicate, it may be that women and girls encounter more online aggression in part because of their greater use of these technologies for communication and because there is a perception that the Internet is a digital sphere for men (e.g., the manosphere, a loosely associated network of social media communities that focus on men's issues and aspects of masculinity, suggesting that there is an ongoing crisis of masculinity. These communities range from benign to toxic and misogynistic.; Ribeiro et al., 2021). Other research suggests that online harassment and cyberbullying are primarily perpetrated and experienced by girls and women. Some studies indicate girls are more often victims and perpetrators of cyberbullying (Smith et al., 2008).

More recent reviews of the literature indicate that women and gender minorities are targeted with online harassment and cyberbullying more than men (Backe, Lilleston, & McCleary-Sills, 2018). Furthermore, this work indicates that, relative to cisgender heterosexual men, people from these groups are more likely to be victimized by a wider variety of harassment on social media, including revenge porn (the release of private photos by a jilted former partner) and cyberstalking. Survey data indicate that men report engaging in greater amounts of online harassment relative to women (Donner, 2016). Other research indicates that girls may be more inclined toward cyberbullying (Hinduja & Patchin, 2008), as it aligns with the subtler forms of aggression typically associated with female behavior (Baldry, 1998; Crick & Dodge, 1996; CLapierre & Dane, 2023; Crick, Casas, & Mosher, 1997). Cyberbullying, often a form of indirect aggression, reinforces this trend. Interestingly, cyberbullies often recruit others to target the same victim, allowing them to achieve dominance and social recognition (Shariff, 2009). Despite their harmful behavior, children exhibiting proactive aggression are often seen as charismatic leaders with advanced social skills (Dodge & Coie, 1987).

Overall, the gender differences reported in the literature on social media and aggression suggest that there are gender differences in the reasons why people display aggressive behavior toward others on social media. This literature is somewhat inconsistent, but it does suggest that men and women vary in the ways and reasons why they target others for online harassment. More research is needed to better understand the situations in which people's sex and gender affect the likelihood that they are targeted by an online harasser.

Culture

As the section on the prevalence of cyberbullying and online harassment above demonstrated, experiencing aggression through social media appears to be more common in the United States than in other parts of the world. This does not include people who troll or harass as part of their job (e.g., IRA employees, Chapter 5)—that is a very different type of aggression and one that is instrumental. Professional trolls are aggressive online because they are being paid to do so.

Research on cyberbullying and online harassment outside of the US has revealed similar motivations for engaging in the behavior as US samples. For instance, Renati, Berrone, and Zanetti (2012) study on Italian teens identified four key roles in bullying: bullies, victims, bully victims, and uninvolved individuals. They found that both bullies and victims exhibited high levels of moral disengagement and both proactive and reactive aggression. Cyberbullies, in particular, showed a notable lack of emotional empathy, setting them apart from traditional bullies. Similarly, Menesini et al. adapted traditional bullying criteria, adding public versus private actions and anonymity. They found that, across 6 european countries, power imbalance was the most critical factor in cyberbullying, with repetition being less relevant due to the persistent nature of digital harassment (Menesini & Nocentini, 2009).

Research in China on cyberbullying and online harassment between co-workers illustrated that victims of this type of aggression experienced more job strain (Zhang, Xiao, Zhang, & Zheng, 2022). Another study compared samples from the United States and China and assessed their responses to hypothetical workplace harassment scenarios and filled out the social dominance orientation scale (SDO; Wang, 2022). The results revealed that the United States and Chinese samples were quite similar in their responses. Across both samples people who scored higher in social dominance orientation were more likely to respond to the scenarios with cyberbullying behavior (Pratto, Sidanius, Stallworth, & Malle, 1994), a personality characteristic that assesses people's preferences for specific hierarchies in groups and the belief that some groups are higher in status than others. People high in SDO endorse these beliefs more than those low in SDO. Finally, the Chen et al. (2017) meta-analysis described earlier in the chapter found that parental involvement affected cyberbullying rates differentially across cultures in North America, Europe, and Asia. Results indicated that samples in North America reported lower levels of self-reported cyberbullying and online harassment when participants' parents interacted more with the children sampled.

Overall. the literature on culture suggests that there are more similarities than differences in aggression on social media. And, as with gender, more research is needed to better understand how culture and the type of social media used in that culture are related to the propensity to engage in cyberbullying and online aggression.

Why bystanders often do not intervene

Despite the significant long-term effects of cyberbullying and online harassment, it remains puzzling why witnesses often stay passive in the face of it. One explanation is "pluralistic ignorance," where individuals privately disagree with a situation but remain silent, assuming others feel differently (Katz, Allport, & Jenness, 1931). Research shows that people do not speak up because they perceive that their disagreement would violate the social norms of the situation. Another explanation is the "bystander effect," where onlookers do not intervene, thinking someone else will act (Latane & Darley, 1968). This dynamic worsens with more witnesses, as the individual perceived obligation to help gets diluted and more potential helpers appear (Li, 2007). Online, particularly on social media, inaction by many online connections creates a perception that ignoring online harassment and cyberbullying is normal. Additionally, verbal cyberbullying is often downplayed as harmless "jokes" (Rivers & Smith, 1994; Terasahjo & Salmivalli, 2003).

Several personality traits influence whether bystanders intervene. Those who are more emotionally stable (Tani, Greenman, Schneider, & Fregoso, 2003) possess stronger cognitive skills (Pozzoli & Gini, 2012) and hold stronger antibullying values (Salmivalli & Voeten, 2004) are more likely to step up and intervene. These defenders also show high empathy (Caravita, Pöyhönen, Rajala, & Salmivalli, 2011; Gini, 2008) and have confidence in their ability to intervene (Salmivalli, Voeten, & Poskiparta, 2011). Interestingly, younger children, especially girls, are often more likely to defend victims (Caravita et al., 2011; Salmivalli & Voeten, 2004).

Prevention of cyberbullying and online harassment

While there is a growing literature on interventions to reduce the prevalence of cyberbullying and online harassment, there are also significant barriers. First, not all countries have laws outlawing cyberbullying and online harassment. Second, while social media platforms have rules prohibiting aggressive behavior, the specific guidelines vary by platform. Not all harassment is reported, and reports of harassment are also not taken seriously. Given that the literature illustrates that the long-term consequences of being targeted by cyberbullying and online harassment are extremely detrimental to a victim's mental health, there is much room for improvement in how individuals, corporations, and nations respond to bullies and trolls.

First, among children, research indicates that parental involvement with their children's social media use is important for the prevention of cyberbullying and online harassment. Similarly, social support is extremely important to victims in aiding their recovery from negative experiences on social media due to aggression (Ademiluyi et al., 2022).

Antibullying programs have become more commonplace, only some targeting cyberbullying (Bhat, 2008). Surprisingly, many educators do not perceive cyberbullying and online harassment as a critical issue, and some even see the experience as a useful life lesson (Stauffer, Heath, Coyne, & Ferrin, 2012). This mindset potentially undermines the efficacy of antibullying initiatives and impedes incident reporting. To improve, strategies like specialized training for educators or designating "safe rooms" could be employed, similar to safe spaces designated for LGBT support. Peer-led intervention and education have also been shown to help reduce cyberbullying (Palladino, Nocentini, & Menesini, 2016).

To reduce the incidence of cyberbullying, certain steps are critical. For instance, Campbell (2005) recommends awareness campaigns, consistent school policies, supervision, and specialized programs. Initial challenges might include the school's denial of bullying's existence (Besag, 1989). Adopting school-wide policies can standardize responses to bullying (Smith & Sharp, 1994). Adult supervision can limit face-to-face bullying, and integrating "netiquette" and empathy into the curriculum could be beneficial. Researchers emphasize education's role and also highlight the legal dimensions of cyberbullying (Butler, Kift, & Campbell, 2009). Key aspects involve teaching children what constitutes bullying and identifying bullying's emotional toll (Mishna, 2004).

All of the above suggestions are focused on teaching children and adolescents not to engage in cyberbullying and online harassment. Other research suggests that deterrents to online aggression can also be built into the design of online spaces. For instance, Matias (2019) explored the impact of visible community rules as a source of on online behavior and participation. In a large-scale experiment involving a science discussion group on Reddit with 13 million subscribers, the research found that prominently displaying community norms reduced harassment and increased participation, especially from newcomers. The study showed that posting clear rules increased rule compliance by over 8 percentage points and boosted newcomer engagement by 70%. The results suggest that clear social norms not only discourage negative behavior but also create a more welcoming environment for new participants. Thus providing clear normative guidelines for user behavior on social media platforms may also help reduce the prevalence of online aggression.

Summary

While the online harassment of Taylor Swift is ongoing, the distribution of fabricated pornography has stopped. Unfortunately, Ms. Swift is still receiving hateful comments—see Fig. 8.3 in which the 2024 Republican nominee for president responds to her endorsement of his opponent, and Fig. 8.4 in which the CEO of Twitter/X, Elon Musk, senselessly offers to impregnate Ms. Swift as his response to her political endorsement of Harris.

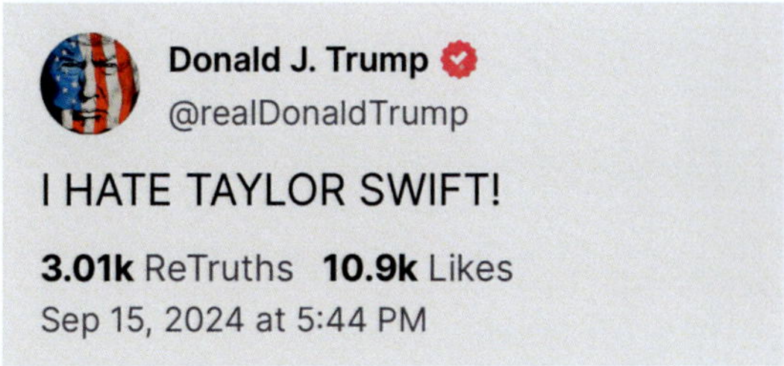

Figure 8.3 Donald Trump cyberbullying Taylor Swift.

Figure 8.4 Elon Musk, the CEO of Twitter and Tesla, Offering to impregnate Taylor Swift.

Public figures should not have to endure this type of harassment nor should less well-known people like Amanda Todd. Regardless of the target, the research reviewed in this chapter highlights the psychological damage that can be caused by this behavior. Both online harassment and cyberbullying, however, can lead to significant emotional distress and contribute to toxic online environments. A regular and open dialog on the subject can deter bullies and empower victims.

References

Ademiluyi, A., Li, C., & Park, A. (2022). Implications and preventions of cyberbullying and social exclusion in social media: Systematic review. *JMIR Formative Research*, *6*(1), e30286. Available from https://doi.org/10.2196/30286.

Amichai-Hamburger, Y., & McKenna, K. Y. A. (2006). The contact hypothesis reconsidered: Interacting via the Internet. *Journal of Computer-Mediated Communication*, *11*(3), 825–843. Available from https://doi.org/10.1111/j.1083-6101.2006.00037.x.

Arseneault, L., Walsh, E., TrzesniewskiZf, K., Newcombe, R., Caspi, A., & Moffitt, T. E. (2006). Bullying victimization uniquely contributes to adjustment problems in young children: A nationally representative cohort study. *Pediatrics*, *118*, 130–138.

Bacchini, D., Esposito, G., & Affuso, G. (2009). *Social Experience and School Bullying*, *32*, 17–32. Available from https://doi.org/10.1002/casp.

Backe, E. L., Lilleston, P., & McCleary-Sills, J. (2018). Networked individuals, gendered violence: A literature review of cyberviolence. *Violence and Gender*, *5*(3), 135–146. Available from https://doi.org/10.1089/vio.2017.0056.

Baldry, A. C. (1998). Bullying among Italian MIDDLE school students: Combining methods to understand aggressive behaviours and victimisation. *School Psychology International*, *19*, 155–168.

Besag, V. (1989). *Bullies and victims in schools*. Milton Keynes, UK: Open University Press.

Bhat, C. S. (2008). Cyber bullying: Overview and strategies for school counsellors, guidance officers, and all school personnel. *Australian Journal of Guidance and Counselling*, *18*, 53–66. Available from https://doi.org/10.1375/ajgc.18.1.53, Document Type: journal.Citation.

Bjorkqvist, K. (1994). Sex differences in physical, verbal, and indirect aggression: A review of recent research. *Sex Roles*, *30*, 177–188.

Blair, J. (2003). New breed of bullies torment their peers on the Internet. *Education Week*, *22*, 6–7.

Bosworth, K., Espelage, D. L., & Simon, T. R. (1999). Factors associated with bullying behavior in middle school students. *The Journal of Early Adolescence*, *19*(3), 341–362. Available from https://doi.org/10.1177/0272431699019003003.

Butler, D., Kift, S., & Campbell, M. (2009). Cyber bullying in schools and the law: Is there an effective means of addressing the power imbalance. *eLaw Journal: Murdoch University Electronic Journal of Law*, *16*, 84.

Calvete, E., Orue, I., Estévez, A., Villardón, L. Y., & Padilla, P. (2010). Cyberbullying in adolescents: Modalities and aggressors' profile. *Computers in Human Behavior*, *26*, 1128–1135.

Campbell, M. A. (2005). Cyber bullying: An old problem in a new guise? *Australian Journal of Guidance and Counselling*, *15*, 68–76.

Canning, D. (1990). "Average Behaviour in Learning Models" papers. *Cambridge - Risk, Information & Quantity Signals*.

Caravita, S. C. S., Pöyhönen, V., Rajala, I., & Salmivalli, C. (2011). The architecture of high status among Finnish youth. *British Journal of Developmental Psychology*, *29*(3), 668–679. Available from https://doi.org/10.1111/j.2044-835X.2011.02034.x.

Chen, L., Ho, S. S., & Lwin, M. O. (2017). A meta-analysis of factors predicting cyberbullying perpetration and victimization: From the social cognitive and media effects approach. *New Media & Society*, *19*(8), 1194–1213. Available from https://doi.org/10.1177/1461444816634037.

Chesney, R., & Citron, D. (2019). Deepfakes and the new disinformation war: The coming age of post-truth geopolitics. *Foreign Affairs*, *98*(1), 147–155.

Coyne, S. M., Archer, J., & Eslea, M. (2006). We're NOT FRIENDS ANYMORE! UNLESS': The frequency and harmfulness of indirect, relational, and social aggression. *Aggressive Behavior*, *32*, 294–307.

Crick, N. R. (1995). Relational aggression: The role of intent attributions, feelings of distress, and provocation type. *Development and Psychopathology*, *7*, 313–322.

Crick, N. R., Casas, J. F., & Mosher, M. (1997). Relational and overt aggression in preschool. *Developmental Psychology*, *33*, 579–588.

Crick, N. R., & Dodge, K. A. (1996). Social information-processing mechanisms in reactive and proactive aggression. *Child Development*, *67*(3), 993–1002. Available from https://doi.org/10.1111/j.1467-8624.1996.tb01778.x.

Cullen, M. (2024, September 12). *Taylor Swift inspires record-breaking voter registrations after endorsement ahead of 2024 election*. USA Today.

Darcy, O., & Kazybsky, A. (2024, January 30). Taylor Swift and the Super Bowl fuel right-wing conspiracy theories. CNN. https://edition.cnn.com/2024/01/30/media/taylor-swift-super-bowl-right-wing-conspiracy/index.html.

Dehue, F., Bolman, C., & Vollink, T. (2008). Cyberbullying: Youngsters' experiences and parental perception. *Cyberpsychology & Behavior: The Impact of the Internet, Multimedia and Virtual Reality on Behavior and Society*, *11*(2), 217–223.

Devlin, M. (2024). Twitter trending of Taylor Swift AI should outrage everyone, including the ghost of Jim Henson, January 24*Straight*. Available from https://www.straight.com/music/twitter-trending-of-taylor-swift-ai-should-outrage-everyone-including-ghost-of-jim-henson.

Dodge, K. A., & Coie, J. D. (1987). Social-information-processing factors in reactive and proactive aggression in children's peer groups. *Journal of Personality and Social Psychology*, *53*, 1146–1158.

Donner, C. M. (2016). The gender gap and cybercrime: An examination of college students' online offending. *Victims & Offenders*, *11*(4), 556–577. Available from https://doi.org/10.1080/15564886.2016.1173157.

Epley, N., & Kruger, J. (2005). When what you type isn't what they read: The perseverance of stereotypes and expectancies over e-mail. *Journal of Experimental Social Psychology*, *41*, 414–422.

Erdur-Baker, Ö. (2010). Cyberbullying and its correlation to traditional bullying, gender and frequent and risky usage of internet-mediated communication tools. *New Media & Society*, *12*(1), 109–125. Available from https://doi.org/10.1177/1461444809341260.

Forero, R., McLellan, L., Rissel, C., & Baum, A. (1999). Bullying behaviour and psychosocial health among school students in New South Wales, Australia. *British Medical Journal*, *319*, 344–348.

Galen, B. R., & Underwood, M. K. (1997). A developmental investigation of social aggression among children. *Developmental Psychology*, *33*, 589–600.

Gini, G. (2008). Associations between bullying behaviour, psychosomatic complaints, emotional and behavioural problems. *Journal of Paediatrics and Child Health*, *44*, 492–497. Available from https://doi.org/10.1111/j.1440-1754.2007.01155.x.

Goldbaum, S., Craig, W. M., Pepler, D., & Connolly, J. (2003). Developmental trajectories of victimization: Identifying risk and protective factors. *Journal of Applied School Psychology*, *19*, 139–156.

Guadagno, R. E., & Cialdini, R. B. (2002). Online persuasion: An examination of gender differences in computer-mediated interpersonal influence. *Group Dynamics: Theory Research and Practice*, *6*, 38–51. Available from https://doi.org/10.1037//1089-2699.6.1.38.

Hartman, R., & Stage, S. A. (2000). The relationship between social information processing and in-school suspension for students with behavioral disorders. *Behavioral Disorders*, *25*, 183–195.

Hicks, J. (2021). Global evidence on the prevalence and impact of online gender-based violence. K4D Helpdesk Report. Institute of Development Studies. doi: 10.19088/K4D.2021.140ce.

Hinduja, S., & Patchin, J. W. (2008). Cyberbullying: An exploratory analysis of factors related to offending and victimization. *Deviant Behavior*, *29*(2), 129–156.

Katz, D., Allport, F. H., & Jenness, M. B. (1931). *Students' attitudes; a report of the Syracuse University reaction study*. Oxford, England: Craftsman Press.

Kent, G. (n.d.). Freedom of speech doesn't justify online bullying. Words have power, be careful how you use them. Atomic Quote. https://atomicquote.com/.

Kirby, P. (2023, December 21). Amanda Todd: Dutch court cuts jail term for fatal cyberstalking. BBC. https://www.bbc.com/news/world-europe-67787843.

Kimbrough, A. M., Guadagno, R. E., Muscanell, N. L., & Dill, J. (2012). Gender differences in technology use: Women connect more than do men. *Manuscript under review*.

Kumar, A., & Epley, N. (2021). It's surprisingly nice to hear you: Misunderstanding the impact of communication media can lead to suboptimal choices of how to connect with others. *Journal of Experimental Psychology: General, 150*(3), 595–607. Available from https://doi.org/10.1037/xge0000962.

Lapierre, K. R., & Dane, A. V. (2023). Early adolescents' involvement in anonymous relational and cyber aggression: An evolutionary perspective. *Evolutionary Behavioral Sciences*, *17*(4), 446–464. Available from https://doi.org/10.1037/ebs0000294.

Latane, B., & Darley, J. M. (1968). Group inhibition of bystander intervention in emergencies. *Journal of Personality and Social Psychology*, *10*(3), 215–221. Available from https://doi.org/10.1037/h0026570.

Law, D. M., Shapka, J. D., Domene, J. F., & Gagné, M. H. (2012). Are cyberbullies really bullies? An investigation of reactive and proactive online aggression. *Computers in Human Behavior, 28*(2), 664–672. Available from https://doi.org/10.1016/j.chb.2011.11.013.

Li, Q. (2007). New bottle but old wine: A research of cyberbullying in schools. *Computers in Human Behavior, 23*, 1777–1791. Available from https://doi.org/10.1016/j.chb.2005.10.005.

Lochman, J. E., & Wells, K. C. (2002). Contextual social-cognitive mediators and child outcome: A test of the theoretical model in the Coping Power program. *Development and Psychopathology, 14*, 945–967. Available from https://doi.org/10.1017/S0954579402004157.

Matias, J. N. (2019). Preventing harassment and increasing group participation through social norms in 2,190 online science discussions. *Proceedings of the National Academy of Sciences, 116*(20), 9785–9789.

McKenna, K. Y. A., & Bargh, J. A. (2000). Plan 9 from cyberspace: The implications of the internet for personality and social psychology. *Personality and Social Psychology Review, 4*(1), 57–75. Available from https://doi.org/10.1207/s15327957pspr0401_6.

Menesini, E., & Nocentini, A. (2009). Cyberbullying Definition and Measurement. *Zeitschrift für Psychologie/Journal of Psychology*, *217*, 230–232. Available from https://doi.org/10.1027/0044-3409.217.4.230.

Mier, T. (2023). Taylor Swift's voter registration post helps Vote.org reach record-breaking numbers, September 20*Billboard*. Available from https://www.billboard.com/music/music-news/taylor-swifts-voter-registration-post-record-breaking-voteorg-numbers-1235419640/.

Mishna, F. (2004). A qualitative study of bullying from multiple perspectives. *Children & Schools*, *26*(4), 234–247.

Morton, F. S., Zettelmeyer, F., & Silva-Risso, J. (2003). Consumer information and discrimination: Does the Internet affect the pricing of new cars to women and minorities? *Quantitative Marketing and Economics*, *1*(1), 65–92.

Nansel, T. R., Overpeck, M., Pilla, R. S., Ruan, W. J., SimonsMorton, B., & Scheidt, P. (2001). Bullying behaviors among US youth: Prevalence and association with psychological adjustment. *Journal of the American Medical Association*, *285*, 2094–2100.

Olweus, D. (1991). Bully/victim problems among school children: Basic facts and effects of a school based intervention program. In In. D. Pepler, & K. Rubin (Eds.), *The development and treatment of childhood aggression* (pp. 411–446). Hillsdale: Erlbaum.

Orobio de Castro, B., Veerman, J. W., Koops, W., Bosch, J. D., & Monshouwer, H. J. (2002). Hostile attribution of intent and aggressive behavior: A meta-analysis. *Child Development*, *73*, 916–934.

Owens, L., Shute, R., & Slee, P. (2007). They do it just to show off." Year 9 girls', boys' and their teachers' explanations for boys' aggression to girls. *International Journal of Adolescence and Youth*, *13*, 343–360.

Palladino, B. E., Nocentini, A., & Menesini, E. (2016). Evidence-based intervention against bullying and cyberbullying: Evaluation of the NoTrap! program in two independent trials. *Aggressive Behavior*, *42*(2), 194–206. Available from https://doi.org/10.1002/ab.21636.

Patchin, J. W., & Hinduja, S. (2006). Bullies move beyond the schoolyard: A preliminary look at cyberbullying. *Youth Violence and Juvenile Justice*, *4*(2), 148–169. Available from https://doi.org/10.1177/1541204006286288.

Pellegrini, A. D., & Bartini, M. (2001). Dominance in early adolescent boys: Affiliative and aggressive dimensions and possible functions. *Merrill-Palmer Quarterly*, *47*, 142–163. Available from https://doi.org/10.1353/mpq.2001.0004.

Peter, J., Valkenburg, P. M., & Schouten, A. P. (2005). Developing a model of adolescent friendship formation on the Internet. *CyberPsychology and Behavior*, *8*, 423–430.

Piazza, J., & Bering, J. M. (2009). Evolutionary cyber-psychology: Applying anevolutionary framework to Internet behavior. *Computers in Human Behavior*, *25*, 1258–1269.

Postmes, T., Spears, R., & Lea, M. (2002). Intergroup differentiation in computer mediated communication: Effects of depersonalization. *Group Dynamics*, *6*, 3–15.

Pozzoli, T., & Gini, G. (2012). Why do bystanders of bullying help or not? A multidimensional model. *The Journal of Early Adolescence*. Available from https://doi.org/10.1177/0272431612440172.

Pratto, F., Sidanius, J., Stallworth, L. M., & Malle, B. F. (1994). Social dominance orientation: A personality variable predicting social and political attitudes. *Journal of Personality and Social Psychology*, *67*(4), 741–763. Available from https://doi.org/10.1037/0022-3514.67.4.741.

Renati, R., Berrone, C., & Zanetti, M. A. (2012). Morally disengaged and unempathic: do cyberbullies fit these definitions? An exploratory study. *Cyberpsychology, Behavior, and Social Networking*, *15*, 391–398. Available from https://doi.org/10.1089/cyber.2012.0046.

Ribeiro, M. H., Blackburn, J., Bradlyn, B., De Cristofaro, E., Stringhini, G., Long, S., ... Zannettou, S. (2021). The evolution of the manosphere across the web. In *Proceedings of the international AAAI conference on web and social media*. (15, pp. 196–207).

Rivers, I., & Smith, P. K. (1994). Types of bullying behaviour and their correlates. *Aggressive Behavior*, *20*(5), 359–368. Available from https://doi.org/10.1002/1098-2337(1994)20:5%3C359::aid-ab2480200503%3E3.0.co;2-j.

Ronson, J. (2015). *So you have been publicly shamed*. New York: Riverhead books.

Salmivalli, C., & Voeten, M. (2004). Connections between attitudes, group norms, and behaviour in bullying situations. *International Journal of Behavioral Development*, *28*(3), 246–258. Available from https://doi.org/10.1080/01650250344000488.

Salmivalli, C., Voeten, M., & Poskiparta, E. (2011). Bystanders matter: Associations between reinforcing, defending, and the frequency of bullying behavior in classrooms. *Journal of Clinical Child & Adolescent Psychology*, *40*(5), 668–676. Available from https://doi.org/10.1080/15374416.2011.597090.

Schaeffer, K. (2023, November 17). *9 facts about bullying in the U.S.* Pew Research Center. https://www.pewresearch.org/short-reads/2023/11/17/9-facts-about-bullying-in-the-us/.

Schenk, A. M., & Fremouw, W. J. (2012). Prevalence, psychological impact, and coping of cyberbully victims among college students. *Journal of School Violence*, *11*(1), 21–37. Available from https://doi.org/10.1080/15388220.2011.630310.

Schroeder, J., & Epley, N. (2016). Mistaking minds and machines: How speech affects dehumanization and anthropomorphism. *Journal of Experimental Psychology: General*, *145*(11), 1427–1437. Available from https://doi.org/10.1037/xge0000214.

Shariff, S. (2009). *Confronting cyber-bullying: What schools need to know to control misconduct and avoid legal consequences*. New York: Cambridge University Press.

Smith, P. K., & Boulton, M. (1990). Rough-and-tumble play, aggression and dominance: Perception and behaviour in children's encounters. *Human Development*, *33*, 271–282.

Smith, P. K., Mahdavi, J., Carvalho, M., Fisher, S., Russell, S., & Tippet, N. (2008). Cyberbullying: its nature and impact in secondary school pupils. *Journal of Child Psychology and Psychiatry*, *49*, 376–385.

Smith, P.K., Mahdavi, J., Carvalho, M., & Tippett, N. (2006). *An investigation into cyberbullying, its forms, awareness and impact and the relationship between age and gender in cyberbullying*. Research Brief No. RBX03-06. DfES, London.

Smith, P. K., & Sharp, S. (Eds.), (1994). *School bullying: Insights and perspectives.* London: Routledge.

Solberg, M. E., & Olweus, D. (2003). Prevalence estimation of school bullying with the Olweus Bully/Victim Questionnaire. *Aggressive Behavior, 29*(3), 239–268. Available from https://doi.org/10.1002/ab.10047.

Sourander, A., Helstela, L., Helenius, H., & Piha, J. (2000). Persistence of bullying from childhood to adolescence: A longitudinal 8-year follow-up study. *Child Abuse and Neglect, 24*, 873–881.

Stauffer, S., Heath, M. A., Coyne, S. M., & Ferrin, S. (2012). High school teachers' perceptions of cyberbullying prevention and intervention strategies. *Psychology in the Schools, 49*(4), 352–367. Available from https://doi.org/10.1002/pits.21603.

Tani, F., Greenman, P. S., Schneider, B. H., & Fregoso, M. (2003). Bullying and the big five. *School Psychology International, 24*(2), 131–146. Available from https://doi.org/10.1177/0143034303024002001.

Terasahjo, T., & Salmivalli, C. (2003). "She is not actually bullied" the discourse of harassment in student groups. *Aggressive Behavior, 29*(2), 134–154. Available from https://doi.org/10.1002/ab.10045.

Underwood, M. K., Galen, B. R., & Paquette, J. A. (2001). Top ten challenges for understanding gender and aggression in children: Why can't we all just get along? *Social Development, 10*, 248–266. Available from https://doi.org/10.1111/1467-9507.00162.

Vogels, E.A. (2021, January 13). *The state of online harassment.* Pew Research Center. https://www.pewresearch.org/internet/2021/01/13/the-state-of-online-harassment/.

Wang, J., Iannotti, R. J., & Nansel, T. R. (2009). School bullying among adolescents in the united states: physical, verbal, relational, and cyber. *Journal of Adolescent Health, 45*(4), 368–375. Available from https://doi.org/10.1016/j.jadohealth.2009.03.021.

Wang, Y. (2022). Understanding the role of social factors in cyberbullying at work. *Computers in Human Behavior, 134*, 107325. Available from https://doi.org/10.1016/j.chb.2022.107325.

Ward, C. C., & Tracy, T. J. G. (2004). Relation of shyness with aspects of online relationship involvement. *Journal of Social and Personal Relationships, 21*, 611–623.

Weatherbed, J. (2024, January 25). *Trolls have flooded X with graphic Taylor Swift AI fakes.* The Verge. https://www.theverge.com/2024/1/25/24050334/x-twitter-taylor-swift-ai-fake-images-trending.

Wingate, V. S., Minney, J. A., & Guadagno, R. E. (2013). Sticks and stones may break your bones, but words will always hurt you: A review of cyberbullying. *Social Influence, 8*(2-3), 87–106.

World Health Organization. (2024, March 27). *One in six school-aged children experiences cyberbullying, finds new WHO/Europe study.* https://www.who.int/europe/news/item/27-03-2024-one-in-six-school-aged-children-experiences-cyberbullying-finds-new-who-europe-study.

Zhang, Z., Xiao, H., Zhang, L., & Zheng, J. (2022). Linking cyberbullying to job strain: Roles of ego depletion and self-efficacy. *Journal of Aggression, Maltreatment & Trauma, 31*(6), 798–815. Available from https://doi.org/10.1080/10926771.2021.1933288.

CHAPTER 9

Social media and well-being

The problem with social media is that it's not designed to nurture well-being; it's designed to keep us engaged, even at the expense of our mental health. (Harris, 2017)

In 2023 US Surgeon General Dr. Vivek Murthy released a new advisory addressing the mental health risks posed by social media on children and adolescents. This advisory stated that while social media can offer benefits, it also has potential harms, particularly for young people whose brains are still developing. The advisory calls for urgent action from policymakers, technology companies, researchers, families, and youth to make social media safer and healthier. The advisory referred to studies that show how excessive social media use is linked to poor mental health outcomes, such as anxiety, depression, and body dissatisfaction, especially among teenage girls. The report emphasized the need for further research and immediate steps to protect youth, including stronger safety standards, better privacy protection, and promoting healthy online behavior. Dr. Murthy urges collective action to address the national youth mental health crisis, which is exacerbated by social media.

In addition to the warning from the US Surgeon General, lawsuits from the vast majority of the US states have been filed alleging that social media giant Meta—the umbrella corporation for Instagram and Facebook knowingly created addictive technology (Caldwell, 2023, October 24). Elon Musk's social media application Twitter/X has been permanently banned in Brazil due to the rampant and unchecked misinformation spreading through it. People who use a virtual private network to try to circumvent the ban face a potential penalty of nearly $9000 (Karnitschnig, 2024, September 5). While facing waning support, the United States Congress has been trying to ban the social media platform, TikTok, due to concerns about it being used as Chinese spyware (Pew Research Center, 2024, September 5).

While I have been studying the psychological effects of social media for over 15 years, I do not allow my teenage kids to use it. By the end of this chapter, you will understand why. It all has to do with the question

Psychological Processes in Social Media
DOI: https://doi.org/10.1016/B978-0-12-811320-2.00007-1

of whether social media is a psychologically healthy activity, especially for children and adolescents.

Social media provides people with an opportunity to find geographically distant yet similar others. As a result, people can seek information and social support from others if they suffer from similar illnesses or have similar life challenges, irrespective of their geographical location. This chapter will review the benefits and risks of using social media for this reason and also examine the psychological antecedents of excessive social media use as a mental health and well-being concern. I start by reviewing the psychophysiological effects of social media use, establish what the term psychological well-being means in this literat, discuss the positive effects of social media use, review the results of meta-analyses on the social media use and well-being relationship, review gender differences, and conclude with recommendations for healthy social media use.

The dopamine hit: the psychophysiological effects of social media use

A "dopamine hit" refers to the release of the neurotransmitter dopamine, which is associated with rewards, into the brain (Wachler, 2022). While this can be caused by many things, in the realm of social media, a dopamine hit occurs when people's social media posts are liked, commented on, or shared. The release of dopamine is pleasurable, and it serves to reinforce the behavior that triggered it. So, if a person experiences a dopamine hit from others interacting with their social media content, they will want to repeat the behavior. This can create a fast feedback loop in which people experience nearly instant gratification from people's interactions with their posts, and this makes them want to repeat the behavior in anticipation of another dopamine hit. As a result, people's engagement with social media applications can increase as they seek out the dopamine hit over and over by posting and interacting with more social media content. For some people, this can lead to problematic social media use as these individuals start finding it difficult to disengage from their social media interactions.

What is psychological well-being?

Psychological well-being broadly describes people's emotional and cognitive evaluations of their lives. This includes a person's self-esteem and assessment of how well their life is going. High well-being has been widely shown to be associated with positive emotional and mental health lives (Huppert, 2009; Winefield, Gill, Taylor, & Pilkington, 2012). This includes having good stress management skills, the ability to set and meet goals, and making and maintaining healthy social connections. Psychological well-being is frequently associated with aspects like life satisfaction, having a sense of purpose, independence, and maintaining emotional stability.

Huppert (2009) explored the factors that influence psychological well-being and the outcomes associated with it. The research identified several predictors of well-being, including personality traits, social connections, and environmental influences, as well as the impact of well-being on various life aspects such as cognitive functioning, physical health, and social relationships. The results of this research suggest that high psychological well-being is linked to improved health outcomes, greater life satisfaction, and resilience. Overall, this research emphasizes that both individual and societal factors contribute to well-being, and it underscores the importance of public policy and interventions oriented towards enhancing well-being for public health benefits.

Psychological benefits of social media use

While social media often receives media attention for its potential negative effects on people's behavior and mental health, there are indeed various psychological benefits associated with social media use when approached mindfully. Some of these benefits include a sense of connection and belonging that people experience from being part of a group, social support provided by people who are experiencing similar life circumstances such as illness or divorce, personal or professional development, and learning opportunities afforded by social media applications that are more informational, entertainment from humorous posts, increased awareness, and involvement in social causes, connecting with people who share hobbies and interests, networking opportunities, assuaging loneliness, and exposure to differing views.

For instance, people with rare medical conditions or who spend much of their time serving as caregivers for others may find it difficult to find people sharing their life experiences. Indeed, the results of a longitudinal study suggest that people report receiving more social support as social media users relative to non-users. However, the impact of this social support on well-being and stress was negligible (Utz & Breuer, 2017). This finding is contradicted by other work that has shown a relationship between social support and well-being. In a systematic literature review of 27 studies that examined this relationship, Gilmour, Machin, Brownlow, and Jeffries (2020) reported that social support provided through Facebook did increase people's health and well-being. This review also suggested that the relationship between social support and well-being may be moderated by self-disclosure such that people who engaged in more self-disclosure received more social support which in turn enhanced their well-being. Overall, the literature on social support and social media and how this relates to well-being yields mixed results and this will be a common theme throughout this chapter. More research is needed to better understand the nuances of these relationships.

Social media and well-being

While there have been many studies and meta-analyses that have examined the relationship between social media use and psychological well-being, the complexities of this relationship are unclear. As the meta-analyses reviewed next will demonstrate, this relationship is multifaceted. It has been well-established that people do connect with others on social media in meaningful ways and this can provide people with social support and enhance the positivity in their lives. However, problematic social media use has been shown to increase feelings of loneliness, depression, and anxiety, and has been associated with decreased psychological well-being. As a result, one important implication of the existing research on social media and well-being emphasizes the importance of limiting social media use.

What meta-analyses conclude about well-being and social media use

To date, many meta-analyses have examined the relationship between social media use and psychological well-being and drawn subtlely different conclusions. In this section, I review the results of many of them. The fundamental question to ask is under what conditions is social media use good for people's mental and physical health and well-being.

In an early meta-analysis on this subject, Huang (2017) focused on social media use defined as time spent on social media. Across 61 studies with 19,652 participants, this meta-analysis yielded a small negative correlation between time spent on social media and psychological well-being such that more time on social media was associated with lower well-being. Marino, Gini, Vieno, and Spada (2018) examined problematic Facebook use and its association with self-esteem, considered a component of well-being. Across 56 independent samples with a total of 27,867 participants, the meta-analysis found that problematic Facebook use—defined as Facebook use that is heavier than planned or what is considered typical for people—was associated with lower self-esteem.

Huang (2022) examined data from 133 independent samples with a total of 244,676 participants. This meta-analysis revealed a small but significant relationship between problematic social media use and self-esteem and life satisfaction, both of which are components of well-being. As problematic social media use increased, self-esteem and life satisfaction decreased. This meta-analysis also examined the relationship between problematic social media use and depression and loneliness. Both resulted in a moderate but significant effect such that as problematic social media use increased so did depression and loneliness.

While the meta-analyses reviewed above examined the relationship between social media use and psychological well-being among adults, other meta-analyses have examined this relationship in children, specifically adolescents. In 18 studies with a total of 9269 participants, Shannon, Bush, Villeneuve, Hellemans, and Guimond (2022) reported positive relationships between problematic Facebook use and depression, stress, and anxiety, all of which are counter-indicators for well-being.

Ivie, Pettitt, Moses, and Allen (2020) meta-analytically examined the relationship between children's social media use and depressive symptoms, a counter-indicator of psychological well-being. Across the studies examined, they found a small but significant correlation between social media use and symptoms of depression. Cunningham, Hudson, and Harkness (2021) also conducted a meta-analysis on social media use and depression. Their sample included both children and adults and included 62 studies with a total of 451, 229 participants. Results revealed that there was a small, significant relationship between depression symptoms and both time spent using social media and the intensity of social media use. Problematic social media use was more strongly related to depression. There were no age differences found in their analyses.

Ansari et al. (2024) examined the relationship between problematic social media use and psychological well-being across 51 studies with a total sample size of 680,506 people. Their sample included both adults and children. Results revealed that problematic social media use was negatively associated with psychological well-being. This relationship was stronger for samples of adolescents relative to samples of adults.

What conclusions can be drawn from the results of these different meta-analyses? First, in answer to the question on the nature of the relationship between social media use and psychological well-being, it appears that the primary concern is problematic social media use, as there is a consistent negative relationship between well-being and social media use that is defined as problematic (i.e., excessive or obsessive). Thus one conclusion that can be drawn from these meta-analyses is that when used in moderation, social media use may not be harmful. Second, these results consistently demonstrate a stronger relationship between social media use and counter-indicators of well-being such as depression, especially for adolescents. Because of the correlational nature of these findings, conclusions cannot be drawn about causality. It may be that social media use can increase depression, it may be that people experiencing more depressive symptoms are heavier social media users, and it may be that another variable such as unemployment and loneliness is driving this relationship. Future research should continue to explore this to better understand this relationship. Finally, the results of these metaanalyses do show a consistent pattern that the negative effects of social media use are stronger for children. This suggests that the US Surgeon General and others should be concerned about the impact social media has on children and adolescents.

Culture and gender considerations

Gender

Research on gender and body image suggests that social media use can have a particularly negative impact on girls and women. Studies show that platforms like Instagram and TikTok, which focus heavily on visual content, often promote unrealistic beauty standards that lead to body dissatisfaction and a higher risk of developing issues like low self-esteem, body dysmorphia, and eating disordered behaviors (Markey, August, Gillen, & Rosenbaum, 2024; Marks, De Foe, & Collett, 2020). This is because girls compare themselves to the unrealistic images they see on social media and often do not consider the extent to which these images are curated and edited with software such as Photoshop.

Culture

The question of cultural differences in the relationship between psychological well-being and social media use is a difficult question to answer. This is in part because there are large cultural differences in the types of social media applications commonly used (e.g., Facebook in the United States and WeChat in China). Across these different applications, the design and affordances vary and may produce different results. It is also well established that societal norms vary by culture and this affects the types of behaviors often observed on social media. Nonetheless, there is some published research on this question.

For instance, Boer et al. (2020) examined the relationship between problematic social media use and well-being among 154,981 adolescents across 29 different countries in Europe. Canada was also included in this sample. While the countries differed in the frequency of problematic social media use, across all countries, the results revealed that problematic social media use was associated with lower psychological well-being. In this case, well-being was measured by satisfaction with school and perceived family support such that higher values indicated greater well-being. Other cross-cultural research has yielded similar results. For instance, Khan, Thomas, Karatela, Morawska, and Werner-Seidler (2024) reported that across 40 European and North American countries, problematic social media use among children was associated with difficulty falling asleep. Unfortunately, this research did not include samples from Asia. However, overall these results further highlight the greater concern for children's social media use.

Recommendations for psychologically healthy social media use

To mitigate these potential negative effects of social media use, it is essential for users to be mindful of their social media consumption, set limits, and engage in regular digital detoxes. For children, their parents should be teaching them healthy social media usage patterns. As I stated earlier, I did not allow my children to use social media until they got to an age where I could not stop it (in my case at 16). I kept an open dialog about healthy social media use and also ensured that my children focused more on informational rather than image-heavy social media platforms (Fig. 9.1). It is also important to maintain balance between one's online life and their

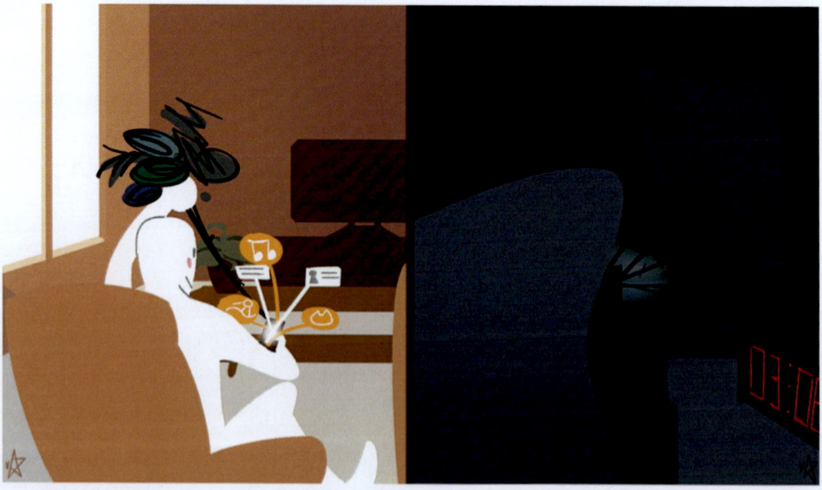

Figure 9.1 Healthy versus unhealthy social media use (Loewald, 2024).

offline world. Thus, in addition to social media, people should work to cultivate offline relationships and hobbies, ensuring a more balanced life. If someone feels overwhelmed or stressed due to their social media use, seeking professional counseling or therapy can also be beneficial.

Summary

Overall, the literature on social media and well-being has yielded somewhat conflicting results. This is in part due to the variation in measurements of psychological well-being and in social media use. More research needs to be conducted to better understand this relationship, particularly experimental research in which causal conclusions can be drawn. For adults, this research suggests that moderate social media use will either have no effect on well-being or even may enhance it, particularly in situations in which a person is seeking social support and is willing to engage in self-disclosure. For children, the research reviewed supports the US Surgeon General and suggests that their exposure to social media should be limited and supervised. Finally, much of this research examined counter-indicators of well-being such as depression but did not expressly study well-being itself (Valkenburg, 2022). Future research should focus more on well-being rather than assessing "ill-being" and assuming that the two concepts are opposite to one another.

References

Ansari, S., Iqbal, N., Asif, R., Hashim, M., Farooqi, S. R., & Alimoradi, Z. (2024). Social media use and well-being: A systematic review and meta-analysis. *Cyberpsychology, Behavior, and Social Networking*. Available from https://doi.org/10.1089/cyber.2024.0001.

Boer, M., Van Den Eijnden, R. J., Boniel-Nissim, M., Wong, S. L., Inchley, J. C., Badura, P., & Stevens, G. W. (2020). Adolescents' intense and problematic social media use and their well-being in 29 countries. *Journal of Adolescent Health*, *66*(6), S89–S99.

Caldwell, S. (2023). *41 states sue Meta, accusing company of harming kids with addictive social media features*. Gizmodo. https://gizmodo.com/states-sue-meta-addicted-kids-social-media-1850954682.

Cunningham, S., Hudson, C. C., & Harkness, K. (2021). Social media and depression symptoms: A meta-analysis. *Research on Child and Adolescent Psychopathology*, *49*(2), 241–253. Available from https://doi.org/10.1007/s10802-020-00715-7.

Gilmour, J., Machin, T., Brownlow, C., & Jeffries, C. (2020). Facebook-based social support and health: A systematic review. *Psychology of Popular Media*, *9*(3), 328–346. Available from https://doi.org/10.1037/ppm0000246.

Harris, T. (2017). *How a handful of tech companies control billions of minds every day* [Video]. TED. https://www.ted.com/talks/tristan_harris_how_a_handful_of_tech_companies_control_billions_of_minds_every_day.

Huang, C. (2017). Time spent on social network sites and psychological well-being: A meta-analysis. *Cyberpsychology, Behavior, and Social Networking*, *20*(6), 346–354. Available from https://doi.org/10.1089/cyber.2016.0758.

Huang, C. (2022). A meta-analysis of the problematic social media use and mental health. *International Journal of Social Psychiatry*, *68*(1), 12–33. Available from https://doi.org/10.1177/0020764020978434.

Huppert, F. A. (2009). Psychological well-being: Evidence regarding its causes and consequences. *Applied Psychology: Health and Well-Being*, *1*(2), 137–164. Available from https://doi.org/10.1111/j.1758-0854.2009.01008.x.

Ivie, E. J., Pettitt, A., Moses, L. J., & Allen, N. B. (2020). A meta-analysis of the association between adolescent social media use and depressive symptoms. *Journal of Affective Disorders*, *275*, 165–174. Available from https://doi.org/10.1016/j.jad.2020.06.014.

Karnitschnig, M. (2024). *Elon Musk's free speech absolutism is costing him—and Brazil*. Foreign Policy. https://foreignpolicy.com/2024/09/05/elon-musk-brazil-x-ban-free-speech/.

Khan, A., Thomas, G., Karatela, S., Morawska, A., & Werner-Seidler, A. (2024). Intense and problematic social media use and sleep difficulties of adolescents in 40 countries. *Journal of Adolescence*.

Marino, C., Gini, G., Vieno, A., & Spada, M. M. (2018). A comprehensive meta-analysis on problematic Facebook use. *Computers in Human Behavior*, *83*, 262–277. Available from https://doi.org/10.1016/j.chb.2018.02.009.

Markey, C. H., August, K. J., Gillen, M. M., & Rosenbaum, D. L. (2024). An examination of youths' social media use and body image: Considering TikTok, Snapchat, and Instagram. *Journal of Media Psychology: Theories, Methods, and Applications*.

Marks, R. J., De Foe, A., & Collett, J. (2020). The pursuit of wellness: Social media, body image and eating disorders. *Children and Youth Services Review*, *119*, 105659.

Pew Research Center. (2024). *Support for a U.S. TikTok ban continues to decline, and half of adults doubt it will happen*. https://www.pewresearch.org/short-reads/2024/09/05/support-for-a-us-tiktok-ban-continues-to-decline-and-half-of-adults-doubt-it-will-happen/.

Shannon, H., Bush, K., Villeneuve, P. J., Hellemans, K. G., & Guimond, S. (2022). Problematic social media use in adolescents and young adults: Systematic review and meta-analysis. *JMIR Mental Health*, *9*(4), e33450. Available from https://doi.org/10.2196/33450.

U.S. Department of Health and Human Services. (2023). *Social media and youth mental health: The U.S. Surgeon General's Advisory*. https://www.hhs.gov/sites/default/files/sg-youth-mental-health-social-media-advisory.pdf.

Utz, S., & Breuer, J. (2017). The relationship between use of social network sites, online social support, and well-being. *Journal of Media Psychology*, *29*(3), 115–125.

Valkenburg, P. M. (2022). Social media use and well-being: What we know and what we need to know. *Current opinion in psychology*, *45*101294.

Wachler, B. B. (2022). *Influenced: The impact of social media on our perception*. Rowman & Littlefield.

Winefield, H. R., Gill, T. K., Taylor, A. W., & Pilkington, R. M. (2012). Psychological well-being and psychological distress: Is it necessary to measure both? *Psychology of Well-Being: Theory, Research and Practice*, *2*(1), 3. Available from https://doi.org/10.1186/2211-1522-2-3.

Index

Note: Page numbers followed by "*f*" and "*t*" refer to figures and tables, respectively.

D

E

Printed and bound by CPI Group (UK) Ltd, Croydon, CR0 4YY
28/01/2025
01827164-0004